# TWO NOTE BOOKS OF
THOMAS CARLYLE

# TWO NOTE BOOKS

## OF

# THOMAS CARLYLE

FROM 23D MARCH 1822
TO 16TH MAY 1832

EDITED BY

CHARLES ELIOT NORTON

PAUL P. APPEL, *Publisher*

MAMARONECK, N.Y.

1972

Originally Published 1898
Reprinted 1972

Published by PAUL P. APPEL
Library of Congress Catalog Card Number 79-162486
ISBN 911858-21-0

# INTRODUCTION.

The Notebooks of Carlyle printed in this volume contain records of his thought and work from March, 1822, to June, 1832 — ten years which in many respects were the most important of his life: for during their course he was married, and his genius discovered its true quality and bent; he wrote his *Life of Schiller*, *Sartor Resartus*, and many of his most characteristic and interesting essays; he became widely known as a new power in literature; he was in friendly relations with Goethe; he formed acquaintance with many of the foremost men of letters in England, and entered into relations with the life of the world outside of Ecclefechan, Edinburgh, and Haddington. At the beginning of the books he is a poor student, without definite prospects or decided aims, without knowledge of his own capacities, and little acquainted with the world or known by it. At the end he is still very poor, but with ascertained powers, already exercising a strong influence on the thought of his time, and with a well-planted and rapidly growing reputation.

The Notebooks display in their irregular entries and miscellaneous contents the wide

## INTRODUCTION.

range of his interests, the general course of his reading, the increase of his intellectual resources, the gradual maturing of his mind. They contain his reflections upon books and men, the first rough jottings of his thought, and the records of current experience, set down not for the eyes of others, but as private memoranda for his own use. They exhibit his unwearied industry, and his mental ardor, vigor, and independence, while they reveal as well the strength of his moral convictions and the tenderness of his affections. To one who knows how to fill out the sketch which they afford, the character of their writer stands plain and impressive in its sincerity, integrity, and originality.

A considerable part of these books was printed by Mr. Froude in his *Life of Carlyle*, but, as was generally the case with his transcripts from manuscript, with many inaccuracies.

Although Mr. Froude's selections were judiciously made, their fragmentary character deprives them of a part of the interest and value which the Notebooks as a whole possess, in their illustration of the disposition and methods of their author. The very triviality of some of the entries which the books contain shows that mingling of trifling incidents and experiences with serious permanent concerns which gives to every life a double aspect. The deep, constant current flows steadily on, while its surface is ruffled by the breath of the moment, brightened by the passing gleam, or darkened by the flitting shadow. The picture of life is complete only when the details, each insignificant in itself, have their due part in the composition.

To the student of the growth of Carlyle's intellectual powers and the development of his opinions, these books afford material of interest hardly inferior to that contained in his *Reminiscences* and in his *Letters*—letters remarkable beyond most others for the fullness of their exhibition of the character of their writer, for their sincerity and directness, and for the union in them of ease and rapidity of composition with excellence of expression. The Notebooks display in like manner, if in less degree, the mastery which Carlyle possessed over his own faculties. He complains often of the difficulty he experienced in writing, but his letters and his journal alike reveal the mental discipline which enabled him to give off-hand an adequate and clear expression to his thought. There is seldom an erasure or defective phrase in his most rapid and instant writing.

## INTRODUCTION.

The reader familiar with his *Essays* will find in the Notebooks many germs of thoughts more fully developed in the published pages; many hints of topics more largely treated in them. Here, too, is the first suggestion of the idea wrought out in *Sartor Resartus;* here the embryo of conceptions which were to take on body in the later writings through which his influence was exerted upon contemporary opinion.

The most striking feature of the comments upon books, men, and events which these Notebooks afford is, perhaps, the integrity and consistency of the moral convictions which they exhibit. The character of Carlyle was based upon moral principle. His vivid imagination was quickened and his insight clarified by moral sentiment. His moral strenuousness was the chief element of his effect upon his own generation, and is the main source of his abiding influence. It is this which accounts for his stern and sometimes harsh judgments of men, for the limitation of his sympathies, for the occasional errors in his estimates of character, for his own self-reproaches.

In the spring of 1822, when the Notebooks begin, Carlyle was living in Edinburgh, occupied with various literary work, and engaged as tutor to Charles and Arthur Buller, who were entered at the University. Carlyle was in his twenty-seventh year. It was through the recommendation of his friend Edward Irving that he had been appointed, with a salary of two hundred pounds a year, "tutor and intellectual guide and guardian" to the Bullers — Charles, then about sixteen years old, Arthur, a year or two younger. "From the first," wrote Carlyle many years later, in his *Reminiscences*, "I found my Charles a most manageable, intelligent, cheery and altogether welcome and agreeable phenomenon; quite a bit of sunshine in my dreary Edinburgh element. I was in waiting for his Brother and him when they landed at Fleming's: we set instantly out on a walk round by the foot of Salisbury Crags, up from Holyrood, by the Castle and Law-Courts, home again to George's Square; and really I recollect few more pleasant walks in my life! So all-intelligent, seizing everything you said to him with such a recognition, so loyal-hearted, chivalrous, guileless; so delighted (evidently) with me, as I was with him. Arthur, a two years younger, kept mainly silent, being slightly deaf too; but I could perceive that he also was a fine little fellow, honest, intelligent, and kind; and that

## INTRODUCTION.

apparently I had been altogether much in luck in this didactic adventure. Which proved abundantly the fact: the two Youths both took to me with unhesitating liking, and I to them; and we never had anything of quarrel, or even of weariness and dreariness, between us: such 'teaching' as I never did, in any sphere before or since! Charles, by his qualities, his ingenuous curiosities, his brilliancy of faculty and character, was actually an entertainment to me, rather than a labour; if we walked together (which I remember sometimes happening) he was the best company I could find in Edinburgh. I had entered him of Dunbar's Third Greek Class in College. In Greek and Latin, in the former in every respect, he was far my superior, and I had to *prepare* my lessons by way of keeping *him* to his work at Dunbar's. Keeping him 'to work' was my one difficulty, if there was one, and my essential function. I tried to guide him into reading, into solid inquiry and reflection; he got some mathematics from me, and might have had more. He got, in brief, what expansion into wider fields of intellect, and more manful modes of thinking and working, my poor possibilities could yield him; and was always generously grateful to me afterwards; friends of mine, in a fine frank way, beyond what I could be thought to merit, he, Arthur, and all the Family, till death parted us."

The boys had arrived in Edinburgh about the middle of January, and the charge of them took up the better part of every day, "from ten o'clock till about one, and from six till nearly eight." During his free hours one of Carlyle's chief occupations was the translation of Legendre's "Elements of Geometry," a work to which he had been set by Dr. (afterward Sir David) Brewster, who was then editing the "Edinburgh Encyclopaedia," to which Carlyle had contributed various articles, mainly biographical.[1]

But his thoughts were set upon a Book of his own, and he was "riddling Creation" for a subject. Early in 1822 he had well nigh determined to write an Essay on the Civil Wars and the Commonwealth of England; not a history, but a study of the national character as it was then displayed, and it is with notes made with this intention in mind that the Notebooks begin.

---

[1] These articles were respectable compilations, serviceable enough for their purpose, but of no distinguished merit. They have been reprinted in a volume, as a bookseller's speculation, under the title: *Montaigne and other essays, chiefly biographical, now first collected.* By Thomas Carlyle. London, 1897. 8vo.

## INTRODUCTION.

The books have been printed in close conformity with the manuscript. A few corrections of the errors of a hasty pen have been made; a few careless misspellings have been set right, some words in foreign tongues have been italicized, some quotation marks have been supplied. But the integrity of the original writing has been scrupulously preserved, even at the cost of uniformity in printing. The words in brackets, except a few which supply obvious omissions, are not editorial additions, but are bracketed in the manuscript; a few words abridged in the writing are filled out with bracketed letters in the printed text. Some lines, in two or three places, not amounting to a page in all, have been omitted. The manuscript used for the press was a copy of the originals made some years since, but the proof-sheets have been carefully compared with the original Notebooks by Mr. Alexander Carlyle of Edinburgh, their present possessor.

CHARLES ELIOT NORTON.

*Cambridge, Massachusetts,*

The first Notebook is a volume of one hundred and eighty-eight pages of small duodecimo size. It has been carefully preserved, but on some of the pages the ink has now somewhat faded, though nowhere so far as to make the writing indistinct. The second Notebook consisted originally of seventy-six pages of nearly the same size as those of the first, but to its original leaves others were added, of different and somewhat smaller paper, sewn into the cover. Of these additional pages forty-four are occupied with the memoir of James Carlyle (printed in Carlyle's *Reminiscences*), and thirty-four with the entries with which this volume closes.

LIST OF BOOKS CITED UNDER ABBREVIATED TITLES IN THE NOTES.

*Reminiscences.*
    Reminiscences by Thomas Carlyle. Edited by Charles Eliot Norton. 2 vols., cr. 8vo, London, 1887.

*Early Letters.*
    Early Letters of Thomas Carlyle. 1814–1826. Edited by Charles Eliot Norton. 2 vols., cr. 8vo, London, 1881.

*Letters.*
    Letters of Thomas Carlyle, 1826–1836. Edited by Charles Eliot Norton. 2 vols., cr. 8vo, London, 1889.

*Essays.*
    Critical and Miscellaneous Essays by Thomas Carlyle. People's Edition, 7 vols., 12mo, London, 1872.

*Life.*
    Thomas Carlyle. A history of the first forty Years of his Life, 1795–1835. By James Anthony Froude. 2 vols., 8vo, London, 1882.
    Thomas Carlyle. A History of his Life in London. 1834–1881. By James Anthony Froude. 2 vols., 8vo, London, 1885.

1822. (at Edin.ʰ I *suppose*.)¹

# NOTE BOOK.

BEGUN WHILE READING CLARENDON'S HISTORY.

23d March, 1822.²   *Quod bonum, faustum, felix, fortunatum sit!*
Dr. Burgess and Mr. Marshal — who were they ? (page 239).

Oliver Cromwell's remark to L.ᵈ Falkland touching the " Remonstrance " or declaration of grievances voted & printed by the P.ᵗ — about the date of King's return from Scotland. Oliver said "they would have a sorry

¹ Note by Carlyle made in 1866, when, at the time of writing his *Reminiscences*, he looked over this volume.

² At the date of the beginning of this note-book, Carlyle, twenty-six years old, was engaged in reading for a work he had in mind on the Civil War and the Commonwealth. On April 27, 1822, he wrote to his brother Alexander: "Within the last month I have well-nigh fixed upon a topic. My purpose... is to come out with a kind of Essay on the Civil War and the Commonwealth of England — not to write a history of them — but to exhibit, if I can, some features of the national character as it was then displayed, supporting my remarks by mental portraits, drawn with my best ability, of Cromwell, Laud, George Fox, Milton, Hyde, etc., the most distinguished of the actors in that great scene." *Early Letters*, ii. 56. Before the end of the year the design was relinquished under the pressure of other engagements. *Id.* p. 171. But the work done now stood him in good stead twenty years later in the preparation of his *Cromwell*.

debate " — the thing being so plain ; and next day when the debate was done and not *sorrily* — he said, if the question had failed " he w$^d$ have sold his all next morning, and never seen Eng$^d$ more " — so near (quoth Clarendon) was the poor Kingdom to its deliverance (247).

Williams Archbishop of York (formerly Lincoln) seems to have been a *very* queer man (p. 272). He wrote a book against Laud — what was it ?[1]

The King comes to the H. C. to seize the members accused of Treason, viz. Pym, Hambden, Hollis, Hazelrig & Strode — with Lord Kimbolton — all this by advice of Lord Digby (p. 280).

The grant of Londonderry and the adjacent districts had been wrested from the City of London (together with a fine of £50,000) by the Star Chamber (first set up in Harry 7th's time); afterwards restored — but, as the City tho!, more out of fear of the Par! than a sense of justice. This one cause of their Roundheadism.

" Perfunctorily " — " upstart companions."[2]

---

[1] How " queer " Archbishop Williams was appears from Bishop Hacket's Life of him, which Coleridge called " a delightful and instructive book," but which Johnson, in his Life of Ambrose Phillips, described not less truly as " written with such depravity of genius, such mixture of the fop and pedant as has not often appeared."

[2] Words used by Clarendon.

## THOMAS CARLYLE.

25th and 26th March. Read Milton's *Defensio Pop. Angl.* ag![t] the *Def. Reg.* of Saumaise. Exhibits some new shades of John's character — his stern detestation of tyranny — his contempt for his enemies — and perhaps the ordinary tone of his intercourse with them in private life. There is a kind of rude wit mixed up with his fierce invective. But what austerity — what contempt for the mere pomp and circumstance of things! He seems to tear the unhappy pedagogue into a thousand shreds, to trample his remains and beat them into perfect mire — and at last he sends his soul to the infernal shades. *Furcifer, Bipedum nequissime,* etc., etc. — all the terms of indignation and contempt which the Latin affords are exhausted in abusing Salm[asius]. His wife too is said to have " worn the breeks "; & several cuts are made thro' this rent. The whole seems very *ill-bred:* but John was not a man of breeding. No newspapers then & his work is like the concentration of fifty " Couriers " or " Chronicles." Conceive that all the Radicals had " one neck " and put Gifford to strike it off — what a stroke he would fetch ! So is it with Milton. Besides Carolus II was then getting settled in Scotland, and M. naturally feared that the good work would be destroyed and with it all that was worth preserving in England. What is the history of Salmasius? (*Les Daciers, les Saumaises*—Volt. Temple du goût[1]—I must see—am very stupid to-night and *bilious*—*n'importe*, I must along with Clarendon second vol. which I trust will suit me better than the first did.) Milton's mode of reasoning has something curious in it: he appeals to no first principles hardly, but wanders in a wilderness of quotations and examples, summoning to his aid all that Jew or Gentile ever did or said on the subject. Still more is this true of Saumaise, who set the example of this species of disceptation first—an example however readily enough followed by his opponent. Are *our* "first principles" more solid than his? I doubt if they are *so* much more, as we often think. Nine tenths of our reasonings are *artificial* processes, depending not on the real nature of things but on our peculiar mode of viewing things, and therefore varying with all the variations both in the kind and extent of our perceptions. How is this? Truth *immer* WIRD *nie* IST?[2]

Newspapers *did* exist in Milton's time: the first, "Mercurius," was set on foot during the Spanish Armada (See Aikin's Memoirs of Q. Elizabeth—a book about the weight of

[1] "Là j'aperçus les Daciers, les Saumaises,
Gens hérissés de savantes fadaises."
Voltaire, *Le Temple du Goût.*
[2] "Is truth always relative, never absolute?"

McCrie's Knox — which is no immense weight. She[1] talks of revels, masques, courtly vanities, courtly feuds; he of Masses, sol[emn] conferences, synods, books of discipline: each in a peculiar solid prosaic vein — *hebetia ingenia cum aliquanto doctrinae.*[2])

I read the *Defensio* but "perfunctorily." I must read it again, if I persist in *this* work. And Salm.'s too — which is no light matter.

Fleetwood — first a trooper in the Guards sent by Essex to Shrewsbury — with a letter. (See p. 21, notes.)

Stanza by Swift or Rochester on Charles II his spouse Katherine of Portugal —

> Here 's a health to Kate,
> Our Master's mate,
> Of the royal house of Lisbon;
> And the Devil take Hyde,
> And the Bishop beside,
> Who made her bone of his bone!

Such is the power of rhyme, and of one double ending — certainly indeed the happiest possible. (From Southey's travels — the most contemptible, pragmatical — Yet he writes well now: *Esperance!* — I read it 2 weeks ago.) —

Excellent description of the Battle of Edgehill — very excellent (pp. 38, 39.) Edgehill

---

[1] Miss Lucy Aikin.
[2] "Dull natures, with somewhat of learning."

is near Keinton (Kington) on the east border of Warwickshire.

Proposals — osals — osals, all abortive.

Second Battle — at Bradock-Down near Liskard in Cornwall; wherein the P[arliament] forces (under Ruthven a Scot) were defeated by Hopton, in the winter of 1642. Indifferently described.

Third battle in March 1643 (on a Sunday like the first) at Hopton-heath 2 miles from Stafford. P. beat again.

An attempt at treaty in the beginning of 1643 at Oxford; then Reading taken. Waller (the poet) talked & vapoured much and plotted a little for the King — was betrayed by his servant, had Tomkins his brother-in-law hanged with another, and saved his own life by the most abject prostrations, affecting to be "awakened" and listening with great contrition to various ghostly comforters sent to him; then glozing the H. C. with fair speeches (for indeed he had a pleasant wit and could plead very cunningly & movingly) he prevailed on the P. to accept a fine of £10,000, and banish him to the isle of Bermuda — not hang him as he deserved but for his poetry & pregnant parts.— This was in June —'43.

The great Hambden killed at *Chalgrove*-field, between Thame and Oxford on a Sunday morning, having ridden forth with many

## THOMAS CARLYLE.

others to punish Prince Rupert for beating up Essex' quarters, an enterprise contrived by one Hurry a Scot, who had served in the Low Countries, and with the P. at Edgehill, but deserted to the K. after — his abilities not being as he tho! sufficiently rewarded. This Hambden was undoubtedly a great character; & his worth has been sufficiently acknowledged by the affection which his country yet bears to him. Hambden & Washington are the two people best *loved* of any in history. Yet they had few illustrious qualities about them; only a high degree of shrewd business-like activity, and above all that honest-hearted unaffected fearless *probity*, which we patriotically name *English*, in a higher degree than almost any public men commemorated in History. After all "honesty *is* the best policy." Yet to have seen a Cæsar, an Alexander, a Napoleon *honest*—! What a splendid thing — what a difficult not to say impossible one! (fudge!).

Hambden lingered three weeks — his wound was in the shoulder-bone. He seems to have been the ablest and best man of England. To Cæsar, Alex$^r$, Nap. &c. &c. we may pause before assigning any superiority even in talent (whatever they had in fortune) over him — his talents, at least were unrivalled in political management; and for virtuous conduct he has no fellow.— Claren-

don draws his character well (p. 306). Staid, sober, a keeper of his own counsel, resolute yet meek, generous as the Lion, subtle as the serpent. What a "Protector" he would have made had he lived!
Battle at Stratton hill on the w. side of Cornwall, where the P. forces under Stamford are shamefully defeated (16th May 1643).

Birch's "historical and critical account of the Life & Writings of Milton."

Battles of Landsdown near Bath, and of Roundway — down near Devizes — in both of which Sir W. Waller is beaten. July 1643.
Geoffrey Chaucer's house Donnington, within two miles[1] of Newbury — in Wilts. Glo'ster recovered, and the battle of Newbury fought by Essex, both sides claiming the victory. Lord Falkland was killed here. "Of so flowing and obliging a humanity and goodness to mankind, and of that primitive simplicity & integrity of life." Men came to him by his commerce "to examine and refine those grosser propositions, which laziness and consent made current in vulgar conversation." — Beautiful delineation of his character (p. 277): a finer person, as here shadowed forth, than even Hambden.— But it is wrong to set

---

[1] Clarendon says, "within a mile."

two such men at variance in their posthumous reputation, now when the contests that set them at variance in their conduct have passed away into the vast and ever-increasing, ever-stranger ruin of things that *were*. How expressive is that "sad and shrill" tone, with which in the Council he would pronounce the words, *Peace! Peace!* — when there was no peace! I know few finer specimens of men than H. & F. *What* would a man not give to be like them? Vain bargain! these are the favourites of Nature; *we* are made of poorer clay.— F. died in Lord *Byron's* regiment.

"The learned & eminent Mr. Chillingworth" taken at the retaking of Arundel by Sir W. Waller, and *so* ill-treated that he died within a few days *(sic scribit)*. This C. was a sceptic finally, having been a catholic first.

Soon afterwards (29th March 1644) Sir W. defeated the K's army under Hopton & Brentford, at Arlesford — between Winchester & Farnham.

Oliver Cromwell was chosen to command the horse, under Manchester head of the five associated counties, Essex, C[ambridge] N[orfolk] S[uffolk] Bedf. Hunt.[1] — Year 1644

---

1 "This winter arise among certain counties 'Associations' for mutual defense against Royalism and plunderous Rupertism." Carlyle's *Cromwell*, 3d ed. i. 175.

Huntingdonshire was not of the association mentioned in the text.

somewhat fertile in military exploits. King eludes Waller very cunningly at Worcester and comes back to Oxford (Essex being gone to the west, whither the Queen — then with child of the future Duchesse d'Orléans — see Bossuet's *Oraisons funèbres* — had retired); goes out to meet him; fights at Cropredy-bridge (on the Cherwell, Northamptonshire) with moderate success (in June); follows Essex into the West, and forces his foot to capitulate at Lostwithiel, then fights twice within a week at Newbury — the first time, being beaten as it seemed, and the second only showing himself (reinforced) to deliver Donnington castle in which his old dotard drunkard deaf General Brentford (Ruthven) was besieged. He then went to Oxford. Shortly after the skirmish of Cropredy-bridge, the battle of Marston Moor was fought (close to York on the South), Rupert and Newcastle being "on the matter" beaten by Manchester, and chiefly by Cromwell's *iron band* — as the Scots all ran like collies *(fidem detis ?)*. Newcastle went beyond sea immed.— Rupert rode southward; each in a pet with the other: by which means Charles' affairs in the north were completely ruined. This Rupert seems to have been a very boisterous man — brave and impetuous — but somewhat too headstrong and overbearing. His poor father, the Ex-Elector Palatine, Ex-King of Böhmen,

## THOMAS CARLYLE.

&c. &c. was in the meanwhile come to London; had taken the Covenant, and been gifted by a pension. (What became of him at last?)

Goring the Par.'s guardian (and betrayer) of Plymouth (or Portsmouth?) and afterwards the King's general of the horse appears to have been a very sufficient cozener; there is something very clever in him and very original.

The "self denying ordinance" proposed by Cromwell and Sir H. Vane, the object being to get Essex and all Presbyterians ousted from command.

Uxbridge-treaty is graphically delineated. I would have gone some distance to see Mr. Henderson pitted against Bishop Steward — the theological democracy of Σκωτια against the vain hierarchy of the South. It is very curious to see the vehemence wherewith those highly accomplished divines of the Prelatical persuasion still insist upon the continuous transmission of the Episcopal virtue, maintaining it to have passed (like the electric fluid) with undiminished purity and intenseness, thro' all the dark and polluted periods of the Romish superstition, thro' all the Dunstans and Bonars & Gardiners, to rest worthily in the liberal and enlightened souls of Dr. Marsh, Mr. Tomline, and the like — in our own times — and by them to be as happily handed down to worthies destined to follow. There seems little danger that the " Goddess Reason " will ever draw many votaries to her idolatry from the followers of that creed; considering that it is now 1822. Why does not McCrie write a life of Henderson? Dare he not?

Secret history of Montrose as connected with O'Neil and the Earl of Antrim (p. 470 &c). Would not this raid of Montrose's make an admirable history of its kind — somewhat like the Venice *Conjuration* of St.-Réal? Why has [not] Walter Scott seized it!

Battle of Naseby, where the poor King was beaten: here is no bad description of it. Curious anecdote of the Earl of Carnwath laying hold of the K's bridle — when the Guards and he were ready to dash upon Cromwell; and bawling out with a loud Scotch oath: Will you go upon your death in an instant? which exclamation introduced a misconception and a panic; which panic " begot " a flight; which flight &c. &c. The battle was fought in June 1645, Fairfax *imperante*, & Rupert on the other side " a fiery ettercap, a fractious chiel." They found the King's papers here and published them.

> Strange that such disputes should be
> 'Twixt Tweedledum & Tweedledee!

After the loss of Naseby every thing with

## THOMAS CARLYLE.

Charles went to wreck & ruin. Sir Dick Greenvil the Nabal, and Goring the dog kept quarrelling & sparring with all men; there was nothing but agitation confusion, mis-rule & despondency. So that in fine C. retired to Chepstow, thence to Cardiff — thence to various other places — wandering about with a purpose ever-changing, a hope ever-declining — his own servants, even his own nephews, rebelling against him, till nearly all had "forsook" him & fled. He was twice or thrice of mind to go and join Montrose; on one occasion he despatched Lord Digby as General of the North, who carried a little army as far as Dum*freeze*, and then embarked for the Isle of Man, leaving his people to shift for themselves as they chose. Disputes in the West ran higher than ever. Goring drank and vapoured, wavering between insanity & treason, and at length settling into the latter (he went to France, and seemed to aim at selling his army to some foreign prince, and becoming a Condottiere): Sir R. Greenvil intent upon stuffing his own pantry well, acted even more inconsistently than Goring; he levied enormous contributions, squeezed fines out of every one he disliked by imprisonment & hard usage, commanded to-day what he countermanded to-morrow, and after ruining all was at length thrown into prison and allowed to escape beyond seas,— when the L$^d$ Hopton, to whom his army had been delivered, could make no stop to the torrent of ill fortune that swept away all the royalists of the Kingdom. Prince Charles went to Scilly in March, 1646; his father being still at Oxford and trying in vain to obtain a treaty from his Parl., to engage the Scots to his side (by the aid of Montrevil, a French agent), or the Independents, or any one — before he perished utterly. The Generals in the West were Fairfax and Cromwell; there was Poyntz also, and David Lesly who went from Hereford to beat Montrose, & afterwards returned into those parts, his valiant antagonist being defeated at Philipshaugh.

In April 1646, the King surrenders himself to the Scotch army then at Newark which by his direction was given up to them; whereupon they forthwith marched to Newcastle, keeping the K. with g$^t$ respect &c. but as a prisoner. They seem not well to have known what to do: the negotiation for his surrender was managed by Montrevil the French envoy. The prince meanwhile had sailed for Jersey, and thence, after much opposition from his Council, into France.

Third June 1647 King seized at Holmby in Northampt[onshire] by Cornet Joyce — a knight of the needle, who refused to show any authority for so doing but " *That* " (shewing a large pistol), and carried himself rather sturdily than rudely. He acted by order of Cromwell, who having been detected in his dissimulations and crocodile tears, and secretly doomed to be committed one morning to the Tower, had tho$^t$ good to set out to the army before light, where he found indeed that "*the* prejudice entertained against him was less than he supposed." Charles was brought to Newmarket.

One day Ireton and Hollis quarrelled; and the matter went so far that on Ireton's refusal from conscientious motives to fight Hollis, the latter "pulled him by the nose" *(proh pudor!)* and used great plainness of speech to him; which incensed the other officers of the army not a little.

When Charles went to the Scots, old Henderson turned out like a true man to convert him to the Presbyterian persuasion; but succeeded so ill that he was well-nigh converted himself (*credat Apella!*), and soon after died " of a broken heart."

" Clean contrary."

King's treaty with the Scots was signed in Carisbrook castle in December 1647.

Machiavel " as great an enemy to tyranny & injustice in any Gov$^t$ as any man then was or now is." " A man *were* better be a dog "; could not " find in their hearts "; " resolved to *pass* themselves in boats."

In the summer of 1648, the Scots under the Duke of Hamilton made an inroad into England, and were defeated by Cromwell in the most shameful manner, Ham$^n$ himself being taken prisoner at Uttoxeter in Staffordshire, to which place the rout extended after it had begun at Preston. Drivellers!

The business of Pomfret Castle is a very dramatic affair (p. 147. III).

The King was beheaded on the 30th Jan$^y$ 1649, and buried at Windsor without pomp. He had previously been removed from Carisbrook to Hurst Castle, and was conducted to Westminster to the " High Court of Justice," by Harrison who had once been a lawyer's clerk in Cheshire and originally was a butcher's son. Prince C. was in the meantime at the Hague where he had been left by a part of the fleet, which mutinied in his behalf, and was then in Ireland under the command of P. Rupert. There had been various insurrections &c. the year before; all of which were speedily quelled: one in Kent, and then in Essex where Colchester being seized was besieged by Fairfax, and being taken three of the chief officers were shot — Gascoigne (a Florentine) excepted, when his doublet was already off, and his mind made up to die. There are many picturesque incidents in these wars. As to the K., he seems to have been a very good man, tho' weakish and ill-brought up. Cromwell and the rest look much like a pack of fanatical knaves — a compound of religious enthusiasm, and of barbarous selfishness; which made them stick at no means for gratifying both the one and the other. Cromwell is a *very* curious person. Has his character been rightly seized yet? I must peruse the late documents about him.

House of Peers abolished soon after King's Dth. Poor Lord Capel's escape and recapture (p. 212). Duke Hamilton, L$^d$ Holland with him, were beheaded.— L$^d$ Norwich — was he our old friend Goring?

The barbarous execution of Montrose (who appeared in the North for Charles II. & was easily defeated by Strahan — 1649-50) reflects indelible disgrace upon the Scottish Kirk. Montrose is almost, if not altogether, the brightest specimen of a man ever produced by the country. His character is a fine sample of the *heroic* ambitious.

Scots again smashed to pieces at Worcester, 3$^d$ September 1650 — Poor knaves!

The act of Navigation passed in anger at the Dutch about the year 1651 or 2. Whereby all ships are prohibited from bringing into England any commodity not produced in the countries they belonged to. Raynal says this act was passed by King James! — This was the beginning of their quarrel with the English; the mutual spite being aggravated by

various regulations about not " striking flags " & so forth. The Dutch were *dished* we all know. See lives of Blake, Van Tromp, De Ruyter &c. May 1652.
Received " a brush " (p. 360 & elsewhere). " Ludlow " succeeded Ireton, who died of the Plague at Limerick in '50. Was *this* Ludlow the Historian?[1]
Cromwell dissolves the Par! by Force; in about 3 months summons another elected by himself; this (Barebone's Par!) delivered up their commission in about 6 months (December 1653) whereupon he was declared Protector — by the officers of the Army, and as such acknowledged by all the Kingdom. His first Par! was in Sept! 1654, and fairly elected — tho' by a rule different from the common. " Strange man — don't know him — don't."
Lilburn & Wildman curious personages — particularly the former, first a book-binder — persecuted by the Star Chamber, which raised in him a marv[ellous] appetite & inclin. to suffer for the vind. or defense of *any* oppressed Truth; then a soldier taken at Brentford & ready to be condemned; escapes, fights, then attacks the Par! then Cromwell, by whom he was at last tried — acquitted by the jury. This was the Cobbett of those days — but how much better than ours!

[1] He *was* the historian. See Carlyle's *Cromwell*, il. 333.

Cromwell dies $3^d$ September 1658 — a day he always tho$^t$ very propitious to him — having twice been victorious on it formerly. . . .

Fleetwood was the son of Sir Miles Fleetwood, and the "troopers of the Guards" to Essex, among whom was Ludlow, were all gentlemen's sons. (Began Ludlow $9^{th}$ April 1822.)

At the Battle of Edgehill Ludlow's "jaws for want of use had almost lost their natural faculty"!

Milton to be appointed adjutant gen! to Waller.— *When* did Cromwell & Fairfax march thro' the city to quell Brown & Massy? "Progging" "Gobbet."

Saturday 13th April. I have now finished the third volume of Clarendon — of which more afterwards; and the whole of Ludlow's Memoirs, concerning which I can make only a few vague remarks, having read it hastily & without great study. Ludlow is not a man of great parts; but he describes with a ready a modest & a graphic pencil, the scenes in which he took part, presenting a distinct tho' narrow sketch of what himself accomplished in his walk thro' that confused riot, and of what he saw in it on looking to the right hand and to the left. He differs in no important fact from Clarendon; and impresses us with an idea of his frank ingenuousness at least equal to that of his rival; while his stern sense of honesty, his unflinching adherence to principle thro' good and thro' bad report, his disdain of truckling alike to the open enemies as to the unworthy friends of republicanism, tend to inspire us with a higher respect for his heart & mind, than all the ingenious speculation and shrewd watchful sagacity of Clarendon can inspire us with for the mental gifts which they presuppose. I admire Ludlow's patient unaffected calmness very highly. Neither Russell nor Sidney were better men. Did he blanch before the Royalists at Oxford? before Cromwell at London? before Monk & the new "Convention"? And when he fled to Vevay — tho' banished from his friends his country his wife his property and cheated of his just fame, and daily beset with barbarous assassins in a far land — does he whine or make lament? Compare him with Rousseau or Ovid or Necker — he is like a pillar of marble compared with a weeping willow. *How* was it such noble minds were generated in those times? I know not but think it well worth inquiring into.— Ludlow writes rather prettily; he describes graphically the siege of Wardour Castle, the "firing" of a castle in Ireland; the troopers at Marston Moor; &c. His best description however, & that unconsciously, is of himself.— Would it not be right to make out *a list* of the chief personages of that period as well as the chief events?

Ellwood's Life of himself — Read it for the sake of Milton to whom this person was Reader of Latin at one time; but found nothing therein beyond what is recorded in my own Milton. Found however something advantageous and amusing, which I did not at all anticipate — a picture of human nature under a somewhat new aspect, delineated with great liveliness & simplicity & clearness. Ellwood seems to have been a cheerful quick pure-minded rather clever little fellow. His fanaticism is of a curious species: it is obstinacy & enthusiasm without any moroseness or rancour. He suffered persecutions out of number, but cherished no revenge against the authors of them; his share of worldly comfort was small in comparison of what he once might have hoped for; but his heart was clear & healthful, and his life may justly be called happy notwithstanding. What made it so? How came he to shew so complete and consistent & respectable a walk and conversation amid so many drawbacks & obstructions? His *creed* was his support, his all in all. Is it better then to have *a* straight road formed for us, tho' a false one, thro' this confused wilderness of things — than to be waiting asking searching for a true one, if we never find it altogether? Compare Ellwood, a weak man, with Alfieri, Goethe, Voltaire, strong men; & award the palm! What *is* the proper province of Reason?

For the rest Ellwood's book is very amusing. It affords a vivid tho' a brief glimpse of English life in the middle & religious walks of it, during the reign of Charles II. One reads it like a kind of Novel.

Milton's history of Britain. The first part of this is very beautiful — one simile about a traveller setting out amid "smooth & idle dreams" equal to anything I know of.[1] For fine composition in matter & form see also the first invasion of Anglesea, and the revolt of Boadicea. The style is very Latinish, tho' also very perspicuous: the prejudice against woman-rule breaks out on all occasions; some views too of Particular providence, which did he really entertain? Invocation at the beginning. On the whole, however, it is unphilosophically composed. The Saxon period cannot be better — so cannot be well-related by any person upon this plan. Perhaps the moderns *have* improved in their mode of writing history. (See Stewart's life of Robertson?) Milton's history is like a stone-

[1] "By this time, like one who had set out on his way by night, and travail'd through a Region of smooth or idle Dreams, our History now arrives on the Confines, where day-light and truth meet us with a cleer dawn, representing to our view, though at a farr distance, true colours and shapes."— Book i. *ad fin.*

dike of ugly whinstones, numberless, shapeless, joined together with the finest Roman cement. They were not worth the pains; *materiem superat opus:* better to have left the *cairn* as he found it in Hoveden, Mat[thew of] West[minster], Simeon of Durham, Huntington, &c. Here follow some *agates* picked from it.

Estrildis (a small tragedy ?) & her daughter Sabra p. 8. " Severn swift guilty of maiden's death."[1] Boadicea (do ?) p. 28 — She was of the *Iceni* about Norwich. A wild Semiramis. Has not some one sung of her ?[2]

Edwin p. 60. his conversion to Christianity (another ?) — his wavering fortunes, visions, loves, ultimate success — " Harryed the coast " — " felled him " — " to chronicle the wars of kites & crows fighting & flocking in the air " — the sceptre found " too hot " for a man's hand.

Christianity tho! to have come hither A.D. 180.

Monday 15th April 11½ o'clock P. M.  I have this moment finished the perusal of Milton's first publication, entitled " Of Reformation &c." Had he written nothing else whatever, it would have

[1] Milton, "At a Vacation Exercise," v. 96.
[2] Perhaps Carlyle had in mind Cowper's so-called Ode, entitled "Boadicea."

stamped his name with the ineffaceable impress of genius, and shewn him to all the world as a man no less high & solemn in his moral nature than rare and richly gifted in his intellectual powers. There are pieces of as sublime eloquence here as I ever saw: the learning of the piece is great, and the logic of it powerful & as well ordered as in an oration is needful. He begins by alluding to the corruptions of the church; then hails the reformation in a beautiful sentence (p. 250), and tries to point out why it was less complete in England than elsewhere. Solemn protestation (252). Next comes the main gist of the performance, the reasons that obstruct improvement at *this* time. The enemies of it are divided into three classes the *Antiquitarians*, the *Libertines*, the *Politicians*. The two former are discussed in the first book. Difference in the power & dignity of ancient from those of modern bishops — besides, the Fathers full of errors — their works garbled — their example therefore unbinding even when Constantine *had* united the civil to the eccles. power. "How then should the dim taper" (257). Besides themselves refer to the Bible as all sufficient — "homely & yeomanly religion"—Truth — Understanding (p. 260). "Wherefore should they not urge only the Gospel, & hold it ever in their faces like a mirror of Diamond till it dazzle and pierce their misty eyeballs" (p.

261).—Libertines not convincible.— Figures in the II.ᵈ Book about vulgar politics. The Pope's & clergy's small favour to monarchy shown by various instances. Rude fable of a wen (p. 266). Their measures banish many subjects, corrupt & irritate the rest — destroy much revenue, and so disaffect Englishmen — unfitted for peace now make war. Objections answered — Excommunication (272–3). Exuberant & felicitous sarcasm (273). Majestic peroration in the form of a prayer.

progging, fobbing, rooking, sconced,— greasy palm — unctuous paunches — fiery whip — blood diverted from the veins to the ulcers — &c. *Heu quantum ab illo!*

Second pamphlet — "Of Prelatical Episcopacy" against Usher. Judges of the Insufficiency of their "traditional ware" with the skill and indifferentism of a complete connoisseur — acquainted with this & with other sources of truth far purer. Little order — being a reply rather than an oration. "Drag-net" of time (p. 239). Fine simile of the robe of truth & the rags of time's garment (p. 242).

Brerewood — what of him? (p. 201).

Barclay his "Image of minds"? (217).[1]

[1] John Barclay, best known by his *Argenis*, extravagantly praised by Coleridge (*Lectures on Shakespeare, with other Literary Remarks*, 1849, ii, 236). His *Icon Animarum* "Image of Minds," "a delineation of the genius and customs of the European nation," was published in 1614.

The "sovran TREACLE of sound doctrine" (235). "Lin pealing," leave pealing p. 236.

These latter extracts are from "The Reason of Church Gov$^t$," Milton's third pamphlet, which I have just concluded, after many interruptions (22$^{nd}$ April — Saturday) particularly to-day, when idlers not a few have been here to consume my hours vainly.— The general character of this tract is vigour of feeling & thought, clothed in a garb of rich metaphorical and emphatic language — presenting a few large views of polity and morals, and much indignant aversion for everything connected with the sordid carnality & worldlymindedness of Prelates & their office.

The first part is argumentative in the strict sense; endeavoring to prove 1$^o$ that *a* government is established for the Church by divine Wisdom, and that either Episcopacy or Presbytery (which latter point is avowedly assumed without demonstration); 2$^o$ that no argument can be drawn from Moses in favour of E.; 3$^o$ that it does not prevent schisms but breeds them &c. The second book opens with a fine exordium on the Author's own studies and aspirations — by way of apology for engaging in the controversy — then proceeds to shew that Prelacy both in the spirit & form is clean contrary to the religion of the Gospel. — There are many fine ideas

## THOMAS CARLYLE.

& fine delineations scattered thro'out; but the thread of reasoning is not very easily followed — partly perhaps because the whole matter has long ago ceased to be a subject of discussion or interest among men, & so to be capable easily of arresting the attention enough. It is only where we gain a brief glimpse of the vast & sweeping ocean of Milton's mind, with all its wonders, its curious *fata morganas* & stately navies & majestic scenery (wretched figure!) that we feel a complete participation in the beauties of the composition. I never saw so eloquent a person. What boundless store of metaphors! What infinitude of thoughts! What strong & continuous fervour of soul! — Upon the whole however I am only beginning to see Milton: I must have him far more intimately present to me, must feel as it were with his great spirit — or it will never do. The men Symmons & Hayley[1] praise him loudly enough — but it is nearly all flattery. I like Hayley better: he is better-natured & almost as readable a kind of person as his rival. Indeed neither of them pass in this last quality; & Symmons is a very egotistical, pragmatical, verse-scanning, gerund-grinding pert sentimental little companion: I love him not.

" Axle of Discipline " (p. 202.— Milton no

[1] Hayley's *Life of Milton* was first published in 1794, Symmons's in 1806.

leveller or Radical).— fine comparison about the formation of a statue & that of any great social improvement — both leave chips & rubbish (p. 217) — Merchandize of Truth — good (p. 219) — likening of the King to Samson — good (p. 237).— bitter conclusion.

N. B. I am far too much of a *critic* — too little of an *artificer* in all points; always asking How? or only *saying* Thus — No affectation! True feeling once — always true partly.

The last two pamphlets of the year 1641 are "Animadversions on the Remonstrant's defence of Smectymnuus" and the "Apology for Sm." The first proceeds by way of extract and rejoinder; its aim is satire fully more than argument. Milton's wit is sometimes pungent, always unaffected, frequently not of the finest. The Apology is written in a more serious style; it contains many interesting developments of the Author's own feelings & purposes & history & hopes. It is written with more equality than any of the former treatises; and distinguished for a stately march of eloquent ratiocination dressed out in a rich and royal wardrobe of beautiful metaphors & honourable staid enthusiasm.— I am now at the "Divorce." (Must *it*[1] be

[1] "It," that is, the book which Carlyle was thinking of writing.

sketches of English character generally, during the Commonwealth? Containing portraits of Milton, Cromwell, Fox, Hyde, &c., in the manner of De Staël's *Allemagne.* The spirit is willing — but ah! the flesh —!) Prynne's Histrio-Mastix (should see it). Sir James Harrington. Who was Au[thor] of " Oceana "? Foot soldiers gave " four-pence a-piece." (Cromwell's life. 118) — poor fellows! Sir J. Burrow's Anecdotes of Cromwell — Dugdale, Bates, Harris. Milton's " Areopagitica " — just perused (6th May — after a long bout with Cromwell's life, &c.) : it is a stately grave & dignified oration in the manner of the ancients; contains a fair shew of candid argument, generous feeling; and is decked out with the usual unrivalled richness of style, by which this author is distinguished from all others. What I desiderate in Milton is luminousness of arrangement: he never reasons systematically, clearing all the ground before him as he goes, and collecting all the scattered brigades of his arguments to the final assault. It is quite clear that he never studied mathematics very deeply, or political economy — or any subject merely logical. Even in this Areopagitica splendid & powerful as it is, I am clearly of opinion that Brougham or any such person could discuss a similar subject with more practical *effect in the way of persuasion*, than Milton with all his noble eloquence. The perusal of these old giants, and the infirm appearance of their most venerable structures in the department of philosophy & controversy ought surely to make us humble in our estimate of human Reason. *How* is it? The art of Logic seems to come & go & change like the fashion of clothes from age to age!

As to this metaphorical talent, it is the first characteristic of genius — tho' not the only or an indispensable one, see Alfieri. It denotes an inward eye quick to perceive the relations & analogies of things; a ready memory to furnish them when occasion demands; and a sense of propriety & beauty to select what is best, from the immense store so furnished. There is far far more in it than this: but what — I have not time or power to say.

The plan of this Areopagitica (not rigidly adhered to) is fourfold — first that no worthy community ever adhered to it; [1] secondly that reading many bad books is often useful; thirdly that one might as well license fiddlers, tailors &c. &c. as printers; fourth the harm it does. There is no great felicity in this arrangement — but in executing it very very much.

[1] " Ever adhered to *it*," that is, to the prohibition and licensing of books.

## THOMAS CARLYLE.

" Not he who takes up arms for cote and conduct,[1] and his four nobles of Dunegelt." There is the " eagle muing " again. There is a highly sarcastic description of some tradesman's " Religion," & some clergy's preaching. *What* were precisely the things which Milton, Cromwell &c. aimed at so intensely? This should be clearly ascertained *in limine*, more clearly than hitherto.

---

[Thus far was written in August 1822 — what a horrid gap has followed! It is now the 4th of March 1823; and *what* have I been doing since? Fearful question! I will think no more of it. Goethe says it is always wrong to spend time in looking back at the road we have travelled over; it either disheartens us vainly, or puffs us up with a conceit as vain: the best plan is *whatever our hand findeth to do, to do it quickly*. So be it then! — But alas! alas! —]

The old Dramatists, Massinger, Beaumont and Fletcher &c. have disappointed me a good deal. Their language has often an echo of richest melody in it; their characters (particularly of *Rips* and Blackguards in B & F.) are sometimes well conceived and happily

[1] 'Cote' or coat-money was a tax for clothing new levies, imposed on the counties by the King. 'Conduct' a tax for defraying the cost of moving or *conducting* troops from place to place.

presented; there are in short many individual beauties: but no one piece, so far as I recollect, that I read to an end without disgust. What horrid barbarism of taste! what shocking grossness of manners! how little of genuine philosophy or real insight into the depths of human nature. Rich and royal Shakespeare! We should read his cotemporaries in order rightly to prize him.— No this is *not* the way for instructing myself! It is not.

What *should* I think of Goethe? His Wilhelm Meister instructed, disgusted, moved and charmed me. The man seems to understand many of my own aberrations, " the nature and causes" of which still remain mysterious to myself. I do feel that he is a wise and great man. The last volume of his *Life* is good also — gossipping, but full of intellect and entertainment.

Lacretelle[1] is but a flashy superficial historian: he has nothing to tell me that I did not know before. French chivalry — the spirit of honour, and the everlasting Henri Quatre — stuff — very wersh[2] stuff. It is really curious to think how little *knowledge* there is actually contained in these uncountable mountains of books that men have written. A few

[1] Author of many works on the history of France, born 1766, died 1835.
[2] Wersh, *Scottice*, "insipid."

## THOMAS CARLYLE.

general ideas, a few facts in the history of natural phenomena, a few observations on the properties of our minds, a few descriptions of our feelings — the whole repeated in ten thousand times ten thousand forms; — this is what we call philosophy and poetry. Alas! I am not yet past the threshold of instruction! GOTT HILF MIR! as Luther said.

These German critics are curious people. Grüber, Wieland, Doering, Schiller shew curiously beside our Edin[h] and Quarterly Reviews. *How much* better are they? More learned at any rate, more full of careful reflection, displaying greatly more *culture* than is usual among such people this side the water. I rather fear however there is more cry than wool. I must read some of them any way. Herder I have some good hopes of. Here is a place extracted from his *Nemesis*. After mentioning that he thinks the notion of the soul was first suggested by the phenomena of dreams, and preluding a little on the similarity of Sleep and Death and their common relation to Night, he proceeds:

"Beautiful allegory which the Former of our nature, by the alternation of light and darkness of sleeping and waking, has placed in the feelings of the most unthinking man! It seems as if He had wanted to give us a daily emblem of the circuit of our destiny, and had sent us daily to deliver it his messenger, Sleep the brother of Death. Softly do the dark wings of this Ambassador sweep towards us, and overshadow us with the clouds of Night. The Genius sinks his torch, and refreshes us, if the day dazzled our eyes, with some drops of forgetfulness from his ambrosial horn. Tired with the glare of the young Sun, we look to our old Mother Night as she comes with her two children in her arms, shrouded in a dark veil, but circled with a far-glancing crown of Stars. Whilst on the Earth she obscures the eyes of our body, she awakens the eyes of our soul to wide prospects of other worlds. But the views there are but dreams for our earthly spirit; the Mother of Sleep and Rest can give us nothing more." — Is not this a little in the vein of Hervey? Yet there is *something* very sweet in it. Herder writes a Prize-essay about the origin of Speech — Another about the decay of taste, from which Mad. de Staël appears to have borrowed something.

> In voller Jugend glänzen sie (the stars)
> Da schon Jahrtausende vergangen:
> Der Zeitenwechsel raubet nie
> Das Licht von ihren Wangen.
> Hier aber unter unserm Blick
> Verfällt, vergeht, verschwindet alles:
> Der Erde Pracht, der Erde Glück
> Droht eine Zeit des Falles —
>
> *Herder*

(Last line *bad*.)

## THOMAS CARLYLE.

"But as to the place and hour of thy future existence, fret not thyself O man; the Sun which illuminates thy day measures out for thee thy dwelling and thy earthly business, and obscures for thee meanwhile all the stars of Heaven. Soon as he goes down the world appears in its wider form: the sacred Night in which thou once layest shrouded up and wilt again lie shrouded up, covers thy Earth with shades but opens for thee in its stead the shining books of Immortality in the sky. There lie dwellings, worlds, and spaces."

"Unchanged they shine still young as ever
    When thousand years have passed away;
And Time, the all-destroying, never
    May smite their beauty with decay.

"But here while yet one views it
    All fades and falls and mocks the eye;
Earth's pomp — Destruction's foot pursues it,
    To glance of joy is scowl of sorrow nigh.

"That Earth herself will be no more when thou shalt still be, and in other dwelling-places under other forms of existence shalt enjoy thy God and his creation. Already hast thou in this Earth enjoyed much good. In it thou hast obtained that form of being, in which as a son of Heaven it is allowed thee to look around about thee and above. Seek then to leave it in contentment, and bless it as the green field where thou a child of Immortality wert wont to play, and as the school where in sorrow and in joy thou wast reared to manhood. Thou hast no farther claim upon it; it has no farther claim on thee: crowned with the cap of freedom and girt with the girdle of Heaven, take up thy pilgrim staff with cheerfulness, and go on thy way." *Herder.*

Schiller born 10th Nov! 1759 at Marbach on the Neckar in Würtemberg (same year with our Burns). His father a Regiment surgeon made a prayer for the boy — see the Life in his *Werke*. Well answered.— What *were* the regulations in the school at Stuttgard? Who was *Schubart*[1]? (51)— p. 72? Mad[am von] Wollzogen was Schiller's protectress when he fled. *Philosophische Briefe* what vol.? Vol. 4.—His sailing in the Elbe, 100. Went to Weimar, saw Herder and Wieland, and was induced by the latter to take part in the Teutsches Mercur. Invited by the F[rau] Wollzogen to come and see her, he went to Rudolstadt and saw his future wife. First interview with Goethe 106. *Blarney* about history. Garden at Jena 118. Kant's phil. 120. Goethe's *Naturgeschichte und Morphologie.* Jean Paul's Aesthetic. Schiller about to write an epic poem on Fred-

[1] Carlyle answers this question in a long note in the appendix to his *Life of Schiller*, 1825.

erick the Great — 124 Critical remarks — Marries 130 — Garden 132 — Help from Denmark 133 — Schiller's critique on Bürger vol. 8.— The *Xenien?* little Epigrams — are they to be found in S's *Werke?* Musenalmanach? *Horen?* 158. Walks 164. Where is Fr. Schlegel's *Vorlesungen über die neuere Geschichte* to be had? Schiller's triumph at Leipzig 176 — Translate 193 &c. *decent?* 197 Must see the 8 vol. of *W[erke]* —

> Morn, alas! thy radiance tinges
> A dead sepulchral stone.
> And Eve thou throw'st thy crimson fringes
> But o'er his slumber dark and lone.

Must see Jean Paul's *Vorschule der Aesthetik*.

"Schiller was tall in stature, of a strong frame, yet withal very lean. His body appeared visibly to be suffering under the keen emotions of his spirit; but from his pale countenance, from his softly kindling (animated) eye, there gleamed a still enthusiasm; and his high free brow announced the deep thinker. His cheeks and temples were hollow, the lips a little prominent, the chin rather long and projecting. The colour of his hair was inclined to reddish.

"In his external appearance there was little to recommend him. In walking he kept his eyes constantly bent on the ground; he often failed to notice the salutations of acquaintances that passed him, but on hearing such he caught hastily at his hat and gave his cordial *Guten Tag.*"

His rather stiff and slow gait, and plain apparel were not calculated to draw attention towards him; and there was farther in his manner a sort of painful backwardness visible in large companies, and especially at court. In such situations he felt himself oppressed by a certain constraint, he saw outward show made the ruling principle; and both were at variance with the inmost feelings of his nature.

It was in the circle of his family or of a few intimate friends that he became unembarrassed, talkative, mirthful with all that loved mirth. He enjoyed no little recreation in a club which had been formed at Weimar, and for which he and Goethe composed some social songs.

To the noisy and tumultuous pleasures of life Schiller was nowise inclined. Among the few public places which he used to frequent the Playhouse was the only one on which he bestowed any positive attention. It was especially his pleasure and concern to communicate instruction to the actors. The first reading of the new pieces was always gone thro' in his or Goethe's house; a circumstance which of itself must have had the most beneficial influence on many a player of talents. Schiller indeed required much; he made strict demands on professors of the art. Yet after the successful exhibition of any of his later dramatic works, he was wont to invite the more distinguished players to a supper in the Town-house, where they had merry songs, improvisoes, and all kinds of jokes and diversion.[1]

Schiller was in the highest degree benevolent and the friend of men. His heart felt the sorrows of another like his own. He often said he wished for nothing more than to see all men happy and contented with their lot.

As a proof how upright his feelings were, how far from petty self-interest, I may give this example. A well-known Bookseller hearing that Schiller was busied with Wallenstein waited upon him at Weimar, and offered him 12 gold Carolins per sheet for the property of the piece. The price was considerably higher than Cotta of Tübingen, with whom he was then treating on the same subject, used to give; but Sc[hiller] did not for that reason think of changing his publisher: "Cotta" he said "deals honestly (*solide*) with me, and I with him," and sent the Bookseller

[1] Among other things the player Genast used at S's request to recite the Capuchin's speech out of Wallenstein. T C.

away without even the hope of any future trade with him.

Schiller has delineated himself with very striking correctness. "The childlike character" he observes "which genius expresses in its works, it shews also in its morals and private life. It is *bashful*, for nature is ever so; but it has not the art of *concealment*, for concealment is taught of perversion alone. It is *wise*, for nature never can be otherwise; but it is not *crafty*, for that can by Art alone be. It is true to its character and inclinations, but not so much because it walks by principles as because nature with all her aberrations ever returns to her former aim, ever brings back her original desire. It is *prudent*, nay *timid*, for genius ever remains a secret to itself; but it is not anxious, not knowing the dangers of the path it treads. We know little of the private life of the greatest geniuses; but even that little as it has been transmitted to us proves the truths here stated."[1]

Schiller[2] seems to have been a very worthy character, possessed of great talents, and fortunate in always finding means to employ

---

[1] From "*Naive und Sentimentalische Dichtung.*" The passage was much better translated by Carlyle in his *Life of Schiller*, 1825, p. 299.

[2] The following passage is cited by Mr. Froude, in his *Life of Carlyle*, Vol. i, p. 196, but inaccurately; for example, instead of "Schiller seems to have been," he prints, "Schiller was."

them in the attainment of worthy ends.  The
pursuit of the Beautiful, the representing of
it in suitable forms, and the diffusion of the
feelings arising from it, operated as a kind of
religion in his soul.  He talks in some of his
essays about the *Aesthetic's* being a *necessary*
means of improvement among political socie-
ties : his efforts in this cause accordingly
not only satisfied the restless activity, the
desire of creating and working upon others,
which forms the great want of an elevated
mind, but yielded a sort of balsam to his
*conscience ;* he viewed himself as an Apostle
of the sublime.  Pity that he had no better way of satisfying it !  A play-house shews
but indifferently as an arena for the Moralist: it is even inferior to the synod of the
theologian.  One is tired to death with his
and Goethe's *palabra* about the nature of the
fine arts.  Did Shakespeare know aught of
the *aesthetic ?*  Did Homer ?  Kant's philosophy has a monstrously gigantic appearance
at a distance — enveloped in clouds and darkness, shadowed forth in types and symbols
of unknown and fantastic derivation, there is
an apparatus and a flourishing of drums and
trumpets and a tumultuous *Marktschreyerei*
as if all the Earth were going to renew its
youth; and the *esoterics* are equally allured
by all this pomp and circumstance, and re-
pelled by the hollowness and airy nothing-

ness of the ware which is presented to them. Any of the results which *have* been made intelligible to us turn out to be like Dryden in the Battle of the Books, a helmet of rusty iron large as a kitchen-pot and within it a head little bigger than a nut.[1] What is Schlegel's great solution of the mystery of life — "the strife of necessity against free-will"?[2] Nothing earthly but the old, old story that all men find it difficult to get on in the world; and that one never can get all his humour out! They pretend to admit that nature gives people dim intimations of true beauty and just principles in Art; but the *bildende Künstler* and the *richtende*[3] ought to investigate the true foundations of these obscure intimations and set them fast on the basis of reason. Stuff and nonsense? I fear it is. The people made finer pieces of workmanship when there was not a critic among them. Just as people do finer actions when there was no theory of the moral sentiments among them. Nature is the sure guide in all cases; and per-

[1] Carlyle changes Swift's imagery. "The Helmet was nine times too large for the Head, which appeared Situate far in the hinder Part, even like the Lady in a Lobster, or like a mouse under a canopy of State, or like a shrivled Beau from within the Pent-house of a modern Perewig." *The Battle of the Books*, 1704, p. 263.

[2] For "free-will" Mr. Froude prints "the will," and five lines below, for "dim intimations" he substitutes "true intimations."

[3] "The artist and the critic."

was no theory of the moral sentiments among them. Nature is the sure guide in all cases; and perhaps the only requisite is that we have judgement enough to apply the sentiment implanted in us without our effort to the more complex circumstances that will meet us more frequently as we advance in culture, or move in a society more artificial. Poor silly sons of Adam! you have been prating on these things for 2 or 3000 years, and you have not advanced a single hair's breadth towards the conclusion. Poor fellows! and poorer me! that take the trouble to repeat such insipidities and truisms.

But what if I do not proceed? Why then terar still, —dum I cannot help it! This is the end and beginning of all

(marginal drawing labeled: TERAR DUM PROSIM)

haps the only requisite is that we have judgement enough to apply the sentiment implanted in us without our effort to the more complex circumstances that will meet us more frequently as we advance in culture, or move in a society more artificial. Poor silly sons of Adam! you have been prating on these things for 2 or 3000 years, and you have not advanced a single hair's breadth towards the conclusion. Poor fellows! and poorer me! that take the trouble to repeat such insipidities and truisms.

But what if I do not *prodesse?* Why then *terar* still,—*dum* I cannot help it! This is the end and beginning of all philosophy— known even to Singleton the Blacksmith— "we *must* just do the best we can, boy!" Oh most lame and impotent conclusion.

Welch eine Lage! von tausend ängstlichen Trieben herumgejägt, von Bedürfnissen, Thätigkeiten, zu wirken gefodert, gefodert, gefodert; und *kann nichts* thun! Armseliger Narr! Ich möchte tollwerden — und was denn? Schweige![1]

Herder hated the new philosophy and wrote against it bitterly. Wieland did the same, for it shattered into powder the gim-crack

---

[1] "What a condition! driven by a thousand disquietudes, by necessities, by actualities, obliged to work, obliged, obliged, and can do *nothing!* Poor fool! I am ready to go mad — and what then? Silence!"

palace of French *rationality* which he had been chopping and putting together all his life for *Teutschland*. Goethe was wiser than either; he was clear for "letting it have its time as everything has." This was right, old Goethe, and I respect thee for the solid judgement of this saying. Herder was not deterred by the terror of novelty, or yet by too strong a rational faculty, too keen a judgement. He believed in & greatly prized the *sculldoctrine* of D$^r$ Gall! But Gall had borrowed his fundamental ideas from Herder's *Ideen zur Phil.*— *there* it lay! — and the new philosophy was driving fiercely butting like a wild Bull against the orthodox creed of Germany. The poor divinity-students returned from the prelections of Fichte and Reinhold at Jena full of the most undigestible conceptions; and appeared before the *Consistoriums* in a state approaching to derangement, and like deranged people frequently out-argued the old stagers who believed orthodoxly. Great scandal thereby; and severe reprehensions. One young divine shot himself at Weimar. Fichte appears actually to have been a metaphysical atheist. I wish I fully understood the philosophy of Kant! Is it a chapter in the history of human folly or the brightest in the history of h. wisdom? Or of both mixed? And in what degree?

That distinction of Coleridge's (which he

## THOMAS CARLYLE.

has borrowed or may have borrowed from Woltmann) about *talent* and *genius* is completely *blarney*,— futile, very futile.— I am tired and stupid and almost *red-wud*.[1]

   Farewell my books & pens and papers
      My studies great and small!
   Most pitiful sickly farthing tapers
      Are the sciences one and all.

   Oh once your flaring light inspir'd me
      I certainly thought you moons or suns
   And I ran to catch what somehow fir'd me
      As many a crack-brained ninny runs.

   And when at length nigh broken-winded
      I approached thro' many a *glarry*[2] way
   The *glim was nearly douced*[3] or I was blinded
      I strained my eyes, knew nought to think or say.

   Forsooth ye are most worthy rare devices
      How clearly ye tell us all we know!
   And where we know not, still your art supplies us
      With excellent words and terms to come & go.

      [1] Distracted.
      [2] Miry.
      [3] The light was nearly sunk.

## NOTE BOOK OF

Oh that the *old one* had you to make
A kirk and mill of if so inclined!
And this accursed queasy grumbling stomach
Would cease to trouble an ignorant mind!
March, 1823.            Andrew Macnay.[1]

Poet should preach or poetize for his *age*, should elevate and beautify the ideas which are current in *it:* be *Zeitbürger* as well as *Staatsbürger.*—[Schiller] Review of Bürger.

" What went before and what will follow me I look at as at two black imperforable curtains, which hang down at the two extremities of human life, and which no living man has yet drawn aside. Many hundreds of generations already stand before them with their torches and guess and guess about what lies behind. Many see their own shadows the forms of their passions enlarged and put in motion on the curtain of futurity; they shrink in terror at their own image. Poets, philosophers and founders of states have painted it with their dreams — more smiling or more dark as the sky above them was gloomy or cheerful; and their pictures deceive at a distance. Many jugglers too make profit of this universal curiosity, and by

---

[1] On the margin against the preceding verses the following note is written: "At Mrs. Wilkie's, near Pilrig Street, Leith walk; I still dimly remember the night. (*May*, 1866!)—"

their strange disguisings (*Vermummungen*) have set the outstretched Fantasy in astonishment. (But) a deep silence reigns behind this curtain; none once within it will answer those he has left without; all you can hear is a hollow echo of your question, as if you shouted into a chasm. To the other side of this curtain we are all bound, and men catch it with shuddering, uncertain who may stand behind to receive them, *quid sit id, quod tantum morituri vident.*[1] Some incredulous persons there have been who maintained that this curtain but made a fool of men, and that nothing could be seen because nothing *was* behind it; but to convince these persons, the rest pushed them hastily behind." *Schiller, Geisterseher.* [Vierter Brief.] IV. 350.

---

    As gentle shepherd in sweet eventide
When ruddy Phœbus gins to welk in west
High on a hill, his flock to vewen wide,
Marks which do bite their hasty supper best.
              Faery Queen B. 1. c. 1. [st. 23.]

    A little lowly hermitage it was
Down in a dale hard by a forest's side,
Far from resort of people that did pass
In travel to and fro: a little wyde (distant?)
There was a holy chapel edified,

---

[1] 'What that may be which only those see who are about to die.'

> Wherein the hermit duly wont to say
> His holy things each morn and eventide:
> Thereby a chrystal stream did gently play,
> Which from a sacred fountain welled forth
> away.               (*Do.*) [st. 34.]

Error (battle with) graphical but beastly — Morpheus' establishment is well done. " Bold bad man " is Spenser's — it might have been anybody's.

> By this the northern waggoner had set
> His sevenfold teme behind the stedfast starre
> That was in ocean waves yet never wet,
> But firm is fixt, and sendeth light from farre
> To all that in the wide deep wandring arre:
> And chearefull chaunticlere with &c.
>                     B. i. c. ii. [st. 1.]

> At last the golden orientall gate
> Of greatest Heaven gan to open fayre;
> And Phœbus fresh as bridegroom to his mate,
> Came dauncing forth shaking his deawie hayre
> And hurld his glistring beams thro' gloomy
> ayre          B. i. c. v. [st. 2.]

This Spenser pleaseth me well: he is a *dainty body* as ever I met with.

---

*Hactenus* in May 1823: it is now November;[1] six weary months have passed away,

---

[1] 3 Nov.ʳ 1823. (at Kinnaird! with Bullers.) [T. C. 1866.] Since the spring of 1822 Carlyle had remained in Edinburgh as tutor of Charles and Arthur Buller. In May, 1823, the Buller family removed to Kinnaird House,

another portion from my span of being; and
here am I, in a wet dreary night, at Kinnaird,
with no recollections or acquisitions to fill
up that space with; but the recollection of
agonized days and nights, and the acquisition
of a state of health worse than it ever was!
My time! my time! My peace and activity!
My hopes and purposes! Where are they?
I could read the curse of Ernulphus,[1] or something twenty-times as fierce, upon myself and
all things earthly. What *will* become of me?
Happiness! Tophet must be happier than
this: or they — But *basta!* It is no use talking. Let me get on with Schiller; then with
Goethe. "They that meaned at a gowden
gown gat aye the sleeve." I shall not even
get the listing.— These remarks are interesting to read some months after date: I will
continue them. Schiller is in the wrong vein.[2]
Laborious, partly affected, meagre, bombastic:
too often it strives by lofty words to hide
littleness of thought. Would I were done
with it! Oh Carlyle if ever thou become
*happy*, think on these days of pain and darkness; and thou wilt join trembling with thy
mirth! Forth! Forth! 3d November 1823.

a beautiful place near Dunkeld on the Tay, and here Carlyle resided with them till, in 1824, they removed to London. See *Life*, Vol. i.; *Early Letters*, Vol. ii.

[1] See *Tristram Shandy*, Book iii. c. 11.

[2] The *Life of Schiller* which he was now engaged in
writing.

List of French books — to be read if ever I have leisure and fall in with them. I transcribe them from the back óf an old Recipe (the *Bumming* Doctor's — which I recollect well) about three years of age. Some one or two I have read since then, and omit here. I suppose they must originally have been taken from Chenevix' Articles in the Edin[r] Review; but I am not certain.

Malebranche, Recherche de la vérité.
Condillac, La Logique.
Bonnet, Psychologie.
De Gerando, Des Connaissances humaines.
De Tracy (on Grammar, Ideology &c.)
Garat ? Charron ? La Mothe Le Vayer ?
Nicole, Essais de Morale.
St Lambert (weak I understand). Principes de morale chez toutes les nations.

Servan, Dupaty, Calonne, Siéyès, Lebrun, Roederer, Marbois, Neucours, Garnier, Perreau, Bexon, Bourguignon, Pastoret, Lacretelle, De Bonald.

These are marked "*polit.*" in the List: except Siéyès and Lacretelle and Calonne I never before heard their names, and know nothing about them. Lacretelle I have read one work of, the *Religious Wars:* it is a poor flashy performance, readable because its subject is interesting; and the author tho' half a puppy has been *among* thinkers in the 19th century.

THOMAS CARLYLE.

Cardinal de Retz.   Mémoires
Brantôme.
Froissart (this I should like best)
Seyssel (who is *he ?*)   Velly, Mezeray.
Vertot, D'Orléans, Dubos, Anquetil (bad)
Rulhière, Thouret, Royou (short hist. of France)

I should also like to have Montaigne; the vol. of his Essais that I read was very good — at least very curious.— Here are some rhymers:

Marivaux, Malherbe, Balzac, Voiture, Scuderi, Scarron, &c. I have long wished to read *Grammont:* the parts of it known to me are excellent. What of Mad. de La Fayette, her Princesse de Clèves? Abbé Prévost his Cleveland? Laclos? Louvet? Pigault-le-Brun? — These I fear are but of the small deer I have too long been used to. There is something in a weak or dull book very nauseous to me. Reading is a weariness of the Flesh; after reading and studying about two scores of *good* books, there is no new thing whatever to be met with in the generality of libraries; repetitions a thousand times repeated of the same *general idea;* feelings, opinions and events — all is what we might anticipate. No man without Themistocles' gift of *forgetting* can possibly spend his days in reading.[1] Generally about the age

[1] "Vain was the prayer of Themistocles for a talent of Forgetting." *Sartor Resartus,* Book i. ch. viii. The

of five and twenty he should begin to put the little knowledge he has acquired (it *can* be but little) from books to some practical use. If I could *write*, that were *my* practical use. But alas! alas! Oh! Schiller what secret hadst thou for creating such things as Max and Thekla when thy body was wasting with disease? I am well nigh *done* I think. To die is hard enough at this age; to die by inches is very hard. But I *will* not, tho' all things human and divine are against me, I will not.

Schiller Part II. is off to London three weeks ago: it was very bad. Part III. I am *swithering* to begin: would it were finished. I spent ten days (wretchedly) in Edin[r] and Had[n]; I was consulting doctors, who made me give up my dear *nicotiana* and take to mercury. I sometimes think I shall recover. December 14th.

I am to write letters and then *begin* Schiller. May God bless all my Friends — my poor Mother at the head of them! Oh it sometimes comes over me like the shadow of Death — the thought that we ARE all parting from one another — each moving his several his destined inevitable way, Fate driving us on, inexorable dead relentless Fate! No deliverance? (*mit dem Fusse stämpfend*).[1] No

saying of Themistocles is reported by Cicero, *De Oratore*, ii. 74.
[1] "Stamping with the foot."

## THOMAS CARLYLE.

help? Alas poor sons of Adam! But no more of this.

31st December 1823. The year is closing; this time eight and twenty years I was a child of three weeks old lying sleeping in my mother's bosom.
>Oh little did my mither think
>That day she cradled me,
>The lands that I should travel in
>The death I was to die.[1]

Another hour and 1823 is with the years beyond the flood. What have I done to mark the course of it? Suffered the pangs of Tophet almost daily, grown sicker and sicker, alienated by my misery certain of my friends, and worn out from my own mind a few remaining capabilities of enjoyment, reduced my world a *little* nearer the condition of a bare haggard desart, where peace and rest for me is none. Hopeful youth Mr. C.! Another year or two and it will do; another

---

[1] To this, Carlyle in 1866 appended the words "Extract by Burns —*first* came to me thro' T. Murray."

The stanza is from the beautiful ballad, of much discussed origin, known as "Mary Hamilton," or "The Queen's Marie." See Child's *English and Scottish Popular Ballads*, Vol. iii. p. 379 and Vol. v. p. 246. "We first hear of the Scottish Ballad," says Professor Child, "in 1790, when a stanza is quoted in a letter of Robert Burns." The letter is to Mrs. Dunlop, 25th Jan. 1790. See Currie's *Works of Burns* 1800, ii. 290.

year or two and thou wilt *wholly* be the *caput mortuum* of thy former self, a creature ignorant, stupid, peevish, disappointed, brokenhearted; the veriest wretch upon the surface of the globe. My curse seems deeper and blacker than that of any man: to be immured in a rotten carcass, every avenue of which is changed into an inlet of pain; till my intellect is obscured and weakened, and my head and heart are alike desolate and dark. How have I deserved this? Or is it merely a dead inexorable Fate that orders these things, caring no jot for merit or demerit, crushing our poor mortal interests among its ponderous machinery, and grinding us and them to dust relentlessly? I know not; shall I ever know? "Then why don't you kill yourself Sir? Is there not arsenic? Is there not ratsbane of various kinds, and hemp and steel?" Most true, Sathanas, all these things *are:* but it will be time enough to use them when I have *lost* the game, which I am as yet but losing. You observe Sir I have still a glimmering of hope; and while my friends (my *friends*, my Mother, Father, brothers and sisters) live, the duty of *not* breaking their hearts would still remain to be performed when hope had utterly fled. For which reasons, even if there were no other (which however I believe there are), the benevolent Sathanas will excuse me. I do not design to be a *suicide:*

## THOMAS CARLYLE.

God in Heaven forbid! That way I was never tempted.[1]

But where is the use of going on with this? I am not writing like a reasonable man: if I am miserable, the more reason there is to gather my faculties together, and see what can be done to help myself. I want health, health, health. On this subject I am becoming quite furious: my torments are greater than I am able to bear. If I do not soon recover I am miserable for ever and ever. They talk of the benefit of ill-health in a moral point of view.[2] I declare solemnly without exaggeration that I impute nine tenths of my

---

[1] "From Suicide," says Teufelsdröckh, "a certain aftershine (*Nachschein*) of Christianity withheld me: perhaps, also, a certain indolence of character; for was not that a remedy I had at any time within reach?"
*Sartor Resartus*, Book ii. ch. vii.

[2] In later years Carlyle wrote, in recalling this period of his life, "Other things might have made me hopeful and cheerful as beseemed my years,— had not *Dyspepsia*, with its base and unspeakable miseries, kept such fatal hold of me, which, perhaps, needed only a *wise* Doctor, too, as I found afterwards, when too late! Heavy, grinding, and continual has that burden lain on me ever since to this hour, and will lie; but I must not complain of it, either; it was not wholly a *curse*, as I can sometimes recognize, but perhaps a thing needed, and partly a *blessing*, though a stern one, and bitter to flesh and blood." *Early Letters*, ii. 114, note. See also in regard to his sufferings from dyspepsia, *Reminiscences*, ii. 107, 110, 113, 115, 140. The evil was augmented by *unwise* doctors, who dosed him with active but ineffectual drugs, weakening his health without remedying the specific trouble.

present wretchedness, and rather more than nine tenths of all my faults to this infernal disorder in the stomach. If it were once away I think I could snap my fingers in the face of all the world. The *only* good of it is the *friends* it tries for us and endears to us! Oh! there is a charm in the true affection that suffering cannot weary, that abides by us in the day of fretfulness and dark calamity — a charm which almost makes amends for misery. Love to my friends — Alas! I may almost say relations! — is now almost the sole religion of my mind.

In a month we quit this place; they[1] with a view to amusement, I in the hope of getting *Meister* printed.[2] I have better hopes of *Meister* than I had; tho' still they are very

[1] The Bullers.
[2] In the spring of 1823 Carlyle had engaged with an Edinburgh bookseller to translate *Wilhelm Meister*. In a bit of reminiscences, printed in his *Early Letters*, ii. p. 201, note, Carlyle, describing his life at Kinnaird House, says: "I lodged and slept in the *old* mansion, a queer, old-fashioned, snug enough, entirely secluded edifice, sunk among trees, about a gunshot from the new big House; hither I came to smoke about twice or thrice in the daytime; had a good oak-wood fire at night, and sat in a seclusion, in a silence not to be surpassed above ground. I was writing *Schiller*, translating *Meister;* my health in spite of my diligent riding, grew worse and worse; thoughts all wrapt in gloom, in weak dispiritment and discontent, wandering mournfully to my loved ones far away; *letters* to and from, it may well be supposed, were my most genial solacement. At times, too, there was something of noble in my sorrow, in the great solitude among the rocking winds, but not often."

faint. *Schiller* P. III. I began just three nights ago. I absolutely could not sooner. These drugs leave me scarcely the consciousness of existence. They take away all ambition, all wish for aught beyond deep sleep if that might by any means be made to fall upon me. I am scribbling not writing Schiller: my mind *will* not catch hold of it; I skim it, do as I will, and I am anxious as possible to get it off my hands. It will *not* do for publishing separately: it is not in my natural vein. I wrote a very little of it tonight, and then went and talked ineptitudes at the house. Also there is mercurial powder in me, and a gnawing pain over all the organs of digestion — especially in the pit and left side of the stomach. Let this excuse the wild absurdity above.

Half past eleven! The silly Denovan[1] is coming down (at least so I interpreted his threat) with punch or wishes; which curtails the few reflections this mercury might still leave it in my power to make. To make none at all will perhaps be as well. It exhibits not an interesting but a true picture of my present mood — stupid, unhappy, by fits wretched, but also dull, dull and very weak.

> Now fare thee well old twenty-three!
> No power, no art can thee retain

[1] Probably the butler of the Bullers.

Eternity will roll away — Eternity!
And thou wilt *never* come again.

And welcome thou, young twenty-four,
Thou bringer to men of joy and grief!
Whate'er thou bringest, in sufferings sore
The patient heart in faith will hope relief.

— Here thou art by Jove! Denny is not come. Good night! "To whom?"

There is a good explanation of the *aequo pulsat pede* in Swinburne's travels: it seems creditors and other aggrieved persons still signify their determined hostility and resolution to be avenged by *kicking at the door of the debtor.*

I have sometimes been reading Boswell's Life of Johnson lately: Johnson talked well but not more wisely than a common man; at least very little more. Also his conversation is only *intellectually* felicitous; he has no strange ideas to shew, no curious modes of feelings; he only does well what every one can do in some way. I figure Goethe or even Coleridge to be more curious persons. Poor Goethe is "again dangerously ill" the papers say. *Basta!*

7th January [1824]. Such three days I have had with the introduction to *Schiller!* — and then to reject it all! I must insert some of it here to-morrow, for it cost me labour, and should not be totally lost. To-night I am going to write to Hadn.[1]

Last Sunday came the Times newspaper with the commencement of *Schiller* Part II extracted. So Walter[2] thought it on this side zero! I believe this is about the first compliment (most slender as it is) that ever was paid me, by a person who *could* have no interest in hoodwinking me. I am very weak: it kept me cheerful for an hour; even yet I sometimes feel it.— Certainly no one ever wrote with such tremendous difficulty as I do. *Shall* I learn to " write with ease "—*ever* learn ?

I have got half a new idea to-day about history: it is more than I can say for any day the last six months.

---

CONFESSIO FIDEI *of Wallensteins Jäger* (23)

    purposed
I mean to be quite easy and gay,

To see something new on each [new] day,
  In    joys of the          sharing
To the moment merrily trusting,
      [On the past or the future] not thinking or caring
No thought on the past or the future casting.

So, look, to the Kaiser I sold my bacon

And by him let the charge of all needful be taken

[1] To Miss Welsh, at Haddington.
[2] The proprietor of the *Times*.

## NOTE BOOK OF

          mid       thickest
Order me on to the whistling cannon shot
      Rhine's wild roaring tide
Over the red and roaring Rhine,

The second man must go to pot,—
              not minding a jot
I mount and ride without loss of time.
      d'ye see
But farther I humbly beg and pray,
           you'd let me be
That in other things I may have my way.

*Marketenderin.*

    Cousin! since then I've been wide and far,

    To-day we come, to-morrow we go,
        the rough rude
    As it happens the besom of war
        Pleases to shove us
    Shakes one and sweeps one to and fro

*Wallenstein.*

    Our life was but a battle and a march,

    And like the wind's blast, never-resting, homeless,

    We stormed across the war-convulsed earth.

*Kürassier—*

    This sword of ours is no plough or spade

    You cannot delve or reap with the iron blade;
      falls
    For us there springs no seed, no cornfield grows

## THOMAS CARLYLE.

The soldier no home nor kindred knows,

Must wander over the face of the earth,

Must warm his hands at another's hearth,
From              must onward roam
To the pomp of towns he bids adieu,

In the village green with its cheerful game,
    laughing times of
In the vintage [time] or harvest-home,

No part or lot can the soldier claim.
    In the place of goods of worth or pelf
Tell me then what goods or worth he has
What has he unless
If the soldier cease to honour himself?
    naught to call
Leave him nothing of his own, what wonder
  fellow
The creature should burn and kill and plunder?

VERSES TO MRS. BULLER ON SEEING HER IN A HIGHLAND DRESS—

By Dr. John Leyden.
[From a copy in Mrs. B.'s handwriting—
Jan.y 1824.]

That bonnet's pride, that tartan's flow,
  My soul with wild emotion fills;
Methinks I see in fancy's glow
  A princess from the land of hills.

O for a Fairy's hand to trace
  The rainbow tints that rise to view!
That slender form of sweeter grace
  Than e'er Malvina's poet drew!

NOTE BOOK OF

> Her brilliant eye, her streaming hair,
> Her skin's soft splendour to display
> The finest pencil must despair
> Till it can paint the solar ray.
> Calcutta, 1811.

"It must be night ere Friedland's star will beam."

21st September, 1825. Hoddam Hill.[1] *A hiatus valde deflendus!* Since the last line was written, what a wandering to and fro, how many sad vicissitudes of despicable suffering and inaction have I undergone! This little book and the desk that carries it have passed a summer and winter in London, since I last opened it; and I their foolish owner have roamed about the brick-built Babylon, the sooty Brummagem, and Paris the Vanity-fair of our modern world! My mood of mind is changed: is it improved? *Weiss nicht.*[2] This stagnation is not peace, or it is the peace of Galgacus' Romans: *ubi*

---

[1] A little Farm, not far from Ecclefechan, with a cottage for dwelling-house where "at noon-day (26th May, 1825) I established myself, set up my Books, and bits of implements and *Lares;* and took to doing *German Romance* as my daily work." "This year at Hoddam Hill . . . lies now like a not ignoble russet-coated Idyll in my memory; one of the quietest on the whole, and perhaps the most triumphantly important of my life." *Reminiscences,* ii. 178.

[2] "I know not."

## THOMAS CARLYLE.

*solitudinem faciunt pacem appellant.*[1] How difficult it is to free one's mind from *cant;* how very seldom are the principles we act on clear to our own reason! Of the great nostrums " forgetfulness of self " and " humbling of vanity," it were better therefore to say nothing: in my speech concerning them I overcharge the impression they have made on me, for my Conscience like my sense of Pain or Pleasure has grown dull, and I secretly desire to compensate for laxity of *feeling* by intenseness of *describing.* How much of these great nostrums *is* the product of necessity? *Am* I like a sorry hack *content* to feed on heather while rich clover seems to lie around it at a little distance, *because* in struggling to break the tether it has almost hanged itself? O that I *could* " go out of the body to philosophize!" That I could even feel as of old the glory and magnificence of things till my own little *me* (*mein kleines Ich*) were swallowed up and lost in them! (partly cant!) But I cannot, I cannot! Shall I ever more? *Gott weiss.* At present I am but an *abgerissenes Glied*, a limb torn off from the family of Man, excluded from activity, with Pain for my companion, and Hope that comes to all rarely visiting me, and what is stranger rarely desired with vehemence!

[1] " Where they make a solitude they call it peace." Tacitus, *Life of Agricola*, c. 30.

Unhappy man in whom the body has gained mastery over the soul! Inverse Sensualist, not drawn into the rank of beasts by pleasure, but driven into it by pain! Hush! Hush! Perhaps this *is* the Truce which weary Nature has conquered for herself to re-collect her scattered strength! Perhaps like an Eagle (or a Goose) she *will* " mew her mighty youth " and fly against the sun, or at least fish paddocks with equanimity, like other birds of a similar feather; and no more lie among the pots, winged, maimed and plucked, doing nothing but chirp like a chicken in the coop for the livelong day. " Jook and let the jaw gae by,"[1] my pretty Sir: when this solitude becomes intolerable to you, it will be time enough to quit it for the dreary blank which society and the bitterest activity have hitherto afforded you. You deserve considerable pity Mr. C.; and likewise considerable contempt. Heaven be your comforter my worthy Sir, you are in a promising condition at this present; sinking to the bottom, yet laid down to sleep; Destruction brandishing his sword above you, and you quietly desiring him to take your life but spare your rest! *Gott hilf Ihnen!* — Now for Tieck and his Runenberg: but first one whiff of generous narcotic! How gladly " we love to wander on the plain with the summit in our eye! "

[1] " Duck, and let the wave go by."

## THOMAS CARLYLE.

Ach Du meine Einzige, die Du mich liebst und Dich an mir anschmiegst, warum bin Ich Dir wie ein gebrochenes Rohr! — Sollst Du *niemals* glücklich werden! Wo bist Du heute Nacht? Mögen Friede und Liebe und Hoffnung deine Gefährten seyn! Leb' wohl![1]

3d December 1826.  Comley Bank. Married! Married! — *Aber still davon!*[2] — and of a thousand other things. I am for business.[3]

Read Sir T. Browne's *Religio Medici* and *Urne Burial* lately; his *Vulgar Errors* I had already seen at Kew. The *Urne Burial* I think (with little C. Lamb) the best; tho' much of it is little edifying at this time of day, or perhaps rather to *this* sort of reader. Disquisitions on all imaginable modes of sepulture; of mummies, bones, cremation, inhumation, &c., &c., not without here and there a straggling tone of pathetic feeling, or a gleam of philosophic thought. But the conclusion of the Essay is absolutely beautiful. A still, elegiac mood; so soft, so deep,

---

[1] "Ah, mine only one, thou that lovest me and clingest to me, why am I but as a broken reed for thee. Art thou never to be happy! Where art thou to-night? May Peace and Love and Hope be with thee! Farewell!"

[2] "But of that no words."

[3] Carlyle's marriage had taken place on October 17; and he and his wife were established at Comley Bank, a house in the northwestern suburbs of Edinburgh, where they lived till they went to Craigenputtock, in 1828.

so solemn and tender, like the song of some departed Saint flitting faint under the everlasting canopy of Night! An echo of deepest meaning from "the great and famous nations of the Dead." Browne must have been a good man. What was his history? What the *real* form of his character? for as yet I see him only thro' a glass darkly. "*Abiit ad plures*, he hath gone to the greater number." Life of him by Dr. Johnson. *Qualis?*

Two infants reasoning in the womb about the nature of *this* life might be no " unhandsome " type of two men reasoning here about the life that is to come.[1]

*Lux Jovi, tenebrae Orco*,[2] one stroke up, the other stroke down.

These bones have slept quietly "beneath the drums and trampling of three conquests."[3]

The *Quincunx* I like worst: full of learning, but of a kind little to my taste, tho' I blame not the taste of it in him. The last chapter is better than all the rest. "The hunters are up in Persia"[4] has been quoted

---

[1] "A dialogue between two infants in the womb concerning the state of this world, might handsomely illustrate our ignorance of the next." *Urn Burial*, ch. 4.

[2] "Light unto Pluto is darkness unto Jupiter." *Garden of Cyrus, or the Quincuncial Lozenge*, ch. 4. "Lux Orco, tenebrae Jovi; tenebrae Orco, lux Jovi." Hippocrates *de Dieta;* S. Hevelii *Selenographia*. These references are from Wilkin's note on the passage in his edition of Browne's Works, iii. 436. [3] *Urn Burial*, ch. 5.

[4] "To keep our eyes open longer were but to act our

already in some Magazine. Browne stands midway between a poet and an orator.

His *Religio Medici* is most readable of any, and indeed contains many true and praiseworthy things; only he gives *himself* far too good and orthodox a character, thereby leaving us no refuge but to envy him in despair of doing so likewise; or, what will be a more common resource, to disbelieve in and reject him as a moral *dandy*.

I should like to know more of him; but I ought to understand his *time* better also. What *are* we to make of this old English Literature? Touches of true beauty are thickly scattered over these works; great learning, solidity of thought; but much, much that now cannot avail any longer. Certainly the *spirit* of that age was far better than that of ours; is the *form* of our literature an improvement intrinsically, or only a form better adapted to *our* actual condition? I often think, the latter. Difficulty of speaking on these points without affectation. We know not what to think, and would gladly think something very striking and pretty.

Sir W. Raleigh's *Advice to his Son;* worldly-wise, solid, sharp, farseen — The motto: " Nothing like *getting on !* " — Of Burleigh's Advice the motto is the same; the execution, if

Antipodes. The huntsmen are up in America, and they are already past their first sleep in Persia." *Garden of Cyrus*, ad fin.

I rightly remember, is in a gentler and more loving spirit. Walsingham's *Manual*[1] I did not read. These men of Elizabeth's are like so many Romans or Greeks. Were we to seek for the Cæsars, the Ciceros, the Pericles', Alcibiades' &c. of England, we should find them nowhere if not in that era. Wherefore are these things hid? Or worse than hid, presented in false tinsel colours, originating in affected ignorance and producing affected ignorance? Would I knew rightly about it, and could present it rightly to others! For hear alas! this mournful truth, nor hear it with a frown:[2] *There*, in that old age, lies the *only* true *poetical* literature of England. The poets of the last age took to pedagogy (see Pope and his School) and shrewd men they were; those of the present age to ground and lofty tumbling, and it will really do your heart good to see how they vault!

[1] A book attributed to Elizabeth's crafty and unscrupulous minister, Sir Francis Walsingham, entitled *Arcana Aulica or Walsingham's Manual of Prudential Maxims*. It was not published till long after Walsingham's death.

[2] Dr. Johnson's impromptu while Miss Reynolds was pouring tea:

"Yet hear, alas! this mournful truth,
Nor hear it with a frown,
Thou can'st not make the tea so fast
As I can gulp it down."

Hawkins' *Life of Johnson* (1787), p. 345, and Dr. Birkbeck Hill's *Johnsonian Miscellanies* (1897), ii. 315.

## THOMAS CARLYLE.

It is a damnable heresy in criticism to maintain either expressly or implicately that the ultimate object of Poetry is sensation.[1] That of Cookery is such, but not that of Poetry.

Sir W. Scott is the great *Restaurateur* of Europe: he might have been numbered among their Conscript Fathers; he has chosen the worser part, and is only a huge *Publicanus*. What is his novel, any of them? A bout of champagne, claret, port or even ale drinking. Are we wiser, better, holier, stronger? No: we *have been* — amused. O Sir Walter, thou knowest too well, that *Virtus laudatur et* alget.[2]

Byron, good, generous, hapless Byron! And yet when he died he was only a *Kraftmann*, *Power-man* as the Germans call them. Had he lived he would have been a Poet.[3]

---

I have read Shaftesbury's *Characteristics* (same date), but found it wofully difficult to keep my attention fixed on him. He is not at all a man according to my heart; yet I would not deny him the credit of being a

[1] "Sensation, even of the finest and most rapturous sort, is not the end but the means." "State of German Literature" (1827), *Essays*, i. 47, where the true nature of Poetry is discussed.

[2] "For Virtue is but drily prais'd and starves." Dryden, Translation of Juvenal's *Satires*, i. 113.

[3] "With longer life all things were to have been hoped for from Byron." "State of German Literature," *Essays*, i. 59.

*man,* that is a person conscious of himself and his actions, fixed and determined on all sides, not walking in darkness as others lead him, but in light as he leads himself. He is a Ciceronian sceptic, a philosopher of the eclectic school; the child of Culture not of Nature; except to the men of his own age, therefore, or to the historian of them, he has little to say. Scarce a thought of his dwells with me, I am sorry to say; for which tho' I and my circumstances are partly, we are *not* wholly to blame.

"Pinch" for strait; "anything worth"; "for good and all" &c. &c.—

What shall I say of Herder's *Ideen zur Philosophie der Geschichte der Menschheit?*[1] An extraordinary Book, yet one which by no means wholly pleaseth me. If Herder were not known as a devout man and clerk, his book would be reckoned atheistical. Everything is the effect of circumstances and organisation: *Er war was er seyn konnte!*[2] The breath of life is but a higher intensation of Light and Electricity! This is surely very dubious, to say no worse of it. Theories of this and kindred sorts deform his whole work here and there.— Immortality not *shewn* us, but left us to be hoped for, and believed by Faith. Yet this world, as he thinks,

[1] "Ideas on the Philosophy of the History of Mankind."
[2] "He was what it was possible for him to be."

## THOMAS CARLYLE.

sufficiently explainable without reference to another: *Humanität* the great object of Nature in all her arrangements of society; from the Troglodytes to the wits of Paris and Weimar. *How* true is this? At least this ought to be *our* object. On the whole Herder shews much of it himself. If any thing he has a leaning to the *East.* But indeed he loves all men and all things: his very descriptions of animals and inanimate agencies are animated, cordial, affectionate; much more so those of *men* in their varied *Thun und Treiben*,[1] tho' perhaps the former are not less poetical.

Strange ideas about the Bible and Religion; passing strange we think them for a clergyman. Must see more of Herder: he is a new species in some degree; a sort of *Browne redivivus?*— O Athens, *modern* Athens! Andrew Thomson *versus* J. Gottfried Herder; the "Apocryphal Controversy" *versus* the Philosophy of Man! Certainly we are the most intellectual people in nature at present.—

Tieck's *Genoveva* is a poetical play. Golo,[2] I think, is best. Grimoald even has some touch of beauty. Genoveva second best. Martel one of the worst; and all the Saracens.

[1] "Doing and dealing."
[2] Golo, Grimoald, and the rest are characters in the play.

Plan of it imitated from *Götz von Berlichingen?* Too much beautiful description of nature. Fine scene with the witch in Strasburg. Benno's death, &c., &c.

Good Märchen, *Melusine*, in his own style follows.— Tieck is next to Goethe — now that Richter is gone.

Hans Sachs is a curious fellow; both in age and character; full of humour, reading, honesty, good nature; of the quickest observation, three hundred years old, and — a shoemaker, what a strange medley may we not expect![1] Is his way of treating Heaven, Christus, &c. like that of our old Mysteries? See the *Tailor with the flag; St. Peter and the Landsknechts*, &c.— Story of the water-doctor which I have heard applied to *Habbie Bell of Shortrig!*[2] In like manner the *Monk and Miller's wife:* so stories travel.— The *Narrenschneiden* I think the best of his pieces: the *Holen-Krapfen*[3] is curious but more local in its interest.— What of these poetical *Zunfts?*[4] Where are they to be learned of?

*S. Ranisch* life of Hans Sachs (Altenb. 1765); Reformationsalmanach, 1821, by Chr. Niemeyer. Büsching has edited Sachs.—

---

[1] See Carlyle's essay on the "State of German Literature" (1827), *Essays*, Vol. i.

[2] Shortrig is the name of a farm in Dumfriesshire; Habbie Bell most likely the tenant of it. A. C.

[3] Das Krappfen-holn.   [4] "Guilds."

## THOMAS CARLYLE.

Books recommended in Herder.

Beausobre, Mosheim, Brucker, Walch, Jablonski, Semler (writers on the Church opinions; the three last unknown to me).

Caylus, St. Palaye — their writings collected from the Acad. des Inscriptions.

Pfeiffer (on Church matters).

Koch's Table des revolutions (trivial?)

Fischer, Sibirische Geschichte

Whiston (What are his hist. & theological works?)

Rösler's Bibl. der Kirchenväter.

Praise of Gibbon, p. 340 note.

Gatterer's Abriss der Universalgeschichte (Göttingen 1773).

Mascou's Geschichte der Deutschen (Leipz. 1727).

Lucan, Mela, Columella, two Senecas, Quintilian, Martial, Florus, Columella — Spaniards.

Velasquez, History of Spanish poetry — in German also (Göttingen 1769).

Ferrara's Hist. of Spain.

Mannert's Geographie der Griechen und Römer (much praised).

F. C. J. Fischer, Sitten und Gebräuche der Europäer im 5 und 6 Jahrhundert (1784).

Fischer's Geschichte des deutschen Handels (The same Fischer?)

Le Bret's History of Venice.

## NOTE BOOK OF

Möser's Osnabrückische Geschichte.
Curne de Ste. Palaye, Chivalry of the Middle Ages (in various treatises).
{ Reiske (orientalist), zum Thograi.
{ Cardonne (do)
Poiret, Arnold (writers on *Mystik*).
Füssli, Geschichte (Ketzer- und Kirchen-) of the middle age.
Middleton's Life of Cicero praised p. 203.
Grellmann, Historisch Versuch über die Zigeuner.
Historical materials for the Slavonians, p. 290. Müller, Sulzer only known to me.
Meierotto über die Sitten und Lebensart der Römer. Berlin, 1776.
Paruta (who was he? Wrote on the Romans like Machiavel).
Winckelmann, Geschichte der Kunst. (Must see that work).
Heyne, Demster, Buonarroti on the Etruscans — also Paralipom. Passerii (!) Florence 1723-67.
Spon, Stuart, Chandler, Riedesel's Travels in Greece.
Heyne, Opuscula Academ.
Meiners, Geschichte der Wissenschaften in Griechenland und Rom.
Gillies has translated Lysias and Isocrates.
Parrhasius painted the *Demon Atheniensium* (strange mixture), Pliny.
The Chest of Cypselus (Heyne's Essay on)

— his mother hid him in a κυψέλη (chest) & saved him from the Bacchiadae.
　Eichhorn, Ges. des Ostindischen Handels.
　Anquetil du Perron (orientalist).
　Pallas, Nordische Beiträge.
　Maillac, Hist. générale de la Chine.
　Camper, Dutch comparative anatomist — facial angle.
　Forster, Zimmermann, Geographers.
　Chardin, Voyages en Perse.
　Reimarus (a naturalist. *Triebe der Thiere* (are there two R's?)
　Blumenbach de varietate gen. hum.
　Linnaei Amoenitates Academ.

5th Dec<sup>r</sup>. To-morrow I write out a Prospectus for a "Literary Annual Register." Not at all likely that the Bibliopolists will undertake such a thing at present; however we will try.

To-day I have done, thought, said or seen — nothing. *So fliehen meine Tage!*[1] Why are the *hommes bornés* so happy? Or is their happiness rather *cause* than *effect?* Willie Bell of Newfield[2] is not *happy;* yet he is *limited* enough.

Few men have the secret of being at once determinate (*bestimmt*) and open; of know-

---

[1] "Thus my days fly."
[2] Newfield, a farm near Ecclefechan and Hoddam Hill.
　　　　　　　　　　　　A. C.

ing what they do know, and yet lying ready for farther knowledge.

Coleridge says, " Many men live all their days without ever having an *idea;* and some of them with thousands of things they CALL *ideas;* but an Idea is not a Perception or Image, it cannot be *painted*, it is infinite." Such was his meaning (not his words): I half or three-fourths seem to understand him.

---

*Literary Annual Register* might be the title of a work performing, for the intelligent part of the reading world, some such service as our many *Forget-me-nots*, *Souvenirs* &c seem to perform for the idle part of it. A work which should exhibit by such means as the Author found most attainable a compressed view of the actual progress of *Mind* in its various manifestations during the bygone year. It might consist:

1. Of Biographical portraits of distinguished persons lately deceased; the year 1827 might contain Byron, Parr, Jean Paul, Talma &c.; delineated with some degree of care and minuteness, in the style of the *German Romance* (ein sehr unbekanntes Werk [1]) only at greater length, and with a more flowing, popular and anecdotic aspect. Not a dead detail of this or that man's actions and writings chronologically arranged, and backed with *pièces*

[1] "A very obscure work."

*justificatives;* but an attempt, at least, to bring a likeness of him before the reader; for which purpose it would naturally be necessary first to have a likeness of him before oneself.

2. Of Essays, Sketches, Miscellanies, of various sorts, but all tending to exhibit the distinctive phases of our existing style of Literature, Morals and Manners, to point out its merits, and not hide its short-comings and perversions; on which points several things might be adduced not a little surprising and perhaps unpalatable to the optimists and mob of gentlemen, that write with ease. *Mechanics' Inst[itutes], Doctrine of Utility* &c. &c.

3. Of Critiques, accompanied with considerable extracts, of the few really good books (or rather of the most considerable books) produced lately in England, Germany, France, Italy. This might be an interesting but ought not to become too extensive a department of the work. By right it should be an " Essence of Reviewing," a spirit of the literary produce of the year.

4. If there was any one (such might perhaps be found) to give a similar account of the *works of Art* for the year; the chief statues, pictures, engravings, a sheet or two might very profitably be allotted to that purpose.

5. In case no better might be, I myself would undertake to say something about

*Science;* to gather from Journals foreign and domestic, something like a view of its actual condition and progress within the year. On this point to obtain help were no difficult matter.

6. Tho' we propose to waive the consideration of political and civil history, restricting ourselves purely to what is intellectual & moral; yet any such incidents, misfortunes, delusions, crimes, heroic actions as seemed strongly to illustrate the spiritual condition of man in our time, it would be well to collect, to sift, and preserve with as much accuracy as might be. The *Prince Hohenlohe,* the *Genevese Persecution,* the *Commercial Joint Stock Mania,* the *Catholic Association* &c. (provided correct information could be obtained regarding them) were well worth a few words.

Such are the leading elements of which this work might consist. These ought not to be arranged in distinct sections (at least not all of them), so much depends upon the particular details of each individual year; but mingled together in such manner as the Author might judge most artist-like, and best calculated to fulfil his object, that of conveying to the reader the truest impression *he* can give him of the general progress of intellect during the past year.

Poetry would not be excluded here and there could such be come at; but from all

## THOMAS CARLYLE.

" Odes written at —" " Lines to —" " Verses on —" &c. &c. and the whole genus of " Songs by a Person of Quality," good Lord deliver *hooz !* [1]

If the Bookseller liked he might add a register of Patents &c. &c. and so recommend his work to " practical men." (N. B. Not do. *Essayons !*) [2]

7th December. "My whole life has been a continued night-mare; and my awakening will be in Hell." — Tieck.

" There is just one man unhappy; he who is possessed by some *idea* which he cannot convert into an *action*, or still more which restrains and withdraws him from action." — Goethe. *Wie wahr !* [3]

"The end of man is an *Action* not a *Thought*." — Aristotle. [4]

How many eulogies of Activity, and Nothing acted!

Adam is fabled by the Talmudists to have

---

[1] Vulgar Scotch pronunciation of "us." A. C.
[2] The project of this *Annual Register* came to nothing.
[3] " How true ! "
[4] " Hadst thou not Greek enough to understand thus much : *The end of Man is an Action, and not a Thought*, though it were the noblest ? " *Sartor Resartus*, Book ii. ch. vi. In his " Wotton Reinfred,"— his unfinished story, written in 1827,— Carlyle again cites this saying, calling it "the wisest thing he [Aristotle] ever said." The doctrine was one of the permanent articles of Carlyle's creed. The original is in the *Ethics*, x. 9. 1.

had a wife before Eve: she was called Lilis (see *Faust — Goldne Hochzeit*); and their progeny was all manner of terrestrial, aquatic and aërial — Devils! — Burton.[1]

Read Zacharias Werner's Life by Hitzig,[2] and his *Mutter der Makkabäer*, a Judaico-Christian Tragedy, attempting very unsuccessfully to represent the spirit of religious martyrdom. The play is surely bad in most respects. No character exhibited in the slightest degree probable; no incident grounded on reality, no interest grounded on anything. Some half score of ghosts figure in the piece: *Salome* and her seven sons have no more life than the wooden characters in the well-known popular drama of *Punch*, *Jason* the renegade Highpriest, *Antiochus*, *Nicanor* (in a less degree) &c. &c. could have been tolerated by no true Artist. This is the only work of Werner's known to me; and surely it has not increased my desire of becoming farther acquainted with him. I doubt much if he was a Poet.

But what of his history? A cloudy, vague, mystic existence it was; the true secret of which I am not sure that I can unravel. To

[1] Cited in *Sartor Resartus*, Book i., ch. v.
[2] In 1827 Carlyle published a long article on Werner. See *Essays*, Vol. i. He expresses in it a similar opinion on the *Mutter der Makkabäer* to that which he formed on first reading it.

say that he was mad is saying little: the way in which fools unravel difficulties of that sort. His mother was mad; for she believed herself to be the Virgin Mary, and that her son was the Shiloh promised to the Gentiles: but there is no such fatuity recorded of her son. He had been extremely dissolute, it would appear, in early life; so much so that his character was utterly broken, and his sentient principles (strong at first) had got complete mastery over his intellectual. There is no knowing, in this case, *what* we may be brought to believe. On the whole he was no good man, this Werner: a sensualist, vain, truckling, greedy, bent from first to last not on being *wise* and good but on being *gratified* and what he called happy. Chateaubriand, Schlegel (Friedrich), Werner and that class of men among ourselves, are one of the distinctive features of this time, when Babylon the Great is about to be destroyed (her doom is inevitably appointed) by Infidelity; and Religion (too much interwoven with that same Babylon) has not yet risen on her ruins, but seems rather (only seems) as if about to perish with her.— A curious Essay might be written on the customary " Grounds of human Belief."— Yes, it is true! the decisions of Reason (Vernunft) are superior to those of Understanding (Verstand): the latter vary in every age (by what laws?), while the former last forever, and are the same in all forms of manhood.—

O Parson Alison, what an *Essay on Taste* is that of thine![1] O most intellectual Athenians, what accounts are those you give us of *Morality* and *Faith*, and all that really makes a man a man! *Can* you believe that the Beautiful and Good have no deeper root in us than "Association," "Sympathy," "Calculation?" Then if so, whence in Heaven's name, comes this sympathy, the *pleasure* of this Association, the *obbligante* of this Utility? You strive, like the witch of the Seethor (in Hoffmann) "to work from the *outside* inward," and two inches below the surface you will never get.

---

Sir William Temple's works, I read several weeks ago; but for facts or opinions I scarcely find that I have drawn any from him, or indeed aught at all but the elevated, calm, accomplished, mildly sceptical, yet on the whole wise and benignant figure of the man himself. Indeed he was no Artist or speculative Philosopher, but a man of action; almost the *beau idéal* of an English gentle-

[1] *Essays on the Nature and Principles of Taste*, by the Rev. Archibald Alison, Edinburgh, 1790. A second edition in 1811 was reviewed with high praise by Jeffrey in the "Edinburgh Review." Alison's Theory of Taste was based on the principle of "association." Dust lies heavy on the book now.

man in the era of Queen Anne. He is not the best of conceivable characters, but I doubt greatly if we have improved.

---

*Apud se*, "his own man." Burton (strange book that of his, yet full of amusement).[1]

"Conclusum est contra Manichaeos,"[2] cried Thomas Aquinas smiting the table with his fist, and forgetful that he was at supper with — King Louis.

"Ad haras aptius quam ad aras."[3] — "Mould-warps." "A gripe." "Pullus Jovis et gallinae filius albae."[4] "To overshoot himself" — go beyond his means.

"Crambem bis coctam reponere," set out cabbage twice boiled — a nasty enough dish.

The philosophy of Voltaire and his tribe exhilarates and fills us with glorying for a season; the comfort of the Indian who warmed himself at the flames of his — bed.

[1] This and the next entries are derived from *The Anatomy of Melancholy*.
[2] "It is settled against the Manichaeans."
[3] "Fitter for styes than for altars."
[4] "Jove's chick, and the son of a white hen." Festus, in his *de Significatione Verborum*, says, "The ancients were wont to call the boy whom anyone loved his chick *(pullum)*," and gives a curious instance of one Q. Fabius, nicknamed "Ivory" because of the whiteness of his skin, who was called *pullus Jovis*, because scarred on the rump and not otherwise hurt by a thunderbolt. It appears from Juvenal, *Satire* xiii. 141, that the phrase *gallinae filius albae* was used proverbially for a favorite of fortune.

"Deliquium." "Eating his own heart," Homer of Bellerophon. Il. 3. (6 ?)

A clown that killed his ass for drinking up the moon, *ut Lunam mundo redderet*[1] — In Lud[ovicus] Vives. True of many critics of sceptics: the latter have not drunk up the *moon* but the *reflexion* of it in their own dirty puddle; therefore need not be slain.[2] — (Who was Lud. Viv. ? Should have a modern Biographical Dictionary.)

"Inter pontem et fontem, inter gladium et jugulum,"[3] mercy *may* come to suicides.

An asse and a mule went laden over a brook — the former with wool, the latter with salt; which being wetted was much lightened. "He told the Asse, who thinking to speed as well wet his packe likewise at the next water, but it was much the heavier, hee quite tired" — (Camerarius *Emb.*) Burton. 230 —

A fool or a physician at *forty ?* Tiberius thought at *thirty*. Tacit. Annal. 6.[4]

---

[1] "That he might restore the Moon to the world."

[2] Carlyle repeated this story at the end of his essay on Voltaire (1829). *Essays*, Vol. ii.

[3] "Between the bridge and the stream,
Between the sword and the throat,—"
with which compare the distich
"Between the saddle and the ground,
He mercy sought and mercy found."

[4] "He was accustomed to scoff at the arts of physicians, and at those who after they were thirty years old required advice as to what was serviceable or hurtful to their health." *Annals*, vi., 46.

## THOMAS CARLYLE.

" Mosses " (for bogs) "and Marishes."

" Nequaquam nos homines sumus, sed partes hominis; ex omnibus aliquid fieri potest, idque non magnum, ex singulis fere nihil."[1] (*Scaliger.*) Not men but man.

" Sutton Coldfield in Warwickshire (where I was once a grammar Scholar) " — Burton.

" Oldbury in the confines of Warwickshire, where I have looked about me with great delight, at the foot of which hill I was born." — And in a note — " At Lindley in Leicestershire the possession and dwelling-house of *Ralfe Burton* Esquire my late deceased Father."

" Aganella a faire maid of Corcyra " held by some to be the inventor of Tennis; " for shee presented the first ball that ever was made to Nausicaa the daughter of King Alcinous, and taught her how to use it."

" Carew's Survey of Cornwall," sometimes quoted by Johnson.—Ascham.—

Domitian delighted to catch flies; Augustus to play with nuts amongst children; Alexander Severus was often pleased to play with whelps and young pigs.

*Glucupicron. Nocumentum Documentum.*

---

[1] "In no wise are we men, but parts of man; out of all something, at best no great thing, may be made; out of individuals, scarce anything."

NOTE BOOK OF

Julius Caesar Scaliger was born at Ripa near Verona in 1484. His parentage was much contested in his lifetime: he himself (and his son) pretended a descent from the Princes of Verona; but on this matter their assertions were "strongly doubted." Julius led a wandering life; first a page at some Court or other; more than once in the army, then as physician at Agen in France and Paris where he died. He began to study in his 30$^{th}$ year: his first publication was in [his] 47$^{th}$. A man of vehement parts and temper; *malleus scientiae*, who amassed knowledge (of the kind then to be had) without stint; but seems to have been in regard to wisdom very scantily endowed even to the last. There is no life of him that I know except some details by his son Joseph Justus Scaliger, a man also of huge erudition, who removed from Paris to a Professorship at Leyden (with, according to Ménage, a most contemptuous *congé* from Henry IV.) where he wrote Annotations, (Equations of the Calendar?) and Letters concerning the Antiquity and Splendour of the Scaliger family; and after a fair space "deed and did nocht ava'."[1] Has Bayle any Life of him or his father?

---

Roger Ascham's Life has been written by

[1] " Sandy Blackadder, factor at Hoddam (long ago), a heavy, baggy, big, long-winded man, was overheard

## THOMAS CARLYLE.

Dr. Johnson; Edward Grant, the tutor of his son Giles, has likewise printed an *Oratio de Vita et Obitu Rogeri Aschami*. Chief work is his *Schoolmaster* (which I must see); his *Toxophilus;* Letters; Letter on the State of Germany. Born 1515 (at Kirby Wiske near Northallerton): died 1568. Was Queen Elizabeth's Tutor; a Protestant, yet tolerated even favoured by Queen Mary. He seems to have liked good living; and is reported to have been very fond of " dice and cockfighting "! Yet undoubtedly a good sort of man, and one well worth my study, which accordingly by Heaven's grace he shall not fail to have. (18<sup>th</sup> December.)

---

Accipite cives veneti quod est optimum in rebus humanis: res humanas contemnere.[1]— Sebastian Foscarini, Doge of Venice, made this be engraved on his tomb.[2]

one day, in a funeral company which had not yet risen, discoursing largely in monotonous undertones to some neighbors about the doings, intentions, and manifold insignificant proceedings of some anonymous fellow-man; but at length wound up with ' and then he deed and did nought ava.'" *Letters and Memorials of Jane Welsh Carlyle*, i. 315, note.

[1] " Hear, citizens of Venice, what is best in human affairs: to hold them in low esteem."

[2] This inscription may have been engraved on the tomb of a Doge, but no Sebastian Foscarini was ever Doge of Venice. Marco Foscarini was Doge in 1762, but the words cited seem of earlier date.

Ludovicus Vives was a Spaniard, at one time Tutor to Queen Mary, but obliged to leave England on occasion of Queen Catherine his patroness' divorce, which he disapproved. He is buried at Bruges. His works are in two folios (it seems), analogous to those of *les Daciers, les Saumaises*.[1]

Sir T. Browne was born in 1605 at London; father a merchant: he died on his birthday 1682 at Norwich. Knighted by Charles II. The *Religio Medici* made a mighty noise at its first appearance, over all Europe. *Alexander Ross* opposed Browne on this as on all occasions. Whitefoot, a contemporary, has written a life of Browne (prefixed I suppose to some edition of his works): so also has Dr. Johnson (do.). Browne had travelled over Europe; been at Padua university &c.

---

Of Burton the Anatomiser of Melancholy little is to be learned. Materials for a life of him were collected by Peck. (Who *were* these Pecks, Birches, &c.?) He was a younger brother; was born 1576; obtained some little ecclesiastical preferment at Oxford and in the neighborhood; was a melancholic man himself; the saddest in his dark fits and one of the gayest and brightest in his lucid intervals. A firm believer in astrology; and

[1] See *ante*, p. 4.

dying at the very time his horoscope calculated by himself, some people suspected he "had assisted Nature." His book undertaken for his own cure did not cure him: in his black mood he used to go down to the river side (at Oxford?) and listen to the ribaldry of the boatmen, which made him laugh till his sides ached again. *Credat Apella!* If the man had been rightly melancholy, all the ribaldry in nature would have failed to win a smile from him. His Brother (elder) wrote a history of Leicestershire (their native county) for which he is thought worthy of the main article in the *Biog. Britan.*

## FABLE.[1]

Once upon a time a man, somewhat in drink belike, raised a dreadful outcry at the corner of the market place, "that the world was all turned topsy-turvy, that the men and cattle were all walking with their feet uppermost, that the houses and earth in general (if they did not mind it) would fall into the sky; in short that unless the most prompt means were taken, things in general were on the high road to the Devil." As the people only laughed at him, he cried the more vehemently, nay at last began to objure to foam and imprecate, when a goodnatured auditor

[1] "This and the following fables are reprinted, slightly altered, in Carlyle's *Essays*," Vol. i, Appendix.

going up took the Orator by the haunches, and softly inverting his position, set him down — on his feet. The which upon perceiving his mind was staggered not a little. "Ha? Deuce take it!" said he, rubbing his eyes: "so it was not the world that was hanging by its feet, but I that was standing on my head!"

Public Censor, *Castigator Morum*, Radical Reformer, by whatever name thou art called! Have a care! Especially if thou art getting loud, look to it!

Pilpay Junior.

The instruction communicated by Fable is in its nature chiefly *prohibitive;* therefore not the highest species, which latter belongs to the Province of Poetry. (?)

———

Nothing harder than to form a true judgement of foreign minds and forms of character, especially if they are separated from us by diversity of language, institution, date and place. A Bond-street Tailor can pronounce with extreme readiness and certainty about the beauty or deformity of foreign costumes, and his judgement will be satisfactory to other Bond-street Tailors; a Winckelmann with far less readiness and certainty, and other Artists and Critics may dispute or deny his decision after all. For the one only asks himself: Does this differ from the fashion of Lord Petersham? but the other: Does

## THOMAS CARLYLE.

this differ from the fashion of God Almighty?
—You Travellers, Moores, Clarkes, Russels, Morgans! Ye should think of this.

---

What a fine thing a *Life of Cromwell*, like the *Vie de Charles XII* would be! The wily fanatic himself, in his own most singular features, at once a hero and a blackguard pettifogging scrub; and the wild image of his Times reflected from his accompaniment! I would travel ten miles on foot to see his *soul* represented as I once saw his body in the Castle of Warwick.—

" Nave ferar magna an parva, ferar unus et idem." [1]
" Durum et durum non faciunt murum."[2] Two railers elicit no truth?—" Self-do, self-have." (" His ain wand 'll whip him.").— Helena's *Nepenthe*,[3] supposed by some to be Borage, by others to be Opium, by others (me among them) to be — nothing.

### FABLE II.

" Gentlemen," said a Conjuror, one fine starry evening, "these Heavens are a *deceptio*

[1] " Whether borne on a great ship or a small, let me be borne one and the same man."— Horace, *Epist*. II. ii. 200.
[2] " Hard and hard make not a wall."
[3] A drug "which lulls sorrow and strife, and brings forgetfulness of every ill." *Odyssey*, iv. 221.

*visus*, what you call stars are nothing but fiery motes in the air: wait a little I will clear them off, and shew you how the matter really is." Whereupon the Artist produced a long syringe of great force; and stooping over the neighbouring puddle filled it with dirty water, which he then squirted with might and main towards the zenith. The wiser of the party unfurled their umbrellas; but most part looking up in triumph, cried: " Aha, my little stars! are ye out at last? I always thought you cheats: we have long been—" Here the dirty water fell; and bespattered and beblotched these simple persons; and even put out the eyes of several, so that they never saw the stars any more.

Critic! Truth, Beauty, Goodness is the Heaven and the Stars: These, the very meanest of them, no effort of thy syringe is likely to reach: and the higher thy puddle-jet, the weightier and dirtier will be its return! Qui spuit in coelum in se spuit (?)[1]

January, 1827.  Read Mendelssohn's *Phädon*, a half translation, half imitation of Plato's *Phaedon*, or last thoughts of Socrates on the Immortality of the Soul. Plato's work I have never seen but must see. Mendelssohn's is certainly written with great beauty and simplicity: the intro-

[1] "He who spits at heaven spits on himself."

ductory part concerning the *character of Socrates* is almost a model of graceful modest narrative; what follows is in a more difficult style but scarcely less perfect. The work is divided into three Dialogues: the *First* (so far as I can remember) treats of the *highest good* of man, namely wisdom, and proves that it is a *blessing* to get out of the body to *philosophize*. The *Second*, in answer to some objections from two of the interlocutors, endeavours to prove the *immateriality* of the Soul, a necessary condition of its *indivisibility* and *immortality*. It is an answer to the *Freethinkers'* scheme in *Martinus Scriblerus*: "The *Jack* has a meat-roasting *quality;* so likewise, &c."[1] Socrates' arguments turn on this principle: all those *qualities*, indeed all *unity* of any sort perceived in an object, belongs *not* to the object but to the *mind* that sees it; hence this *subject* (the mind) from which all *qualities* originate cannot itself be a quality. (?) It cannot be a *composite* power; because there is in reality no *change* of power produced by a mixture of simple powers, but

[1] "In every jack there is a meat-roasting quality, which neither resides in the fly, nor in the weight, nor in any particular wheel of the jack, but is the result of the whole combination: so in an animal, the self-consciousness is not a real quality inherent in one being (any more than meat-roasting in a jack) but the result of several modes or qualities in the same subject." *Memoirs of the extraordinary Life, Works, and Discoveries of Martinus Scriblerus*, Book 1, ch. 12.

only a *modification*, the secret of which escaping our sense, we call it a *new* power, but falsely. An acid and an alkali produce a neutral salt: what then? Tho' to our eyes, taste, touch &c, the properties of this new substance seem entirely different from those of its component parts, the truth is not so; there is nothing in it, but some virtues of the acid obstructed, forwarded, cancelled, diverted &c., by the virtues of the alkali; and so in *all* corporeal compositions: the *newness* of the power is only in our way of viewing it. Hence the component parts of the soul would be all *souls;* hence the soul is *one;* hence indestructible, indivisible, immortal. The *Third* Dialogue meets the objection of Cebes: How do we know that the soul is not to fall into *sleep* (if not death) forever? It is chiefly Mendelssohn's own; talks of Perfectibility (not of man alone but of the whole universe); Unhappiness of disbelief in these truths, &c. &c; much less scientific and more rhetorical than the foregoing. On the whole, it is a good book;—and convincing? *Ay de mi!* These things, I fear, are not to [be] *proved*, but *believed;* not seized by the Understanding but by Faith. However, it is something to remove *errors*, if not introduce truth; and to shew us that our analogies drawn from corporeal things are entirely inapplicable to the case.

## THOMAS CARLYLE.

For the present, I will confess it, I scarce see how we can reason with *absolute* certainty on the nature or fate of *any*thing; for it seems to me we only see our own perceptions and their relations; that is to say, our soul sees only its own partial *reflex* and manner of existing and conceiving. I should have this cleared up: How does Kant manage it? — (" White men know nothing.")

" A weeping woman is as much to be pitied as a goose going barefoot." — Burton.
" Done to his hand." — South. (What a fierce, dogmatical, sarcastic, unchristian priest is South!)
" Sleeveless errand." — Burton.
" Looks out *at* window." — B. " all out " — quite.
Mali corvi malum ovum;[1] Cat to her kind.
" Non quâ eundum, sed quâ itur."[2]
It was Petronius that wrote that hemistich:—
 Primus in orbe deos fecit Timor.
(Was he the author of the *sentiment?*[3] it is now trite enough.)

[1] " The bad egg of a bad crow." The origin and significance of this proverb are discussed by Erasmus, *Adagiorum* Chil. i. Cent. ix. Prov. 25.
[2] " Not where one should go, but where one is going."
[3] " Fear first made the gods in the world." The words form part of the first verse of a fragment ascribed to Petronius, but they are also part of a verse by Statius,

NOTE BOOK OF

*C'est nos craintes qui ont formé les cieux;* a line at which I once in the Théâtre Français heard all the people standing up raise a vehement shout of approval. Unhappy France! Talma was then acting, Œdipe: he is now dead; one by one the stars go out.

" As common as a Barber's chair."

7 Jany 1827. After a considerable struggle, and not without many interruptions, I have this morning finished Burton's *Anatomy of Melancholy.* What to say of the Book *parum constat.*[1] Dr. Johnson was in the habit of commending it;[2] but chiefly, I should think, from its subject, which with the Doctor was constitutionally interesting. Burton doubtless had " a pleasant wit," a taste also for the Beautiful (especially if it was the Comfortable at the same time) and still more for the Curious; but his mind looks as if he had surveyed the world chiefly from the observatory of his Library in an Oxford College; and found the gratification of these his tastes not so much in actual inspection of things with

*Thebaid*, iii. 661. It is impossible, in the uncertainty concerning the date of Petronius, to say to which poet they actually belong.

[1] " Is hardly clear."

[2] " Burton's 'Anatomy of Melancholy' he said, was the only book that ever took him out of bed two hours sooner than he wished to rise." Reported by the Rev. Dr. Maxwell in his *Collectanea:* printed by Boswell in his *Life of Johnson.*

his simple vision, as with *armed vision*, armed by all the reading that it ever entered into the head of lazy Bookworm to engage with. He is a singular, a thinking, observing, *character-volle* man; but of no admirable gifts (except memory), and of little or no wisdom but what distinguishes the greater part of English country Parsons; a cleanly, comfort-loving, Greek-and-Latin-reading, but often too sectarian and self-conceited, and withal shallow and ill-informed race of persons. As a scientific treatise his Book is worth absolutely nothing: I may say there is no conclusion in it in which *anything* is concluded. Dunce neutralizes Dunce, and one quack prescription stands (like bane and antidote) fronting with hostile visage another as quackish. The work is an *olla podrida ;* you cannot eat the cursed dish as it stands cooked before you; and tho' you pick many a most dainty morsel from it, you wish with your whole soul the man had been contented with *purveying*, and never tried to *cook* the viands at all. (*Schlechtes Bild!* [1]) Burton however is over, and I do not purpose soon to trouble him again.

---

*Sapientia prima est stultitiâ caruisse* [2] "The prime wisdom is to have got rid of folly;" fully

[1] "A bad image."
[2] — sapientia prima Stultitia caruisse. *Horace*, Epist. i. i. 41.

as well thus: *Stultitia prima est sapientiâ caruisse;* the case of all material metaphysicians, most utilitarian moralists, and generally of all *negative* Philosophers, by whatever name they call themselves.

It was God that said Yes: it is the Devil that forever says No.[1]

Leibnitz and Descartes found all Truth to rest in our seeing and believing in God: we English have found our seeing and believing in God to rest on all Truth; and pretty work we have made of it!

Why dost thou despise that ignorant and ill-mannered man, while thou pitiest and helpest that poor and ragged one?— I give the pauper sixpence and my blessing; but if his rags offend the nostril, I contrive to make him go his ways.

Is not Political Economy useful; and ought not Joseph Hume and MacCulloch to be honoured of all men?— My cow is useful, and I keep her in the stall, and feed her with oil-cake and "draff-and-dreg," and esteem her truly: but shall she live in my

---

[1] " The Everlasting No had said: 'Behold, thou art fatherless, outcast, and the Universe is mine [the Devil's].'" *Sartor Resartus*, Book ii. ch. vii.

*parlour?* No, by the Fates, she shall live in the stall!—

## FABLE III.

"It is I that support this household," said a Hen one day to herself: "The master cannot breakfast without an egg, for he is dyspeptical and would die, and it is I that lay it. And here is this lazy Poodle doing nothing earthly, and gets thrice the meat I do, and is caressed all day! By the Cock of Minerva, they shall give me a double portion of corn, or I will strike!" But much as she cackled and creaked, the scullion would not give her an extra grain. Whereupon in dudgeon, she hid her egg in the dunghill, and did nothing but cackle and creak all day. The scullion suffered her for a week; then (by order) drew her neck; and purchased other eggs at six-pence the dozen!

Man! why frettest and whinest thou? This blockhead is happier than thou, and still but a blockhead? So thy services are not adequately repaid? But art thou sure thou dost not overrate them?[1] At all rates it is vain for thee to *strike work* with Providence: He is no Manchester manufacturer; Him thou *canst* not force to thy terms. Believe it he

[1] Cf. *Sartor Resartus*, Book ii. ch. ix., where these reflections are developed.

will do without thee. *Il n'y a point d'homme necessaire.*

16th January, 1827.   *Qui spuit in coelum in se spuit.*[1] (perhaps wrong arranged, for I write from memory.)

Who was Gassendi? and what were his Metaphysics? I have seen his Commentaries on Newton; but know nothing more of him; yet he is said (by Reinhold) to be the father of the existing French Philosophy.

Locke, Hume, Reid &c. &c. are *Empirics;* Descartes, Leibnitz, Kant &c. are *Rationalists.* Which is right? I begin to see some light thro' the clouds in Kantism; tho' Reinhold is somewhat of a Will-o'-wisp guide, I fear. Empiricism, if consistent, they say, leads direct to Atheism!—I am afraid it does.

Yes, Virtue *is* its own reward; but in a very different sense than you suppose, Dr. Gowkthrapple![2] " The *pleasure* it brings "?— Had you ever a diseased liver? I will main-

[1] "Who spits at the sky spits on himself."
[2] "That chosen vessel, Maister Gowkthrapple." *Waverley,* ch. xxix.
In his Essay on Diderot Carlyle speaks of Naigeon, Diderot's biographer, " as a man with the vehemence of some pulpit-drumming Gowkthrapple."

tain, and appeal to all competent judges, that no evil conscience with a good nervous system ever caused *tenth part* of the misery that a bad nervous system tho' conjoined with the best conscience in nature will *always* produce. What follows then? Pay off your moralist, and hire *two* Apothecaries and *two* Cooks. Socrates is inferior to Captain Barclay, and the *Enchiridion* of Epictetus must hide its head before Kitchener's *Peptic Precepts.* Heed not the Immortality of the Soul, so long as you have Beefsteak, Port, and — Blue Pills! — *Das hole der Teufel!* — Virtue is its own reward because it *needs no reward.*

---

The Hildebrands, the Philips and the Borgias
Where are they now? Behind the scene; mute as
The millions whom they butchered in their rage.
Hard task they had, poor men: what was their
    wage?
From God, we know not, but may dread the worst;
From man, a grave and memory forever curst:
Who worships self a foolish thought has ween'd,
Must offer *all,* and find his God — a Fiend.

    (Our cousin Swift has no turn for poetry.)

---

To prove the existence of God as Paley has attempted to do (a Kantean would say) is like lighting a lantern to seek for the Sun: if you look *hard* by your lantern, you may even miss your search.

"My dear Sir," said Captain Esbie, "there is nothing like getting *on*." *Ay de mi!*

"The artist," it has been said, "*collects* beauties and *combines* them; a bright eye from this, a fair round chin from that, a taper form from the other, and so makes up his Venus." Ah no! In this way he will form a bed-quilt or a hearth-rug, but no poem.

A Poem springs, like Minerva from the head of Jove, full armed and complete, if it is to *live* and give life.

---

*Do* we think sometimes, as Schlegel says, without *thoughts?* Or what wind is it that will rend asunder the thick clouds, and shew us the fair golden landscape lying full perfect and ready-formed without our having shaped it, otherwise than in the dark? Yet was not Praxiteles' Jove created in this fashion, when the evening song of the maidens coming from the well *revealed* it to the struggling and long-baffled statuary? There is more in the poet's heart than Mr Alison or Mr Stewart dreams of. Bring it out then an' be hanged!— Eheu!—

### FABLE. [IV]

"What is the use of thee, thou gnarled sapling?" said a young larch-tree to a young oak. "I grow three feet in the year, thou scarcely half as many inches; I am straight and taper as a reed, thou weak and twisted as loosened withe ": — "And thy duration," answered the Oak, " is some third part of man's life; and I flourish for a thousand years. Thou art felled, and sawed into paling, where thou rottest and art burnt after a single summer: of me are fashioned battleships, and I carry mariners and heroes into unknown seas."

The richer a character, the harder and slower in general is its development. Two boys were once of the same class in our Edinburgh school; John ever trim precise and dux, Walter ever slovenly confused and dolt: in due time John became Baillie Waugh, and Walter became Sir Walter Scott.

The quickest and completest of all vegetables is — the Cabbage.

---

The fraction of life will increase equally by *diminishing* the denominator as by *augmenting* the numerator.[1] [March, 1827.]

---

Eschenburg's *Denkmäler altdeutscher Dichtkunst.*

A popular delusion is like smoke: it is vain

[1] " So true it is, what I then said, that *the Fraction of Life can be increased in value not so much by increasing your Numerator as by lessening your Denominator.* Nay, unless my Algebra deceive me, *Unity* itself divided by *Zero* will give *Infinity*." *Sartor Resartus*, Book ii. ch. ix.

to cut into it with swords and maces; leave it alone, and the air will absorb it by degrees. If it is in small quantity, a *fan* may sometimes help you; not if it is in great; but there is *always* hope in the *air*.

---

" Lieber wäre mir's, wenn ich plötzlich stürbe."[1] Winckelmann [letter to Berends] 12 July, 1751.

" Marco Barbarigo and Franc. Trevısano,[2] two *Nobili di Venetia*, whose memory has been preserved in a rare piece of writing," are the only two modern *Friends*, thinks Winckelmann. Where *is* the *Schrift?*[3]

Friendship not once mentioned in the whole New Testament (so also says Hume); und es ist vielleicht ein *Glück* vor die Freundschaft; denn *sonst* bliebe gar kein Platz vor den Uneigennutz;[4] all virtues having there some temporal or eternal *recom-*

[1] "I should be glad if I could die suddenly."
[2] Carlyle cites the baptismal names incorrectly; see the following note.
[3] Letter to Berends, 17 Sept., 1754. The "rare piece of writing" referred to is entitled *Breve racconto dell' amicizia mostruosa in perfezione tra Niccolò Barbarigo e Marco Trivisano*. In Venezia, 1627, in 8vo. A Latin translation seems to have been published the next year.
[4] "And this is perhaps fortunate for friendship, for otherwise there would have been no place for unselfishness." *Id*.

*pense* promised them.— No wonder Goethe calls him a *Heide*.[1]

---

Mein Gott ich wollte sehr gerne sterben, mit grosser Wohllust meiner Seele: so weit habe ich es in der That und Wahrheit gebracht.— Winckel.—[2]

Ich habe nunmehro bald sechs Jahre in Sachsen gelebet, und kann mich nicht entsinnen dass ich recht gelacht habe.[3]

Allein: Erkenntlichkeit verlangen, heisst beynahe — Undank verdienen.[4]

---

Dr. Ebel best traveller in Switzerland.

Villemain, an able writer of *Mélanges*.

Comte de Lacépède — general Hist. of Europe, in 18 vol.— last — 1827. Considerably praised; apparently (from the extract) a *bagpipe*.

Cicognara's History of Sculpture.

---

Spanish writers (from an article in the *Revue encyclopédique*).[5]

---

[1] "Him," that is, Winckelmann, "a heathen."

[2] "My God I would very willingly die, with entire delight of my soul: so far have I attained in deed and truth." Letter to Berends, 17 Sept., 1754.

[3] "I shall soon have lived six years in Saxony, and I cannot recall having once honestly laughed." *Id.*, 6 July, 1754.

[4] "But to require gratitude comes very near deserving unthankfulness." *Id.*, 10 March, 1755.

[5] Tome XXXIII, Feb. 1827. The article is by Muriel.

Leandro-Fernandez de *Moratin* (the younger) regarded here as the restorer of the dramatic art in Spain. Has written five or six Comedies (indifferent apparently and in the style of the French); first in 1788: he seems to be still living.[1]

Barthélemy Torres Naharro — a play-writer of the 16th century.

Pinciano *Philosophy of ancient Poesy.* 1596.

Luzan (*Poetics*, Saragossa 1737) insists on the French principles of taste. Followed up by:

Mayans (*Rhetoric*); Nasarre (prefacer of Cervantes & comedies); Montiano y Luyando (who wrote a comedia of his own).

Nicolas-Fernandez de Moratin (the father) put forth three tragedies — moderates.

Cadahalso, Ayala, Huerta, Palacios wrote plays also about the same time. The best seemingly of only moderate merit; and in imitation of the French.

Sempere (*Best writers under the reign of Charles III.* In Spanish I presume tho' it is not so stated).

"The muses of [Lope de Vega] Montalvan, Calderon, Moreto, Rojas, Solís, Zamora and Cañizares; those of Bazo, Regnard (French?) Laviato, Corneille, Moncin, Metastasio, Comella, Molière, Valladares, Racine, Zabala, Goldoni, Nifo and Voltaire *were astonished at seeing themselves in company*" [p. 469].

[1] He died in 1828.

D. Gaspar Melchior de Jovellanos wrote the *Delinquente Honrado* in 1770; a *drame*, full of honest sentiments, if not of great poetry. *Genre mixte.*

Trigueros, Melendez Valdès, Cristophe-Maria Cortès, had three prizes for plays in 1784. Indifferent.

Tomas Iriarte; a satirist and sensible man, but of no *divine fire.*

Juan de Iriarte — another of the same.

The period between 1780 and 1790 the last years of the reign of Charles III. have been most illustrious; the government anxious to forward improvement in any way, and tho' arbitrary, enlightened and energetic. Here "Jovellanos, Campomanes, Tavira, Roda and Llaguno were at once the pride and the support of philosophy and sound literature."

Boscan and Garcilaso were named *Pétrarquistes*, as their modern successors are called *Gallicistes*.

Hurtado de Mendoza, Saa de Miranda, Montemayor, Herrera (surnamed the *Divine*), Father Louis de Leon, Gil Polo were all Petrarquists, yet "the glory of Spanish Literature."

Abbé Quadrio *Storia poetica* (Italian?) Capmany, Marchena — men of mould?

*What* is the present state of Literature in Spain? How deep and total is our ignorance on that point at present! Is there such a thing as a Madrid Review? A Spanish newspaper would shew to us almost like a Herculaneum one. This should be altered.

N. B. The *Revue Encyclopédique* a review of merit, and worthy to be imitated and improved upon in Britain.

---

Nearly 14 millions of volumes are printed annually in France; of these 400,000 by F. Didot.

665 printing offices in all France; 82 at Paris: in 1825, there were 1550 presses in activity, in Paris 850 of these.

At Paris there are 480 Booksellers, and 84 Boothkeepers; elsewhere 922.

The whole money annually gained in the producing of those 14 to 13 millions of volumes, the Count Daru estimates at 33,750,000 francs; comprehending all from the wages of the ragman to those of the Author. Authors, it seems, come in for a very poor share 500,000 francs being their whole income in France.[1]

In this the newspapers seem *not* to be comprised, at least not the daily ones, the *feuilles quotidiennes.*

---

Grassi, Niccolini, Pezzana, Gherardini, Abbé Romani, Monti, Italian Grammarians of some note.

[1] See *Revue encyclopédique*, xxxiii. 562.

## THOMAS CARLYLE.

Foscolo, Rossetti, Troya, etc., etc. Commentators of Dante, who is at present literally the idol of Italians.

Champollion's system of Phonetic characters has been well received in Italy: Mai, Peyron, Orioli, Valeriani " savans les plus recommendables" do justice to him.

The *Biblioteca Italiana* of Milan and the *Antologia* of Florence contend the first for the *Romantics*, the second for the *Classics ;* a dispute which seems at present to be spreading over most part of Europe. The *Arcadic Journal* of Rome is a *classicist*, but often with more zeal than judgement. The *Anthology* seems to be the best of these three.

Gherardini, the translator and impugner of Schlegel's Dramaturgic lectures.

Manzoni, a poet and romanticist, but who has failed in exemplifying his new theories as applied to the practice of writing tragedies— The *Count of Carmagnola* and *Adelghis* are their titles.

Thomas Grossi a young poet, praised for his *Ildegonda*, has written a new Epic entitled: *The Lombards in the first Crusade ;* which some have said, surpasses *Jerusalem Delivered*. The pamphlets on the subject have been numerous and loud: our French critic asserts modestly that it is neither so good nor so bad as it has been called. Grossi is a *Romantic*.

The town of Milan alone publishes about a score of Journals.

---

Wagner, Weiller, Hegel, Krug, are testators, opposers or commentators of Kant. Eschenmayer also.

Bardili's *Rational Realism*, is it not like the doctrine of Malebranche?

Bouterwek, *System of Virtuality:* "the subjective and objective are nothing without each other."

*Annihilation of the Subject*—Spinosism and materialism.

Fichte's *Transcendental Idealism*, "elimination of the object;" that is deducing the not-me from the me?

Schelling's *Ideal Realism, Philosophy of Nature*, but usually called the *System of Identity;* "because it represents the subject and the object as absolutely identical and commingling and compounding themselves in intellectual intuition."—To this I can attach next to no meaning.

Fichte pretended to have deduced his system from Kant, which Kant eagerly denied. Kant's system of morality is universal in Germany; his metaphysics are disfigured, misrepresented, no longer studied in his own writings, but (says this critic) well worthy of being studied.

Kant reminded me of father Boscovich:

but alas! I have only read 100 pages of his works. How difficult it is to live! How many things to do, how little strength, how little time to do them! T. C.

There is an *Historical Sketch of Industrialism* by one Dunoyer;[1] a political theory this Industrialism of which I have hitherto never heard, and which seems to mean very little if anything. According to the *Industriels* (the chief of whom was one Saint-Simon, reputed mad) the proper object of legislation is not this or that form of political government, but the *means of forwarding useful activity* which is or ought to be the ultimate aim of all existing nations.— God help us! has not this been understood and admitted in *all* systems of political philosophy for the last century. St. Simon was for wonders upon wonders; a sort of priesthood of *Savans*, and what not. "Il se maria pour faire des hommes de genie, et n'eut pas même des enfants."— poor soul!— He said he was descended from Charlemagne. I understand, he is dead. Thierry, Maignien, Auguste Comte are more sensible men, who wrote for him, and allowed themselves to be called his pupils.

---

Mem. To read the Golden Ass of Apuleius. Burney's Life of Metastasio.

[1] In the *Revue encyclopédique*, Feb., 1827.

Of the world, for us, is made a world-edifice; of the Aether a Gas; of God a Power; and of the second world a Coffin.—Jean Paul, *Levana*.

Intellectual Individuality to be respected and maintained; moral Individuality to be modified, but only by strengthening *antagonist* qualities, not weakening those that appear originally in excess. "Thus let Frederick the Only (der Einzige) take his Flute, and Napoleon his Ossian."

"Our present time is indeed a criticising and critical one; hovering betwixt the wish and the inability to believe, a chaos of conflicting times: but even a chaotic world must have some Point, and Revolution round that Point, and Aether too; there is no pure entire Confusion and Discord, but all such presupposes its Contrary, before it can begin."

"But from of old, among nations the Head has outrun and got before the Heart; often by centuries, as in the Negro trade; nay by tens of centuries, as perhaps in war."

Light goes quicker than warmth: hence every new intellectual revolution, seems at first destructive to morality.

"When in your last hour (think of this) all within the broken spirit shall fade away, and die into inanity, Imagining, Thinking, Endeavouring, Enjoying — then at last blooms on the night-flower of Belief alone, and refreshes with its perfume in the last darkness."

---

Heyne's Virgil, Leipzig, 1803, 4 vol. 8vo., the best edition (the 'London ones were mismanaged); there is also a "Hand edition" of 1803 in 2 vol.; but whether it does not want something I know not. This Book I must have.[1]

Tibullus, Pindar, Homer (8 vol. Leipz. & London. 1822)

Sammlung antiquärischer Aussätze. 1778–1779; about the Laocoon, Venus, Pliny's Authorities, &c &c; the *Chest of Cypselus* among the rest.

An immensity of papers in the Göttingen Society. Chiefly upon Art (Etruscan &c.) and the philosophy of Fables and Mythuses. Something of Sparta. Of the influence of sudden increase of wealth in ancient states. Of Babylonian women annually at the Temple of Venus. On Winckelmann's history of Art. &c. &c.

Eloges &c. Michaelis, Müller, Gmelin, Kättner, Gatterer, &c.

Prolusiones Academicae (at London. 1790 no table of contents; but I suppose all included in the)

Opuscula Academica. Götting. 1785–1812. Chiefly on Aesthetical Antiquity. De

---

[1] The following paragraphs contain a list of Heyne's works.

morum vi ad sensum pulchritudinis. De Genio Saeculi Ptolemaeorum. The Doctrine of the most ancient poets. Physical causes of Myths. Use of History. Invention of Bread. Some ancient beginnings of Greek Legislation. Fifteen Prolusions on the states of Magna Graecia and Sicily. On the Arcadians more ancient than the Moon. Life of the most ancient Greeks. Leo the Pope and Attila. Epidemic Fever of Rome called plagues. Rise, decline and fall of Macedonia. Athenian liberty as seen in Aristophanes. Natural History in prodigies. Disease of Proselytising. Critique or Characteristic of Symmachus; of Ausonius; of Ammianus Marcellinus; of six writers of Augustus' history (historiae Augustae?); of panegyric-writers &c. Alexander Severus.

Heyne was born at Chemnitz (the birthplace of Puffendorf) in 1729; his father was the poorest of weavers. The history of the man was a series of misery (he at one time lived on pease-cods and had no bed), till towards the middle of it; and all along of most wonderful diligence. He died in 1812. Little representation of his character comes of this Biography by Heeren his son-in-law, who seems to be no very deep person. Heyne it appears was a sharp-tempered, but good-hearted, peaceable, methodical and well-beloved man. Not great but large. I know only his Virgil, which certainly appeared to me to leave all other commentaries of the sort I had seen very far behind it. The Homer I long to see.— O that I could read it![1]

Schlözer, Spittler, Gatterer, Martens, Woltmann,— mostly men of mould,— are commemorated in the same vol. with Heyne. They were all Göttingen Professors; for a time at least, for in Germany that class of men is essentially *wandering*. Spittler's little book on Church history is highly praised. Martens wrote on trade; and collected a body of *Fœdera* from 1761 to 1819, which must be very useful. Schlözer was a Journalist; the first public *whig* in Germany: he writes of Russia, where he once lived. Gatterer, a strange old virtuoso, wrote various chronologies, universal-history essays or compendiums; it seems on a greatly improved plan. He is said to have been in the habit of getting all the newspapers of the year collected sometime in December, and then reading them at one fell swoop. *Ex uno.* Müller is also sketched here; not well.

Is it not singular that so many men of note

[1] In 1828 Carlyle wrote an admirable account of Heyne, mainly derived from Heeren's Life of him. It appeared in the "Foreign Review," No. 4. See *Essays*, Vol. i.

should have been produced or gathered at Göttingen? Mosheim — Blumenbach. These Germans put us to shame! We have lost our old *honesty;* even in literature we are eye-servants. Go thou, and do *otherwise!*

---

Michaud Histoire des Croisades (recommended — 4$^{me}$ edit.)
Beck's *Repertorium* is unspeakably stupid.

>Der liebste Bube den wir han
>Der liegt in unserm Keller,
>Er hat ein hölzin Röcklein an,
>Und heisst der Muskateller.[1]
>>From "Ballhorn" golden A. B. C. Horn I. p. 88

Erasmus belongs to that species of writers who with all their heart would build the good God a most sumptuous church; at the same time however, not giving the Devil any offence; to whom accordingly they set up a neat little chapel close by, where you can offer him some touch of sacrifice by a time, and practice a quiet household devotion for him without disturbance.

---

>Leser wie gefall ich Dir?
>Leser wie gefällst du mir?
>Reader, how lik'st thou me?
>Reader, how like I thee?
>>T. von Logau.

[1] See p. (177) for translation of this quatrain.

THOMAS CARLYLE.

### Der Mai.
Dieser Monat ist ein Kuss, den der Himmel giebt der Erde,
Dass sie, jetzo eine Braut, künftig eine Mutter werde.[1]

*The same.*

Andreas Gryph died of apoplexy in the Council where he was syndic at Glogau.

Mem. Must read Mignet's French Revol.

The Palm is said to make saws and hatchets *blunt:* hence came it to be a symbol of Peace.

Wolff's most characteristic writing is said to be: *Vernünftige Gedanken von Gott, der Welt und der Seele des Menschen.* Halle. 1720.

Picinelli *Mundus Symbolicus;* a book of mottoes.

Works which I could like to see written:
1. A Biography and History of LUTHER; a picture of the great man himself, and of the great scenes and age he lived in.
2. A History of English Literature; from the times of Chaucer! Warton's Hist. of Eng. Poet. would do something in the way

---

[1] "May.
"This month is a kiss, which Heaven gives to the Earth,
That she, now a Bride, may in time become a Mother."

of help, but nothing as a model. The men ought to be *judged*, not prated of; and the whole environment of their talent, as well as their talent itself, set fairly before the reader.

3. Failing which, I reckon one of the finest Essays of an aesthetic sort that could be written, were an intelligible account of SHAKESPEARE. *How* did that wonderful being live and think and write? We treat him commonly as a *miracle*, and launch out into vague admiration of him, out of which comes nothing. A miracle he was *not*, except as genius is always a miracle; but a *man* that was born and bred as other men, and lived in a strange shrivelled little brick-house, which I have seen at Stratford on Avon; the one end of which, repaired and new-bedizened was then (1825) inhabited by a — Butcher. Would I *saw* the Poet and knew him, and could then fully understand him!

———

*Luther's Werke,* herausgegeben von Walch, 1724.

Mascov's Geschichte der Deutschen;

Bünau's Teutsche Kaiser-und-Reichshistorie; best books of that sort (says Horn) at their *time.*

Should see Möser: why have I not catalogue?

Dr. Althof's *Life of Bürger.*

## THOMAS CARLYLE.

On the silk-worm: —
Arte mea pereo, tumulum mihi fabricor ipse:
Fila mei fati duco, necemque neo.[1]

---

Miller (of Göttingen's?) *Siegwart* the beginning of the sentimental period.

---

The two Stolbergs — F. Leopold became a Catholic. Jung (Stilling's) *Selbstbiographie*. Matt. Claudius; the *Wandsbecker Bote*.— Lichtenberg's writings —

Johann Christian Brandes, Autobiography; said to be interesting.

---

Die Tugend ist das höchste Gut,
Das Laster Weh dem Menschen thut.[2]
Puppenspieler Jahrm arktfest.

1. *Weisheit auf der Strasse*, a Book of Proverbs, relating many of them to the time of the Reformation.

2. Möser, *Osnabrückische Geschichte;* a very good history. *Fantasienstücke*, by the same.

3. Raumer, *Geschichte der Hohenstauffen;* said to be very good.

4. Ritter a writer on statistics, of great merit; professor at Berlin.

These four recommended by Mr. Aitken.

---

[1] "By my own art I die, for myself I make my tomb; I spin the thread of my own fate, and weave my own death."

[2] "Virtue is the highest good,
While Vice does harm to man."

With regard to the right and left bank of a river, you keep your face *down* the stream.

---

Genus hominum, quod in civitate nostra semper et retinebitur et vetabitur.— Tacitus.[1]

---

A countryman (*Bauer*) one morning knocked at Gellert's door, and asked if "he was the man that wrote those fine Fables?" Being answered in the affirmative, the Bauer added that "here was a cartload of wood which he had brought to warm him thro' winter, as an acknowledgement for the pleasure he (the B.) had got from those writings;" and so saying, he tumbled up his cargo of billets, and with best compliments, took his leave. This was worth a dozen *Reviews*.

---

Quicunque solitudine delectatur aut fera aut deus est.[2]

---

[1] Mathematici "genus hominum ... quod in civitate nostra et vetabitur semper, et retinebitur." *Hist.* i. 22. "Astrologers, a class of men which will always be prohibited in our city and always maintained."

[2] Bacon begins his essay "Of Friendship" with the words: "It had been hard for him that spake it to have put more truth and untruth together in few words, than in that speech, *Whosoever is delighted in solitude is either a wild beast or a god.*" The adages which follow are cited in the same essay. Bacon's reference was undoubtedly to the well-known passage in Aristotle, *Politics*, i. 2, which is to the effect that "he who is unable to live in

## THOMAS CARLYLE.

Magna civitas, magna solitudo.[1]
Cor ne edito (eat not your heart), *Pythag.*
(These are from Bacon.)

---

Stag-heads in Fontainebleau under which stood inscribed; "Louis so-and-so did me the honour to shoot me." Richter, *Levana.*

Turba medicorum perdidit Cæsarem.[2]
　　　　　　　　　　Hadrian's epitaph.

Anton, Geschichte der Deutsche Nation.
Schmidt's　"　　"　　"　　"
Lévesque, Moralistes anciens.
(Somebody's) "　　" Français.
Suard, Mélanges Littéraires.
Duval, Mémoires sur le royaume de Naples.
Varillas, Histoire secrète de la Maison de Médicis.

---

Tasso's Essay Del Poema Eroico.[3]

society, or who has no need because he is sufficient for himself, must be either a beast or a god,"— but Bacon gives the words a false turn, and then proceeds to argue, on the basis of his own error, against the position which he ascribes to Aristotle. Carlyle had obviously been reading the essay in the Latin translation published by Dr. Rawley in 1638.

[1] "A great town is a great solitude."
[2] "The crowd of doctors killed Cæsar."
[3] In a letter to his brother John, Oct. 25, 1827, Carlyle wrote: "Meanwhile I am beginning (purpose seriously beginning to-morrow) an article on *Zacharias Werner* . . . I design afterwards, if Jeffrey is willing, to

NOTE BOOK OF

Ultimate object of the Poet is to *profit* (prodesse as *super*ordinate to delectare). p. 350.— very clear and logical, *giovar dilettando*.

(An Historian must write (so to speak) in *lines ;* but every event is a *superficies ;* nay if we search out its *causes*, a *solid :* hence a primary and almost incurable defect in the art of Narration; which only the very best can so much as approximately remedy.— N. B. I understand this *myself*. I have known it for years; and written it *now*, with the purpose perhaps of writing it at large elsewhere.)[1]

Curious (p. 367) division of Theology. The *mistico* much the same as *Vernunft?*[2]

*Instar omnium Plato*, said Antimachus Clarius, when only this *one* vote went in his favour; " Plato is worth them all."[3]

give a Discourse on Tasso." *Letters*, i. 90. The article on Werner was written, and is to be found in Carlyle's Essays; the proposed discourse on Tasso seems not to have been accomplished.

[1] This purpose was fulfilled in his paper "On History" published in Fraser's Magazine, in 1830. See *Essays*, ii. 258.

[2] For the definition of *Vernunft* " Reason," as used by the Kantists, and its relation to Mysticism, see "State of German Literature" (1827), *Essays*, i. 69.

[3] —"dixisse Antimachum, Clarium poetam, ferunt, qui quum convocatis auditoribus legeret eis magnum illud, quod novistis, volumen suum, et eum legentem omnes, præter Platonem, reliquissent, 'Legam' inquit 'nihilo minus; Plato enim mihi unus instar est omnium millium.'" Cicero, *Brutus*, 51.

THOMAS CARLYLE.

*Convien ch'uom poggi;* man should ascend.
I have gone over (not regularly read) the Essay *Del Poema Eroico*. Must not say that I have derived *any* benefit from it generally; or even specially any great insight into the individuality of Tasso himself. It is unspeakably diffuse, and appeals to no principles of a scientific sort; the main source of his light being Aristotle and the practice of ancient poets. One gathers only that he was a serious man, and *had* high views of the dignity and moment of Epic poetry; tho' *how* from so complicated and generally so barren a system of rules he modulated so harmonious a whole as the *Gerusalemme* seems nowise clear.— On the whole I have not strength to study Tasso at present, nor even to express what I have studied concerning him.

Tasso was a *mystic*, as we should call him: Must not every true poet be so? That is to say, must he not have a sense of the Invisible Existences of Nature, and be enabled as it were to read the symbols of these in the visible? Can any man delineate with *life* the figure even of a Trinculo or Caliban otherwise? For is not the poorest nature a *mystery;* the most grovelling street-porter, the most arid *Kanzlerverwandte* a type in some obscurer sense and an emanation from the Land of wonders? Is he not an INDIVIDUAL; and who shall explain all the significance of that one word? — Not one of Scott's *Fair-services* or *Deanses* &c. is *alive*. As far as prose could go, he has gone; and we have fair *outsides;* but within all is rather hollow, *nicht wahr?* — Alas! I do not see into this, and must talk rather falsely of it, or "altogether hold my peace," which perhaps were better.— Jan$^y$ 8$^{th}$ 1828.—

---

*La Bruyère* I have found, for the second time, strive as I might, *exceedingly* shallow. "He has point and brilliancy; but so has a brass pin." — Yet I do not *know* the French: what *do* I know? —

The courtesies of polished life too often amount to little more than this: "Sir, you and I care not two brass farthings the one for the other, we have and can have no *friendship* for each other or for aught else in nature; nevertheless let us *enact* it, if we cannot practise it; do you tell so many lies, and I shall tell so many, and depend on it the result will be of great service to both. For is not this December weather very cold? And tho' our *grates* are full of *ice*, yet if you keep a *picture of fire* before yours, and I another before mine, will not this be next to a real coal-and-wood affair?

---

Goethe has been called ill-bred, a low and vulgar man by certain British Critics. He is of all past and present writers the farthest from this. Except himself, I might say, there is *no* man of books known to me, who can delineate a *Gentleman*, or even so much as conceive him. Scott goes as far as the Upholsterer and Gentleman-Usher go; but little farther: his highest gentleman (at all events) might be a *writer to the Signet:* Bonaparte himself becomes a sort of Parliamenteering, game-preserving, Road-commissioning Country-Squire in his hands. Put together a Gentleman as e.g. Burns can put together a Peasant! They give us a sort of *shell* of one; but the kernel is not there.

———

What is the unhappiest quality in man? For his moral worth, malignity (excess of emulation *corrupted*); for his civic prosperity, *irresolution.* How long halt ye between two opinions?

———

To be read:
  Mill's History of Chivalry.
        "   " Crusades.
    "   Theodore Ducas?
  Sharon Turner's Anglo-Saxons.
    "     "    England.
    "     "    Henry VIII.
Works of Ritson (never seen by me)
Percy's Relicks (almost forgotten)
Ellis I have read and partly esteemed.

What of all these *Memoirs* by Lucy Aikin, Miss Benger, and Mrs. Thomson? I will take down their names.
    Lucy A's Queen Elizabeth.
    "  " King James I.
    Miss B's Queen of Bohemia (Eliz. Stuart)
    "  " Mary Q. of Scots
    "  " Anne Boleyn.
    "  " Henri IV. [II. ?]
    "  " Mrs. Hamilton.
    "  " Mr. Tobin.
    Mrs. T.'s Henry VIII.

---

The Saxon Chronicle (translated) by J. Ingram.
Coxe's Memoirs of Duke Marlborough.
    "    "    " Sir R. Walpole.

---

Goethe (Dichtung und Wahrheit II. 14) asserts that the sublime is natural to all young persons and peoples; but that day-light (of reason) destroys it, *unless* it can unite itself with the Beautiful, in which case it remains indestructible.— A fine obs.

p. 39. Grotius said he read Terence otherwise than Boys do. "Happy limitedness of youth! nay of men in general, that at all moments of their existence they can look upon themselves as complete; and ask neither for the True nor the False, the High nor the Deep, but simply what is suitable to them."

## THOMAS CARLYLE.

— Alles was daher von mir bekannt geworden sind nur Bruchstücke einer grossen Confession, welche vollständig zu machen dieses Buchlein ein gewagter Versuch ist. p. 109.—[1]

Banier's Mythology.

Finished a Paper on *Burns*. September 16, 1828; at this Devil's Den, Craigenputtock.

Ersch his Handbuch der deutschen Literatur seit der Mitte des 18$^{ten}$ Jahrh. bis auf die neueste Zeit. 2 Bde. Amsterdam & Leipzig. 1812–14. There has been a second and better Edition.
'Das Kind mit dem Bade ausgeschüttet!'
— Killed instead of curing? [" Fling out not the *dirty water* only but y$^r$ washed *child!*" A very pretty proverb.][2]
Der Deutsche Improvisator? Two Books of him published at Gera. The man Goethe speaks of?

F. Schlegel's Philosophy of Life. Literat. Zeit. März, 462. *rather* sensible.

[1] "All my pieces which have thus become known are only fragments of a great confession which this little book is a venturesome attempt to make complete."
[2] "The Germans say, You must empty out the bathing-tub, but not the baby along with it." 'Nigger Question,' 1849. *Essays*, vii. 97.

NOTE BOOK OF

Camillo Ugoni Hist. of Italian Literature
—goodish? 175-1800 is its *Spielraum*.[1]
Corniani has also written a *Secoli della Let.
It.* in nine volumes.

Giuseppe Tartini Italian Fiddler dreamed one night that he had made a paction with the Devil, who 'did, nay surpassed' all his bidding. In particular he (the Devil) played (by request) such a *Sonata* as for beauty was never played before; the ravishments of which indeed woke poor Tartini, who clutching his fiddle tried at least to retain some tones of this Devil's Sonata; but almost in vain, so unearthly was it. However he did what he could; and his best is still called the *Devil's Sonata*. Beppo died at Padua 1770.

Boscovich died mad! 1787.

Passeroni *cooked for himself*—in Milan; an old woman made his bed: he himself was to be seen with cap and apron. He wrote a Poem [*Il*] *Cicerone* in six volumes, containing 11,047 stanzas (octave). This *great* and very good humoured Author died—perhaps about 1800.

Baretti was born at Turin (1719). *Would* not be an Architect, and so ran off from home at the age of 16. London (1757)—from Venice.—He travelled thro' Spain and Portugal *home* (1760); but came back to Lon-

[1] "Area."

don, where he died (1789). Three fellows, (robbers seemingly) attacked him on the street (of L.) and he killed one of them with a silver knife (!) Burke, Reynolds, Johnson, Fitzherbert (quotha) *got him off.* His works are

*Frusta Litteraria* (Literary Scourge).
The Italians.
Travels. *Discorso* on Shakesp. &c. partly in Italian, partly in English. He is a rugged hard keen man — as his Dict. itself shows.[1]

Galiani, a Neapolitan Abbé — See Grimm.

---

Gries has translated Tasso, Ariosto, Calderon — the latter as I partly know *well.*

---

Palestrina, Scarlatti. Italian (earliest) musicians.
Händel, Bach, Hasse.
Darstellungen aus der Geschichte der Musik, by Krause — Göttingen.

---

Millot, Histoire Littéraire des Troubadours.
Raynouard, Choix des Poésies des Tr.

---

Geschichte der Jungfrau von Orleans by Fouqué — 1826. Berlin, 2 vol.

[1] Boswell has conferred immortality on Baretti, by the frequent mention of him in his *Life of Johnson.*

Et sibi res non se rebus submittere tentat.
(Hor.)[1]
*Pièce à tiroir;* a Play of detached scenes.

Has the mind its cycles and seasons like Nature, varying from the fermentation of *werden*[2] to the clearness of *seyn;*[3] and this again and again; so that the history of a man is like the history of the world he lives in? In my own case, I have traced two or three such vicissitudes: at present if I mistake not, there is some such thing at hand for me. Feb$^y$ 1829.

---

Above all things, I should like *to know England*, the essence of social life in this same little Island of ours. But how? No one that I speak to can throw light on it; not he that has worked and lived in the midst of it for half a century. The blind following the blind! Yet each cries out: What a glorious sunshine we have! The 'old Literature' only half contents me: it is ore and not metal. I have not even a *history* of the country, half precise enough. With Scotland, it is little better. To me there is

---

[1] The verse in Horace runs:
Et mihi res, non me rebus, subjungere conor.
*Epist.*, i. i. 19.
"I strive to master things, not let them master me."
Compare Emerson's
"Things are in the saddle, and ride mankind."
[2] "Becoming."    [3] "Being."

## THOMAS CARLYLE.

nothing poetical in Scotland, but its Religion. Perhaps because I *know* nothing else so well. England with its old Chivalry, Art and 'creature comfort' looks beautiful, but only as a cloud-country, the distinctive features of which are all melted into one gay sunny mass of hues. After all, we are a world 'within ourselves'; a 'self-contained house.'

---

The English have never had an Artist, except in Poetry; no Musician, no Painter; Purcell (was he a native?[1]) and Hogarth are not exceptions, or only such as confirm the rule.

---

He who would understand England must understand her Church, for that is half of the whole matter. Am I not conscious of a *prejudice* on that side? Does not the very sight of a shovel-hat in some degree indispose me to the wearer thereof? shut up my heart against him? This must be looked into: without love there is no knowledge.[2]

---

Do I not also partly despise partly hate the Aristocracy of Scotland? I fear, I do, tho' under cover. This too should be remedied.—On the whole, I know little of the Scottish Gentleman; and more than enough

[1] Purcell was born in Westminster.
[2] This thought is more fully written out in 'Biography' (1832). *Essays*, iv. 62.

of the Scottish *Gigman*.— All are not mere rent-gatherers and game-preservers.

———

Have the Scottish Gentry *lost* their national character of late years, and become mere danglers in the train of the wealthier English? Scott has seen certain characters among them; of which I hitherto have not heard of any existing specimen.

———

Is the true Scotchman the Peasant and Yeoman; chiefly the former?

———

Shall we actually go and *ride* thro' England to see it? Mail-coaches are a mere mockery.

———

A national character, that is, the description of one, tends to realize itself, as some prophecies have produced their own fulfilment. Tell a man that he is brave, and you help him to become so. The 'national character' hangs like a pattern in every head; each sensibly or insensibly shapes himself thereby, and feels pleased when he can in any measure realize it.

———

Is the characteristic strength of England its Love of Justice, its deep-seated, universally-active sense of Fair Play?— On many points it seems to be a very stupid people;

but seldom a hide-bound, bigoted, altogether unmanageable and unaddressable people.

---

The Scotch have more enthusiasm and more consideration; that is, at once, more sail and ballast: they seem to have a *deeper* and *richer* character as a nation.—The old Scottish music, our Songs &c., are a highly distinctive feature.
Must see Southey's *Book of the Church* & Tytler's *History of Scotland.* Also Sir W. Scott's *Tales of a Grandfather.*

---

Read *Novalis Schriften* for the second time some weeks ago, and wrote a Review of them. A strange, mystic, unfathomable Book; but full of matter for most earnest meditation. What is to become (next) of the world and the sciences thereof? Rather, what is to become of *thee* and thy science? Thou longest to *act* among thy fellow men, and canst (yet) scarcely *breathe* among them.

---

Friedrich Schlegel dead at Dresden on the 9th of January!— Poor Schlegel what toilsome *seeking* was thine: thou knowest now whether thou hadst *found* — or thou carest not for knowing!

---

What am I to say of *Voltaire?* (His *name*

has stood at the top of a sheet for three days, and no other word!) Writing is a dreadful Labour; yet not so dreadful as Idleness.

---

Every living man is a visible mystery: he walks between two Eternities and two Infinitudes (said already!)[1]— Were we not blind as moles we should value our Humanity at $x$, and our Rank, Influence &c. (the trappings of our Humanity), at $o$. Say, I am a man; and you say all: whether King or Tinker is a mere appendix. — (" very true, Mr. Carlyle, but then " — we must believe *Truth* and practise Error?)—[2]
— Pray that your eyes be opened, that you may *see* what *is* before them! The whole world is built as it were, on Light and Glory; only that our *spiritual* eye must discern it: to the bodily eye Self is as a perpetual *blinder*, and we see nothing but darkness and contradiction.

---

Luther, says Melanchthon, would often, tho' in robust health, go about for *four days* eating and drinking — nothing!— " Vidi continuis quatuor diebus, cum quidem recte valeret,

[1] " In any point of Space, in any section of Time, let there be a living man; and there is an infinitude above him and beneath him, and an Eternity encompasses him on this hand and on that." ' State of German Literature,' *Essays*, i, 73.
[2] In this paragraph lies the germ of *Sartor Resartus*.

## THOMAS CARLYLE.

prorsus nihil edentem aut bibentem. Vidi saepe alias multis diebus quotidie exiguo pane et halece contentum esse"— content for many days with a little piece of bread and herring. O tempora! O mores!

---

Luther's last words:

"'Mein himmlischer Vater, ewiger barmherziger Gott, du hast mir deinen lieben Sohn, unsern Herrn Jhesum Christum offenbaret; den hab ich geleret, den hab ich bekandt, den liebe ich und den ehre ich für meinen lieben Heiland und Erlöser, welchen die Gottlosen verfolgen, schenden und schelten. Nim meine Seele zu dir.' Then he repeated thrice: 'In manus tuas commendo Spiritum meum; redemisti me, Deus veritatis. Also hat Gott die Welt geliebet'[1] &c. repeating these prayers several times, he was called away by God into his eternal school, and eternal blessedness; where he enjoys the presence of the Father, Son, Holy Ghost; of all the Prophets and Apostles. Ah! the chariot and chari-

---

[1] "My heavenly Father, eternal and merciful God, Thou hast revealed to me thy dear Son, whom I have followed and known, and whom I love and honor as my beloved Saviour and Redeemer, whom the godless persecute, revile and abuse. Take Thou my soul to Thyself"

"Into thine hand I commit my spirit; Thou hast redeemed me, O Lord God of truth." (Psalm xxxi. 5.)

"God so loved the world." (John iii. 16.)

NOTE BOOK OF

oteer of Israel is departed; he who guided the church in this last old age of the world."
—Melanchthonis (p. 33.) de vita Martini Lutheri Narratio — a very brief, meagre, and unsatisfactory performance. I must try to see Seckendorf Historia Luth. (a large Latin book, but said to be authentic).—
Keil's *Leben der Aeltern Luther's.*
Keil's *M. Luther's merkw. Lebensumstände.*

"Ich bin eines Bauern Sohn," says Luther. "Mein Vater, Grossvater, Ahnherr sind rechte Bauern gewest. Darnach ist mein Vater gen Mansfeld gezogen, und daselbst ein Berghauer geworden."[1] Luther used to say, in miner fashion, to the last: *wohlauf!* instead of *wohlan!*
Mathesii *Histor. Luth.* (ed. 1576).

Motschmanus in his *Erfordia literata* (Literary Erfurt) has diligently narrated Luther's proceedings while in that town — as student and monk.

Luther was a monk for fifteen years: "Ein frommer Münch bin ich gewesen, und habe so theure meinen Orden gehalten dass ich sagen darf, ist jemahls ein Münch gen Himmel gekommen durch Müncherey, so wollte

[1] "I am a peasant's son. My father, grandfather, and forefather were mere peasants. After a time my father went to Mansfeld, and there became a miner."

## THOMAS CARLYLE.

ich auch hinein gekommen seyn. Dies werden mir zeugen alle meine Kloster-Gesellen de mich gekennet haben. Denn ich hätte mich, wo es länger gewähret hätte, zu Tode gemartert mit Wachen, Beten, Lesen und anderer Arbeit." [1] Luther was born Nov. 10$^{th}$ 1483; he died Feb. 18$^{th}$ 1546 — aged 63: his disease was *Cardiaca* (the last fit, apparently some sort of Colic.) Tetzel's business came on 1517 — when L. was 34 years old. Worms Diet 38.

---

Luther's character appears to me the most worth discussing of all modern men's. He is, to say it in a word, a great man in *every* sense; has the soul at once of a Conqueror and a Poet. His attachment to Music is to me a very interesting circumstance: it was the channel for many of his finest emotions; for which words, even words of prayer, were but an ineffectual exponent. Is it true that he *did* leave Wittenberg for Worms 'with nothing but his Bible and his Flute'? There is no scene in European History so splendid

[1] "I was a pious Monk, and held my Rule so dear that I venture to say that if ever a monk got to Heaven through monkery, I ought to have got there. All my cloister companions who have known me will testify this of me. For I should have tormented myself to death, if it had lasted much longer, with vigils, prayers, readings, and other labor."

and significant.— I have long had a sort of notion to write some life or characteristic of Luther. A picture of the public Thought in those days, and of this strong lofty mind over-turning and new-moulding it, would be a fine affair in many senses. It would require immense research.— Alas! alas! — When are we to have another Luther? Such men are needed from century to century : there seldom has been more need of one than now.

---

Wrote a Paper on *Voltaire* for the Foreign Review (sometime in March & April 1829). It appears to have given some (very slight) satisfaction : pieces of it breathe afar off the right spirit of composition. When shall I attain to write wholly in that spirit?

---

Paper on *Novalis* for F. R. just published; written last January amid the frosts. Generally poor. Novalis is an Anti-Mechanist; a deep man; the most perfect of modern spirit-seers. I thank him for somewhat.

---

Also just finished an Article on the *Signs of the Times*, for the Ed[r] Review; as Jeffrey's last speech.[1] Bad in general; but the best I could make it under such incubus influences.

---

[1] Jeffrey was on the point of giving up the editorship of the Edinburgh Review.

## THOMAS CARLYLE.

(August 5. To *see* Jeffrey at Dumfries the day after to-morrow).

---

Every age appears surprising and full of vicissitudes to those that live therein; as indeed it is and must be: vicissitudes from Nothingness to Existence; and from the tumultuous wonders of Existence forward to the still wonders of Death.

---

Politics are not our Life (which is the practice and contemplation of Goodness), but only the *house* wherein that Life is led. Sad duty that lies on us to *parget* and continually repair our houses: saddest of all when it becomes our *sole* duty.

An Institution (a Law of any kind) may become a *deserted* edifice; the walls standing, no life going on within, but that of bats, owls and unclean creatures. It will then be pulled down if it stand interrupting any *thoroughfare :* if it do not so stand, people may leave it alone till a grove of natural wood grow round it, and no eye but that of the adventurous antiquarian may know of its existence, such a tangle of *brush* is to be struggled thro' before it can be come at and viewed.

---

All Language but that concerning *sensual*

objects is or has been figurative.[1] Prodigious influence of metaphors! Never saw into it till lately. A truly useful and philosophical work would be a good *Essay on Metaphors*. Some day I will write one!

———

Begin to think more seriously of discussing *Martin Luther*. The only Inspiration I know of is that of Genius: it was, is, and will always be of a divine character.

———

Wonderful Universe! Were our eyes but opened, what a 'secret' were it that we daily see and handle, without heed!

———

Understanding is to Reason as the talent of a Beaver (which can build houses, and uses its tail for a trowel) to the genius of a Prophet and Poet. Reason is all but extinct in this age: it can never be altogether extinguished.[2]

———

Books:
  *Must* see Thomas a Kempis.

[1] "Examine Language; what, if you except some few primitive elements (of natural sound), what is it all but Metaphors, recognized as such, or no longer recognized: still fluid and florid, or now solid-grown and colourless?" *Sartor Resartus*, Book i. ch. xi.
  *Sartor* itself may be regarded as the fulfilment of the intention one day to write 'a good *Essay on Metaphors*.'
[2] Cf. "State of German Literature." (1827.) *Essays*, i. 86.

## THOMAS CARLYLE.

Webster's Dramatic Works.
Marston's do. (Never heard of him.)
Life of Sir T. More.
Thoms' *Collection of Ancient English fictions.*
(One Nicholas Harris Nicolas seems to be a determined English Antiquarian.)
(These Books are all in Pickering's List.)

---

What a strange thing is that Quarterly Review! How insular, how lawn-sleeved! What will the world come to?

---

Das Seligseyn ist um eine Ewigkeit älter als das Verdammtseyn.[1]— Jean Paul.

---

"The mixture of those things by speech which by nature are divided is the mother of all error."—*Hooker*, p. 61.—

---

Error of Political Economists about improving waste lands as compared with manufacturing: the manufacture is worn and *done* (the machine itself dies); the improved land remains an *addition* to the Earth *forever*. What is the amount of this error? I see not; but reckon it something considerable.

---

Is it true that of all quacks that ever quacked (boasting themselves to be somebody) in any

[1] "Salvation is by an Eternity older than Damnation."

age of the world, the Political Economists of this age are, for their intrinsic size, the loudest? Mercy on us what a quack-quacking; and their egg (even if *not* a wind one) is of value simply one half-penny! —

Their whole Philosophy (!) is an Arithmetical Computation — performed in words; requires therefore the intellect not of Socrates or Shakespear but of Cocker or Dilworth. Even if it were right! which it scarcely ever is, for they *miss* this or the other item, do as they will, and must return to practice and take the *low* posteriori road after all.

The question of money-making, even of National Money-making, is not a high but a low one: as they treat it, among the lowest. Could they tell us how wealth is and should be *distributed*, it were something; but they do not attempt it. Political Philosophy! Pol. Ph. should be a scientific revelation of the whole secret mechanism whereby men cohere together in society; should tell us what is meant by "country" (*patria*), by what causes men are happy, moral, religious, or the contrary: instead of all which, it tells us how "flannel jackets" are exchanged for "pork hams," and speak much about the "land last taken into cultivation." They are the hodmen of the intellectual edifice, who have got upon the wall, and will insist on building, as if they were masons.

## THOMAS CARLYLE.

The Utilitarians are the "crowning mercy" of this age: the summit (now first appearing to view) of a mass of tendencies which stretch downwards and spread sidewards over the whole intellect and moral of the time. By and by, the clouds will disperse, and we shall see it all, in dead nakedness and brutishness; and Utilitaria will pass away with a great noise. You think not? — Can the Reason of man be trodden under foot forever by his sense; can the Brute in us prevail forever over the angel! —[1]

---

The Devil has his Elect.[2]

---

Pero digan lo que quisieren (los historiadores) que desnudo nací, desnudo me hallo, ni pierdo ni gano, aunque por verme puesto in libros y andar por ese mundo de mano en mano, no se me da un higo que digan de mí todo lo que quisieren.— says Sancho — Quixote 4. 117.[3]

[1] Compare with this passage, *Sartor Resartus*, Book iii. ch. vi.

[2] "Let us offer sweet incense to the Devil, and live at ease on the fat things *he* has provided for his Elect." *Sartor Resartus*, Book ii. ch. vii.

[3] "But let them [the historians] say what they will, for naked was I born, naked I am, I neither lose nor gain, and though I find myself put into books, and passing from hand to hand through the world, I care not a fig, let them say of me what they will." *Don Quixote*, Part ii, ch. 8.

NOTE BOOK OF

What is the *Censura Literaria?*
Granger's Biographical History of England.

———

"The wishers and woulders were never good householders."— Greene (in Drake[1]).
"Hell is paved with good resolutions."

———

This is the only way to make a woman dum:
To sit and smile and laugh her out and not a word but mum.
L[eonard] Wright (from D[rake].)[2]

———

Capel Lofft's Aphorisms of Shakespeare.
Beloe's Anecdotes of Literature (and) Scarce Books.
Oldys' British Librarian.
Brady's Clavis Calendaria.
Brand (or Bourne's) Popular Antiquities.
Burnett's Specim. Eng. Prose writers.
Orford's Royal & Noble Authors.

———

Die Möncherei oder geschichtliche Dar-

---

[1] "Drake" refers to the well-known "Shakespeare and his Times," by Nathan Drake, London, 1817. 2 vols., 4to. The saying here cited (vol. i, p. 490) is from Greene's tract, entitled "Never Too Late," 1590. Greene says "thinking this old sentence to be true *The wishes*, etc." He writes it as prose, but it must originally have been a couplet, "woulders" written and pronounced after the 16th century fashion "wolders," rhyming with "holders."

[2] *Id.*, p. 513. The couplet is from Wright's "Display of Dutie," 1589.

stellung des Klosterwelt (Stuttgard, 1820, 3 Bde.)
See also *Hermes* no. 15. for a Review of it.

---

Dr. Berkenhout (the English son of a Dutch Leeds merchant) has published a 4$^{to}$ vol. which treats of the Lit. Hist. of England, prior to Elizabeth; with what merit I know not.

---

It is the sharpest (black) Frost I have seen for some years. 14$^{th}$ Jan$^y$ 1830.—I am quite idle. Eheu!

My worthy Uncle "Sandy" is dead, and to be buried to-morrow "The heaviest-laden wayfarer at length lays down his load." Uncle Sandy's widow survived him but a week; their eldest son lay sick of fever, and at the time insensible.[1]

The week following died my Aunt Mary (Stewart), after eight years of ill health and weary dreary Death-in-Life.

---

March (perhaps 1st.) I am occupied writing a *History of German Literature* (save the mark!) which will nowise fashion itself into any shape in my hands.[2] Few men have attempted a

[1] [Now (1866) Ja$^s$ Aitken, Husband of his cousin, my sister Jean.]

[2] In October, 1829, the proposal had come to Carlyle, already known, by his *Life of Schiller* and by articles in

compilation under such circumstances: no Books, continual disappointments from Book-agents, etc., etc. But what boots complaining? Bear a hand, and let us do our best; the strongest can do no better.

Does it seem hard to thee that thou shouldst toil, in dullness, sickness, isolation? Whose lot is not even this? Toil, then, *et tais-toi.*

Either I am degenerating into a *caput mortuum*, and shall never think another reasonable thought; or some new and deeper view of the world is about to arise in me. Pray Heaven, the latter! It is dreadful to live without *vision:* where there is no light the people perish.—

With considerable sincerity I can pray at this moment: Grant me, O Father, enough of wisdom to live well; prosperity to live happily (easily) grant me or not, as Thou

---

the *Foreign* and *Foreign Quarterly Review*, to be competent for the task, to write a History of German Literature, for publication in the series of volumes of the *Cabinet Cyclopædia*. His plan for it is set forth at length in a letter to Goethe of May 23, 1830. The first volume was then complete. But on August 31, he writes that the plan had fallen through, after he had brought down the narrative, in the space of a volume and a half, to the Reformation. See *Correspondence between Goethe and Carlyle*, pp. 159, 187, 207. The book was never completed. Some parts were made into independent articles and printed in the Reviews; of these were the essays on "The Nibelungen Lied," and on "Early German Literature," which are now to be found in Carlyle's *Essays*.

seest best.—A poor faint *prayer*, as such, yet surely a kind of wish; as indeed it has generally been with me: and now a kind of comfort to feel it still in my otherwise too withered heart.—

I am a 'dismembered limb'; and feel it again too deeply.[1] Was I ever other? Stand to it tightly, man; and do thy utmost. Thou hast little or no hold on the world; promotion will never reach thee; nor true fellowship with any active body of men: but hast thou not still a hold on Thyself? *Ja, beym Himmel!* —

Religion, as Novalis hints, *is* a social thing. Without a Church there can be little or no Religion. The action of mind on mind is mystical, infinite; Religion, worship can hardly (perhaps not at all) support itself without this aid. The derivation of *Schwärmerey* indicates some notion of this in the Germans. To *schwärmen* (to be enthusiastic) means, says Coleridge, to *swarm*, to crowd together, and excite one another.—

What is the English of *all* quarrels that have been are or can be between man and man? Simply this: Sir you are taking more

---

[1] "For thee the Family of Man has no use; it rejects thee; thou art wholly as a dissevered limb; so be it; perhaps it is better so!"

*Sartor Resartus*, Book ii. ch. viii.

NOTE BOOK OF

than your share of Pleasure in this world, something from *my* share; and by the gods, you shall not; nay I will fight you rather. Alas! and the whole lot to be divided is such a beggarly account of empty boxes; truly a 'feast of shells,' not eggs, for the yolks have all been blown out of them! Not enough to fill half a stomach, and the whole human species famishing to be at them! Better we should say to our Brother: Take it, poor fellow, take that larger share, which I reckon mine, and which thou so wantest: take it with a blessing: would to Heaven I had but enough for thee![1]— This is the Moral of the Christian Religion: how easy to write, how *hard* to practice! (Suggested itself one wet evening, on the Trailtrow moss,[2] as I came from Annan, in 1825; or perhaps I only mentioned it to Jack then, as a thing I had lately seen.— I love to be particular.)

I have now almost done with the Germans. Having seized their opinions, I must turn me to inquire *how* true are they? That truth is in them, no lover of Truth will doubt: but how much? And after all, one needs an intellectual Scheme (or ground plan

[1] The foregoing paragraph appears, with some verbal changes, in *Sartor Resartus*, Book ii. ch. ix.
Near Ecclefechan. A. C.

of the Universe) drawn with one's own instruments.—

I think I have got rid of Materialism: Matter no longer seems to me so ancient, so unsubduable, so *certain* and palpable as Mind. *I* am Mind: whether matter or not I know not—and care not.—Mighty glimpses into the spiritual Universe I have sometimes had (about the true nature of Religion, the possibility, after all, of 'supernatural' (really natural) influences &c. &c.): would they could but stay with me, and ripen into a perfect view!

— Miracle? What is a Miracle?[1] Can there be a thing more miraculous than any other thing? I myself am a standing wonder. It is 'the inspiration of the Almighty that giveth us understanding.'—

What is Poetry? Do I really love Poetry? I sometimes fancy almost, not. The jingle of maudlin persons, with their mere (even genuine) 'sensibility' is unspeakably fatiguing to me. My greatly most delightful reading is, where some Goethe musically *teaches* me. Nay, *any* fact, relating especially to man, is still valuable and pleasing.—

My Memory, which was one of the best, has failed sadly of late years, (principally the last two): yet not so much by defect in the faculty, I should say, as by want of earnest-

[1] Cf. *Sartor Resartus*, Book iii. ch. viii. "What specially is a Miracle?"

ness in using it. I *attend* to few things as I was wont: few things have any interest for me; I live in a sort of waking dream.

Doubtful it is in the highest degree, whether ever I shall make men hear my voice to any purpose or not. Certain only that I shall be a *failure* if I do not, and unhappy: nay unhappy enough (that is with suffering enough) even if I do. My own talent I cannot in the remotest attempt at estimating. Something superior often does seem to be in me, and hitherto the world has been very kind; but *many* things inferior also; so that I can strike no balance. — Hang it, *try;* and leave this *Grübeln!* [1]

*What we have done* is the only mirror that can show us what we *are*.

---

One great desideratum in every society is a man to hold his peace.

---

O Time, how thou fliest,
False heart, how thou liest;
Leave chattering and fretting,
Betake thee to doing and getting!

I must have a whiff of tobacco, first! God help me!

---

Wer vom treuen stirbt, dem soll man mit Furtzen zum Grab läuten (Epist. obs. viror.

[1] "Speculating."

449). Wer vom Dräuen stirbt, dem &c. mit Fürzen . . . läuten ! ! !—[1]

Wrote a Letter to the Dumfries *Courier*, about poor Tom Bell's Massacre at Knockhill, and the Public Prosecutor's neglect to indict his Slayer.[2] Can say that I did it from a feeling that it was necessary. Whether the man will print it or not I shall know to-morrow; in the negative case, I must send it to the *Journal;* and then have done with it. The word is spoken, if they see good to shut the public ear against it; *à la bonne heure!* I have other work to follow.

[1] These words may be found in Boecking's edition of Hutten, Op. Suppl. i. 278, ll. 26 sqq. The context is as follows: "Item Bilibaldus nescio quis, qui debet esse in Nurmberga: ipse fecit multas minas dicens quod realiter vult expedire Theologos scriptis suis. Tunc ego dixi: ' Qui moritur minis, Ille compulsabitur bombis,' *teutonice*, Wer von trewen stirbt, den sol man mit furtzen zum grab leutten." I owe this reference to my friend Professor von Jagemann, who says: " The Latin context makes it clear that Carlyle's second version was intended only as a modernization of the first; but even the first version is in a form quite modern as compared with the original." The words are too coarse to translate.

[2] This letter is printed by Froude, *Life*, ii. ch. 3: " The young man [Tom Bell] it appeared had been engaged in some courtship with one of the maid servants of the house; had come that night to see her in the fashion common, or indeed universal, with men of his station in that quarter, was overheard by the butler, was challenged, pursued, and, refusing to answer any interrogatory, but hastening to escape, was shot dead by him on the spot." Knockhill was near Ecclefechan.

NOTE BOOK OF

Got dreadfully ill on with a most tremendous speculation on *History*, intended first as an introduction to my German work; then found at last that it would not do there; so cut it out (after finishing it) and gave it to my Wife.

I carry less weight now, and skim more smoothly along (April 12): why cannot I write books (of that kind) as I write letters? They are and will be of only temporary use.

---

A man writes me out of Kent (the Rev.[d] G. R. Gleig the "Subaltern"[1]) wanting a Life of Goethe; then still more anxious for one of

[1] *The Subaltern*, published in 1825, is a story founded on incidents in the Peninsular War, in which Gleig had served. The book was a good one of its kind, and brought reputation to its author, who had left the army and taken orders. In 1846 he became Chaplain-general of the army. He died in 1885. The *Lives* which he wanted were for some "Library of General Knowledge" of which he was editor. In a letter to Eckermann of March 20, 1830, Carlyle wrote: "The other day there came a letter to me . . . earnestly requesting a 'Life of Goethe.' Knowing my correspondent as a man of some weight and respectability in literature, I have just answered him that the making of Goethe known to England was a task which any Englishman might be proud of; but that, as for his Biography, the only rational plan, as matters stood, was to take what he himself had seen fit to impart on the subject; and by proper commentary and adaptation, above all, by a suitable version, and not perversion of what was to be translated, enable an Englishman to read it with the eye of a German." *Correspondence between Goethe and Carlyle*, p. 170.

## THOMAS CARLYLE.

*Luther;* — which I have refused. If I write *Luther*, it must be more than a Biographic chronicle or less. Shall we go to Weimar then in winter, and prepare all the documents for that end? — *Manos a la obra!* — Take the task which is *nearest* thee!

---

Francis Jeffrey the other week offered me a hundred a year;[1] having learned that this sum met my yearly wants: he did it neatly enough, and I had no doubt of his sincerity. What a state of society is this; in which a man would rather be shot thro' the heart, twenty-times, than do both himself and his neighbour a *real ease!* How separate Pride from the natural necessary feeling of Self? It is ill to do; yet may be done.

---

On the whole, I have been somewhat in

[1] In his *Reminiscences*, ii, 254, Carlyle, writing thirty-six years later, says: "Jeffrey about this time generously offered to confer on me an annuity of £100; — which annual sum, had it fallen on me from the clouds, would have been of very high convenience at that time, but which I could not, for a moment, have dreamt of accepting as gift or subventionary help from any fellow mortal." He goes on to set forth his motives for refusing the offer in a passage of acute analysis of his own and Jeffrey's feelings in the matter, in which he perhaps hardly does justice to the simplicity of Jeffrey's kind intention. The whole transaction was creditable to both. It reminds one of the Wedgwoods' annuity to Coleridge. The contrast between Coleridge and Carlyle in their respective dealing with a similar matter is striking.

the wrong about 'independence'; man is *not* independent of his brother. Twenty men united in love can accomplish much that to two thousand isolated men were impossible. Know this; and know also that thou *hast* a power of thy own, and standest with a Heaven above even *thee*.—And so, *im Teufel's Namen*, get to thy work then!—

---

Quid mortui viventium legitis epitaphia? [1]

Hutteni opera I. 234 { Hartman v. Kirchberg's Epitaph on himself: he was Abbot of Fulda about 1500.

8th June. Am about beginning the Second Volume of that Germ. Lit. Hist.: dreadfully lazy to start. I know and feel that it will be a trivial insignificant Book, do what I can: yet the writing of it sickens me and inflames my nerves, as if it were a *Poem!* Were I done with this, I will endeavour to *compile* no more.

30th June. On the 22nd of June 1830, my Sister Margaret died at Dumfries, whither she had been removed exactly a week before for medical help. It was on a Tuesday night, about 20 minutes past ten. Alick and

[1] " Why do ye dead read the epitaphs of the living? "

## THOMAS CARLYLE.

I were roused by express about midnight, and we arrived there about four. That solstice night with its singing birds and sad thoughts I shall never forget. She was interred next Saturday at Ecclefechan. I reckoned her the best of all my sisters,— in some respects the best woman I had ever seen. Fain would I have saved her, but it was not to be.—

" Whom bring ye us to the still dwelling?"

" 'Tis a tired playmate whom we bring you: let her rest in your still dwelling, till the songs of her heavenly sisters awaken her." [1]

                    spirit
Thy quiet goodness, [heart so] pure & brave
              now with tears
[With tears] what boots it [here] to tell?
       Peace [Rest]
The path to [God] is thro' the grave;
          take our long
Thou loved one, for a while, farewell! [2]

---

And so this morning (Wednesday), let me

[1] These words are from Wilhelm Meister's Apprenticeship, Book viii. ch. 8. [What a tragedy was this to us; how vivid still in all its details to me! (1866.)], is written on the margin of the Note-book. In his *Reminiscences*, ii. 193-195, Carlyle gives a touching account of his sister's illness and death. It shows the depth and permanence of his affection. It should be read in connection with a letter to his brother John, of June 29, 1830 — a most affecting contemporary narrative. *Life*, ii. 109.

[2] The bracketed words of this stanza are erased in the manuscript.

betake myself *again*, with what energy I can, to the commencement of my task. Work is for the living, Rest is for the dead.

———

Is not the Christian Religion, is not every truly vital interest of mankind (?) a thing that *grows* ?   Like some Nile ' whose springs are indeed hidden, but whose full flood bringing gladness and fertility from its mysterious mountains is seen and welcomed by all.' (from myself!)—

Received about four weeks ago a strange letter from some *Saint-Simoniens* at Paris, grounded on my little *Signs of the Times*.[1] These people have strange notions, not without a large spicing of truth, and are themselves among the *Signs*.  I shall feel curious to know what becomes of them. *La classe la plus pauvre* is evidently in the way of rising from its present deepest abasement: in time, it is likely, the world will be better divided, and he that has the toil of ploughing will have the first cut at the reaping.— I answered these *St. Ss.* and partly expect to hear from them again.[2]

[1] Published a few months before in the *Edinburgh Review*. The thought contained in the preceding paragraph is treated at large in it.

[2] "I forget whether I mentioned last week," writes Carlyle to his mother, "that we had a parcel from Goethe, with pictures of his House, etc. ; and a still stranger parcel from Paris addressed to the Author of the *Signs*

# THOMAS CARLYLE.

A man with £200,000 a year eats the *whole* fruit of 6,666 men's labour thro' a year; for you can get a stout spademan to work and maintain himself for that sum of £30. Thus we have private individuals whose wages are equal to the wages of 7 or 8 thousand other individuals: what do those highly beneficed individuals *do* to society for their wages?

*of the Times.* The people there seem to think me a very promising man, and that some good will come of me. Thus a prophet is not without honor save in his own country. Poor prophet! However, in my present solitude, I am very glad of these small encouragements." *Letters*, i. 226. In a letter of the 31 August, 1830, to Goethe, Carlyle tells of the letter and books sent to him by *La Société Saint Simonienne* and adds: "If you have chanced to notice that Saint Simonian affair, which long turned on Political Economy, and but lately became Artistic and Religious, I should like much to hear your thoughts on it." *Correspondence of Goethe and Carlyle*, p. 215. In his reply on the 17th October, Goethe merely says: "Von der Société St. Simonienne bitte Sich fern zu halten." "From the St. Simonian Society pray hold yourself aloof." *Id.* p. 226.. Writing again to Goethe, on the 22d June, 1831, Carlyle tells of another gift of documents from the Saint-Simonians, and says: "They seem to me to be earnest, zealous and nowise ignorant men, but wandering in strange paths. I should say they have discovered and laid to heart this momentous and now almost forgotten truth, *Man is still Man*, and are already beginning to make false applications of it. I have every disposition to follow your advice, and stand apart from them; looking on their Society and its progress nevertheless as a true and remarkable Sign of the Times." *Id.* p. 258. In *Sartor Resartus*, Book iii. ch. xii, Carlyle repeats his opinion of the Saint Simonians in almost the same words as those he had used concerning them to Goethe.

*Kill Partridges.*[1]  CAN this last? No, by the soul that is in man, it cannot and will not and shall not! —

Our Political Economists should collect statistical *facts:* such as, What is the lowest sum a man can live on in various countries; what is the highest he gets to live on; How many people work with their hands, How many with their heads, How many not at all; — and innumerable such. What all want to know is the condition of our fellow men, and strange to say, it is the thing least of all understood, or to be understood as matters go. — The present 'Science' of Political Economy requires far less intellect than successful Bellows-mending; and perhaps does less good, if we deduct all the evil it brings us. 'Tho' young it already carries marks of decrepitude': a speedy and soft death to it!

---

You see two men fronting each other; one sits dressed in red cloth, the other stands dressed in threadbare blue; the first says to the other: Be hanged and anatomised! — and it is forthwith put in execution, and the matter rests not till Number Two is a skeleton! Whence comes it? These men have

[1] Readers of *Sartor Resartus* will recall that one of the particulars in the famous epitaph of Count Zähdarm is: *Dum sub Luna agebat, quinquies mille Perdrices plumbo confecit.*

## THOMAS CARLYLE.

no *physical hold* of each other, they are not in *contact;* each of the Bailiffs &c. is included within his own *skin*, and not hooked to any other. The Reason is: *Man is a spirit;* invisible influences run thro' *Society*, and make it a mysterious whole, full of Life and inscrutable activities and capabilities. Our individual existence is mystery; our social still more.—[1] Nothing can act but where it is? True, if you will; only *where is it?* Is not the Distant, the Dead, whom I love and sorrow for, HERE, in the genuine spiritual sense, as really as the Table I now write on? Space is a mode of our Sense; so is Time (this I only *half* understand): *we* are — we know not what; light-sparkles floating in the Aether of the Divinity! — So that this solid world, after all, is but an air-image; our *Me* is the only reality, ' and all is Godlike or God.' —[2]
Thou wilt have no Mystery and Mysticism; wilt live in the daylight (rushlight?) of Truth, and see thy world and understand it? Nay thou wilt laugh at all that believe in a Mystery; to whom the Universe is an Oracle and Temple as well as a Kitchen and Cattle-stall? *Armer Teufel!* Doth not thy Cow calve, doth not thy Bull gender? Nay (peradventure)

[1] This paragraph, in fuller development, is embodied in *Sartor Resartus*, Book i. ch. ix.
[2] Cf. *Sartor Resartus*, Book i. ch. vii.

dost not thou thyself gender? *Explain* me that; or do one of two things: Retire into private places with thy foolish cackle; or, what were better, give it up, and weep, not that the world is mean and disenchanted and prosaic, but that thou art vain and blind.—[1]

Is anything more wonderful than another, if you consider it maturely? *I* have *seen* no men rise from the Dead; I have seen some thousands rise from Nothing: I have not force to fly into the Sun, but I *have* force to lift my hand; which is equally strange.[2]

Wonder is the basis of worship: the reign of Wonder is perennial, indestructible; only at certain stages (as the present) it is (for some short season) *in partibus infidelium*.[3]

What is a man if you look at him with the

[1] Cf. *Sartor Resartus*, Book i. ch. x, where this paragraph appears with some enlargement.

[2] "Thus were it not miraculous, could I stretch forth my hand and clutch the Sun? Yet thou seest me daily stretch forth my hand and therewith clutch many a thing, and swing it hither and thither. Art thou a grown baby, then, to fancy that the Miracle lies in miles of distance, or in pounds avoirdupois of weight; and not to see that the true inexplicable God-revealing Miracle lies in this, that I stretch forth my hand at all; that I have free force to clutch aught therewith?"
*Sartor Resartus*, Book iii. ch. viii.

[3] This sentence appears in *Sartor Resartus*, Book i. ch. x.

mere Logical sense, with the Understanding? A pitiful hungry biped that wears breeches. Often when I read of pompous ceremonials, drawing-room levees and coronations, on a sudden the *clothes* fly off the whole party in my fancy, and they stand there straddling, in a half-ludicrous, half-horrid condition!—August 1830.[1]

September 7th Yesterday I received tidings that my project of cutting up that thrice-wretched *Hist. G. Literature* into Review Articles, and so realizing *something* for my Year's work, will *not* take effect. The 'Course of Providence' (nay sometimes I almost feel that there *is* such a thing even for *me*) seems guiding my steps into new regions; the question is coming more and more towards a decision: Canst thou, there as thou art, accomplish aught good and true, or art thou to die miserably as a vain Pretender? It is above a year since I wrote one sentence that came from the right place; since I did one action that seemed to be really worthy. The want of money is a comparatively insignificant affair:[2] were I doing well otherwise, I

[1] Here is the first formal expression of the thought that grew into *Sartor Resartus*. Cf. Book i. chs. ix, x, in which the special fancies of this paragraph have their full play.

[2] "We are very poor at present; but that is *all*, and

could most readily consent to go destitute and suffer all sorts of things. On the whole I am a — But tush! —

The Moral Nature of a man is not a composite factitious concern, but lies in the very heart of his being, as his very Self of Selves. The first alleviation to irremediable Pain is some conviction that it has been merited; that it comes from the All-just, from God.—

What am I but a sort of Ghost? Men rise as Apparitions from the bosom of Night, and after grinning, squeaking, gibbering some space, return thither. The earth they stand on is Bottomless; the vault of their sky is Infinitude; the Life-*Time* is encompassed with Eternity. O wonder! And they buy cattle or seats in Parliament, and drink coarser or finer fermented liquours, as if all this were a City that had foundations.[1]

———

I have strange glimpses of the power of spiritual Union, of Association among men of like object. Therein lies the true Element of Religion: it is a truly supernatural climate. All wondrous things, from a Pennenden Heath, or Penny-a-week Purgatory So-

we will get over that. Fear nothing: we mean nothing but honest things, and must and will prosper in them, seeing the very effort is success." Carlyle to his brother John, Aug. 6, 1830. *Letters*, i. 230.

[1] Cf. *Sartor Resartus*, Book i. ch. iii.

THOMAS CARLYLE.

ciety, to the foundation of a Christianity, or the (now obsolete) exercise of magic, take their rise here. Men work godlike miracles thereby, and the horridest abominations. *Society* is a wonder of wonders;[1] and Politics (in the right sense, far, very far from the common one) *is* the noblest Science.
*Cor ne edito!*[2] Up and be doing! Hast thou not the strangest grandest of all talents committed to thee; namely LIFE itself? O Heaven! And it is momently rusting and wasting, if thou use it not. Up and be doing; and pray (if thou but can) to the Unseen Author of all thy Strength to guide thee

[1] Cf. *Sartor Resartus*, Book iii. ch. ii.
[2] See *ante*, p. 121. This injunction is among the sayings ascribed to Pythagoras by Diogenes Laertius in his Life of the philosopher, § 18. Plutarch cites it in his essay 'Of the Training of Children.' "Eat not thy heart; which forbids to afflict our souls, and waste them with vexatious cares." But, as was long since pointed out, the conception of eating one's own heart is to be found in Homer, in the pathetic verses describing Bellerophon:
— οἷος ἀλᾶτο,
Ὂν θυμὸν κατέδων, πάτον ἀνθρώπων ἀλεείνων.
"He wandered solitary, eating his own heart, avoiding the path of men." *Iliad*, vi. 201-2; and again in the ninth book of the *Odyssey*, vv. 74, 75, "There," says Ulysses, "for two nights and days we lay, eating our hearts because of toil and trouble." Carlyle had experienced the bitterness of this diet. "It was my own heart . . . that I kept devouring," says Teufelsdröckh, *Sartor Resartus*, Book ii. ch. viii. And in *Wotton Reinfred*, Carlyle wrote, "He hurried into the country, not to possess his soul in peace as he had hoped, but, in truth, like Homer's Bellerophon, to eat his own heart." P. 43.

and aid thee; to give thee if not Victory and Possession, unwearied Activity and *Entsagen*.—
Is not every Thought properly an Inspiration? Or how is one thing more *inspired* than another? Much is in this.—

Why should Politeness be the peculiar characteristic of the Rich and Well-born? Is not every man *alive;* is not every man infinitely venerable to every other? 'There is but one Temple in the Universe' says Novalis, 'and that is the body of man.'[1]—

Franz von Sickingen was one of the noblest men of the Reformation Period. He defended Ulrich von Hutten; warred against perfidious Würtemberg; was the terror of evil doers the praise of whoso did well. Hutten and he read Luther together: Light rising in Darkness! He also stood by Götz von Berlichingen, and now walks in Poetry. But why I mention him here is his transcendent good-breeding. He was at feud with his superior the Bishop of Triers, and besieged by him, and valiantly defending himself against injustice, at the moment when he received his death-wound. His Castle was surrendered; Triers and others

[1] *Novalis Schriften*, ii. 126. Berlin, 1826. The preceding entry is developed in *Sartor Resartus*, Book iii. ch. iv.

approached the brave man over whose countenance the last paleness was already spreading. He took off his cap to Triers, there as he lay in that stern agony. What a picture! — " He had feud with the Archbishop of Trier, whom the Elector Palatine, the Landgraf of Hessen, and a large portion of the German Nobles were assisting. His castle *Landstein* was besieged by these Allies in 1523; the hero defended it night and day with unflinching steadfastness and valour. At last he was struck on the roof (*Dachmauer*) by a musket ball, and fell. He lived four and twenty hours; spoke kindly with the Princes who had conquered him; and tho' already *todtschwach*[1] took off his cap (*Müzze*) to the Archbishop whose vassal he was. Even his Enemies wept at the lordly obsequies that in the Church at Landstein were rendered him." *Ulrich von Hutten* by Wagenseil (page already lost in turning to the Title!) — *Landstuhl* the Conv. Lexicon calls the Castle. Münch, *F. von Sickingen's Plane, Thaten, Freunde und Ausgang* is in two volumes. Should like to see it.—

*Nulla dies sine linea!* — Eheu! Eheu! Yesterday (Monday) accordingly I wrote a thing in dactyls, entitled the *Wandering Spirits*, which now fills and then filled me

[1] "Faint with death."

'with detestation and abhorrence.' No matter: to day I must do the like. *Nulla dies sine linea!* To the persevering, they say, all things are possible. Possible or impossible, I have no other implement for trying.

Last night I sat up very late reading Scott's *History of Scotland*. An amusing Narrative, clear, precise and I suppose accurate; but no more a *History* of Scotland than I am Pope of Rome. A series of Palace intrigues, and butcheries and battles little more important than those of Donnybrook Fair; all the while that *Scotland*, quite unnoticed, is holding on her course in Industry, in Arts, in Culture, as if *Langside* and *Clean-the-Causeway* had remained unfought. Strange that a man should think he was writing the History of a Nation, while he is chronicling the amours of a wanton young woman called Queen, and a sulky booby recommended to Kingship for his fine limbs, and then blown up with gunpowder for ill-behaviour. Good Heaven! let them fondle and pout and bicker *ad libitum :* what has God's fair Creation, and man's immortal Destiny to do with them and their trade ?—

One inference I have drawn from Scott: that the people in those old days had a singular talent for nicknames: King *Toom-Tabard*, *Bell the Cat* (less meritorious), the *Foul Raid*, the *Roundabout Raid*, *Clean-the-Causeway*, the

## THOMAS CARLYLE.

*Tulchan* Prelates,[1] &c. &c. Apparently there was more Humour in the national mind then than now. For the rest, the Scottish History looks like that of a Gypsey encampment: industry of the rudest, largely broken by sheer indolence; smoke, sluttishness, hunger, scab and — blood. Happily, as hinted, Scotland herself *was not there.* Lastly it is noteworthy that the Nobles of the country have maintained a quite despicable behaviour, from the times of Wallace downwards. A selfish, ferocious, famishing, unprincipled set of hyaenas, from whom at no time and in no way has the country derived any benefit. The day is coming when these our modern hyaenas (tho' *toothless*, still mischievous, and greedy beyond limit) will (quickly I hope) *be paid off.* " *Canaille fainéante, que faites-vous là ?* Down with your double-barrels; take spades, if ye can do no better, and work or die!"

---

The quantity of Pain thou feelest is indication of the quantity of Life, of Talent, thou hast: a stone feels no Pain.—(' Is that a fact ? ')

[1] A *tulchane* is, according to Jamieson, *Dictionary of the Scottish Language*, "a calf's skin stuffed with straw, and set beside a cow, to make her give milk;" and a Tulchane Bishop, "one who received the episcopate on condition of assigning the temporalities to a secular person."

Thursday, 9th September   Wrote a fractionlet of verse entitled THE BEETLE[1] (a real incident on Glaisters Moor), which alas! must stand for the *Linea* both of Tuesday and Wednesday. To day I am to try I know not what. Greater clearness will arrive; I make far most progress when I *walk*, on solitary roads — of which there are enough here.

Last night came a whole Bundle of Fraser Magazines &c.: two little Papers by my Brother in them; some (small-beer) Fables by me; and on the whole such a hurlyburly of rhodomontade, punch, loyalty, and Saturnalian Toryism as eye hath not seen. This out-Blackwoods Blackwood. Nevertheless the thing has its meaning: a kind of wild popular Lower-Comedy; of which John Wilson is the Inventor: it may perhaps, for it seems well adapted to the age, carry down his name to other times, as his most remarkable achievement. All the Magazines (except the New Monthly) seem to aim at it: a certain quickness, fluency of banter, not excluding sharp insight, and Merry-Andrew Drollery, and even Humour, are available here; however, the grand requisite seems to be Impudence, and a fearless committing of yourself to talk in your Drink.— *Literature* has *nothing* to do with this, but Printing has; and Printing is

[1] See *Essays*, i., Appendix, for these verses.

now no more the peculiar symbol and livery of Literature than writing was in Gutenberg's day. —

Great actions are sometimes historically barren; smallest actions have taken root (in the moral soil) and grown like banana-forests to cover whole quarters of the world. Aristotle's Philosophy and the Sermon on the Mount (and both too had *fair trial*); the *Mécanique Céleste* and the *Sorrows of Werter;* Alexander's Expedition, and that of Paul an Apostle of the Gentiles! Of these, however, Werter is half a *gourd*, and only by its huge *decidua* (to be used as manure) will fertilize the Future. So too with the rest; all are *deciduous*, and must at last make manure; only at longer dates. Yet of some the *root* also (?) seems to be undying.

What are Schiller and Goethe, if you try them in that way? As yet it is too soon to try them. No true effort *can* be lost.

One thing we see: the moral nature of man is deeper than his intellectual; things planted down into the former may grow as if forever; the latter as a kind of drift mould produces only annuals. What is Jesus Christ's significance? *Altogether moral.*

What is Jeremy Bentham's significance? Altogether intellectual, logical. I name him as the representative of a class, important only for their numbers; intrinsically wearisome, almost pitiable and pitiful. Logic is their sole foundation, no other even recognized as possible: wherefore their system is a *Machine*, and cannot *grow* or endure; but after thrashing for a little (and doing good service that way) must thrash itself to pieces, and be made fuel.— Alas poor England, stupid, purblind, pudding-eating England! Bentham with his *Mills* grinding thee out Morality; and some Macaulay, also be-aproned and a grinder, testing it and decrying it, because it is not his own Whig-established *Quern*-morality! I mean that the Utilitarians *have* Logical Machinery, and do grind fiercely and potently, *on their own foundation;* whereas the Whigs have no foundation but must stick up their handmills, or even pepper-mills, on what fixture they can come at, and there grind as it pleases Heaven. The Whigs are Amateurs, the Radicals are Guild-brethren.

The Sin of this age is Dilettantism; the Whigs, and all 'moderate Tories,' are the grand Dilettanti: I begin to feel less and less patience for them. This is no world where a man should stand trimming his whiskers, looking on at work, or touching it with the point of a gloved finger. *Man sollte greifen zu!*[1] There is more hope of an Atheist Utilitarian, of a Superstitious Ultra, than of such a

[1] "One must grip hold."

lukewarm, withered mongrel. He would not believe tho' one rose from the dead. He is wedded to his idols, let him alone.

---

September (about the 28th). Rain! Rain! Rain! The crops all lying tattered, scattered and unripe; the winter's bread still under the soaking clouds! God pity the poor!

---

The Jeffreys were here for about a week.[1] Very good and interesting beyond wont was our worthy Dean. He is growing old, and seems dispirited and partly unhappy.— The fairest cloak has its wrong side, where the seams and straggling stitches afflict the eye! Envy no man; *nescis quo urit*, thou knowest not where the shoe pinches.

Jeffrey's essential talent sometimes seems to me to have been that of a Goldoni; some comic Dramatist not without a touch of true lyrical pathos. He is the best *mimic* (in the lowest and highest senses) I ever saw. All matters that have come before him he has taken up in little dainty comprehensible forms; chiefly logical (for he is a Scotchman and Lawyer) and encircled with sparkles of conversational wit or *persiflage;* yet with deeper

[1] See *Reminiscences*, "Lord Jeffrey," ii. 245, sqq. for Carlyle's recollections of this visit, and his final estimate of his friend.

study he would have found poetical forms for them, and his persiflage might have incorporated itself gracefully with the Love and pure humane feeling that dwells deeply in him. This last is his highest strength, tho' he himself hardly knows the significance of it: he is one of the most *loving* men alive; has a true kindness, not of blood and habit only, but of soul and spirit. He cannot *do* without being loved. He is in the highest degree social; and in defect of this, *gregarious;* which last condition he (in these bad times) has for most part had to content himself withal. Every way indeed he has fallen on evil days: the prose spirit of the world (to which world his kindliness draws him so strongly and closely) has choked up and all but withered the better poetic spirit he derived from nature. Whatever is highest, he entertains (like other Whigs) only as an ornament, as an appendage. The great business of Man he (intellectually) considers as a worldling does: *To be happy*. I have heard him say: 'If Folly were the happiest, I would be a fool.' Yet his daily Life belies this doctrine, and says: 'Tho' Goodness were the most wretched I would be Good.'

In conversation he is brilliant (or rather sparkling), lively, kind, willing either to speak or listen, and above all men I have ever seen, ready and copious. On the whole exceedingly pleasant in light talk. Yet alas light, light, too light! He will talk of nothing *earnestly*, tho' his look sometimes betrays an earnest feeling. He starts contradiction in such cases, and argues, argues. Neither is his arguing like that of a Thinker, but of an Advocate; Victory not Truth. A right *Terrae Filius* would feel irresistibly disposed to 'wash him away.' He is not a *strong* man in any shape; but *nimble* and *tough*.

He stands midway between God and Mammon; and his preaching thro' Life has been an attempt to reconcile these. Hence his popularity; a thing easily accountable when one looks at the world and at him; but little honourable to either. Literature! Poetry! Except by a dim indestructible Instinct, which he has never dared to avow, yet being a true Poet (in his way) could never eradicate — he knows not what they mean. A true Newspaper Critic, on the great scale; no Priest, but a Concionator!

Yet on the whole, he is about the *best man* I ever saw. Sometimes I think he will abjure the Devil (if he live), and become a pure Light. Already he is a most tricksy dainty beautiful little Spirit: I have seen gleams on the face and eyes of the man that let you look into a higher country. God bless him! And I will blab no more. These jottings are as *sincere* as I could write them, yet too dim and inaccurately compacted. I see the nail, but have not here hit it on the head. *Basta!*

I am going to write — Nonsense. It is on " Clothes."[1] Heaven be my comforter! —

It was a wise regulation which ordained that certain days and times should be set apart for Seclusion and Meditation; whether as *Fasts* or not may reasonably admit of doubt, the business being ' to get *out* of the Body to philosophize.' But, on the whole, there is a deep significance in SILENCE. Were a man forced for a length of time but to *hold his peace*, it were in most cases an incalculable benefit to his insight. Thought works in Silence; so does Virtue. One might erect statues to Silence. I sometimes think it were good for *me*, who after all cannot err much in loquacity here, did I impose on myself at set times, the duty — of not speaking for a day. What folly would one avoid, did the tongue lie quiet till the mind had finished, and were calling for utterance. Not only our good Thoughts but our good Purposes also are frittered asunder and dissipated by unseasonable speaking of them. *Words*, the strangest product of our nature, are also the most potent. Beware of speaking. Speech

[1] *Sartor Resartus:* begun at this time, the book was completed in July, 1831. See *Letters*, i. 235, 300.

is human, Silence is divine: yet also brutish and dead; therefore we must learn *both* arts, they are both difficult. Flower-roots *hidden* under soil; Bees working in Darkness, &c. The soul too in Silence.— Let not thy left hand know what thy right hand doeth. Indeed, Secrecy is the element of all Goodness; every Virtue, every Beauty is *mysterious*. I hardly understand even the surface of this.—[1]

Written a strange piece "On clothes": know not what will come of it. October 28th 1830.

See in Goethe's *Werke* B[and] 31, about page 220, for the possible material of an *Article*.

Our loveliest dear doth sit down stairs
Seek well and the gay sweetheart you'll find
A timber gown is the suit she wears,
And her name is the Muscadine.[2]
      Seb. Brandt.

Gutes Pferd
Ist's Hafers werth.[3]
(Myself! November 24th)

Received the 'ornamented Schiller' from

[1] Cf. *Sartor Resartus*, Book iii. ch. iii, where the substance of this entry is reworked.
[2] See *ante* (page 118).
[3] "A good horse is worth his oats."

Goethe, and wondered not a little to see poor old Craigenputtock engraved at Frankfort on the Meyn. If I become anything it will look well; if I become nothing, a piece of kind dotage (on his part).[1]—Sent away the *Clothes*;[2] of which I could make a kind of Book; but cannot *afford* it. Have still *the* Book *in petto* (?) but in the most chaotic shape.

---

The Whigs in office, and Baron Brougham Lord Chancellor! Hay-stacks and corn-stacks burning over all the South and Middle of England! Where will it end? Revolution on the back of Revolution for a

[1] On the sixth of June, 1830, Goethe wrote to Carlyle: " Further you will find in the little box the last sheets of the translation of your *Life of Schiller*. The publication has been delayed, and I wished to make the little work especially pretty, for the sake of the publisher, as well as for its own. I have certainly pleased the public, so may you excuse it. The frontispiece represents your house from a near point of view, the vignette on the title-page, the same from a distance. . . . Outside, on the front cover is a view of Schiller's house in Weimar; and on the cover at the back, a little garden-house [at Jena] which he himself built in order that he might withdraw from his family and all the world." *Correspondence between Goethe and Carlyle*, p. 203. To this volume, which has now become scarce, Goethe prefixed a long preface of much interest, a translation of which forms the first appendix to the above-cited *Correspondence*, occupying pp. 299-323.

[2] It was Carlyle's first intention to make two magazine articles of what became the book *Sartor*. This paper which he sent to Fraser's Magazine was entitled " Thoughts on Clothes." See *Letters*, i. 238, 249.

century yet? *Religion,* the cement of *Society,* is not here: we can have no permanent beneficent arrangement of affairs.

Not that we want *no* Aristocracy, but that we want a *true* one. While the many work with their hands, let the few work with their heads and hearts, *honestly,* and not with a shameless villainy only pretend to work, or even openly *steal.*— Were the Landlords all hanged, and their estates given to the poor, we should be (economically) much happier perhaps for the space of thirty years; but the Population would be doubled then, and again the Hunger of the unthrifty would burn the granary of the industrious. Alas! that there is no Church; and as yet no apparent possibility of one!

The divine right of Squires is equal to the right divine of Kings, and not superior? A word has made them, and a word can unmake.

I have no *Property* in anything whatsoever; except perhaps (if I am a virtuous man) in my own Free-will: of my Body I have only a life-rent; of all that is without my Skin only an accidental Possession — so long as I can keep it. Vain man! are the stars *thine* because thou lookest on them; is that piece of Earth thine because thou hast eaten of its fruits? Thy proudest Palace, what is it but a Tent; pitched not indeed for days, yet for years? The earth is *the Lord's*. Remember this, and seek other Duties than game-preserving, wouldest thou not be an interloper, sturdy beggar, and even thief:—

*Faules* Pferd
Keins Hafers werth.[1]

The Labourer is worthy of his Hire; and the Idler of his also,— namely of Starvation.

———

What *is* Art and Poetry? Is the Beautiful really higher than the Good? A higher *form* thereof? Thus were a Poet not only a Priest but a High-Priest.

———

Examine by Logic the import of thy Life, and of all lives: What is it? A making of Meal into Manure; and of Manure into Meal.[2] To the *Cui-bono* there is no answer from Logic.

———

Clara gives a kiss, is it much for her to do? When she gives one don't she take one too?

———

Canst keep thy own secret
No other will break it.

[1] "The idle horse not worth his oats."
[2] Compare the humorous development of this thought in the epitaph on Count Zähdarm, *Sartor Resartus*, Book ii. ch. iv.

THOMAS CARLYLE.

These two from Logau. A Latin translation of *Mai* in Jördens B[and] 6. (Written here to get rid of a rag of Paper — it is a *sorting* day — Ach!)

29th December 1830. The old year just expiring; one of the most worthless years I have spent for a long time. *Durch eignes und andrer Schuld!*[1] But words are *worse* than nothing. To thy *Review*[2] (Taylor's Hist. Survey.) Is it the most despicable of work? Yet is it not too good for *thee?* O, I care not for Poverty, little even for Disgrace, nothing at all for want of *Renown:* but the horrible feeling is when I cease my own struggle, lose the consciousness of my own strength, and become positively quite worldly and wicked.—

In the paths of Fortune (Fortune!) I have made no advancement, since last year; but on the contrary (owing chiefly to that German Literary History, one way and another) considerably retrograded. No matter; had I but progressed in the other better path! But alas! alas!— Howsoever, *pocas palabras! I* am still here.

Bist *Du* glücklich, Du Gute, dass Du unter die Erde bist? —Wo stehst Du? Liebst Du

---
[1] "Through my own and others' fault."
[2] *Historic Survey of German Poetry*. By W. Taylor of Norwich, 3 vols., 8vo. London, 1830.

mich noch ?[1]— God is the God of the Dead as well as of the living: the Dead, as the Living, are where — HE WILLS.

*Kehret ins Leben zurück!*[2] — Jack[3] writes miserably hurried letters: I fear he is unhappy; there is no doubt he is a little unwise; yet I think him *gathering* wisdom.

This Taylor is a wretched Atheist and Philistine: it is *my* duty (perhaps) to put the flock, whom he professes to lead, on their guard. Let me do it *well!*

In a purse from my wife, yesterday (December 30th 1830); written with pencil on a slip of paper, which I now burn:

Fortunatus' Purse was a mighty fine thing,
Yet a pest, nothing else, to its owner;
For me, neither guineas nor troubles I bring,
My whole worth is the Love of my donor.

Feby 7th 1831. Finished the Review of *Taylor* some three weeks ago, and sent it off: no tidings about it yet. It is worth little, and only partially in a right spirit.—

[1] "Art thou fortunate, thou Good One, in being under the earth? Where art thou? Still lovest thou me?"
[2] "Let us come back to life."
[3] Dr. John Carlyle, then in London.

THOMAS CARLYLE.

Sent to Jack to liberate my *Teufelsdreck* [1] from Editorial durance in London, and am seriously thinking to make a Book of it.[2] The thing is not right, not *Art;* yet perhaps a nearer approach to Art than I have yet made. We ought to try. I want to get it done; and then translate *Faust*, as I have partially promised to Goethe. Thro' *Teufelsdreck* I am yet far from seeing my way; nevertheless materials are partly forthcoming. — Goethe has lost his son, and been on the point of death himself. Venerable old man! Shall I never see thee with these eyes? — A letter of mine will be about this time in his hands.

No sense from the *Foreign Quarterly Review;* have nearly determined on opening a correspondence on the matter of that 'everlasting MS' with Bowring of the *Westminster*. Could write also a Paper on the Saint-Simonians. One too on Dr. Johnson — for Napier. Such are the financial aspects. N. B. I have some £5 to front the world with; and expect no more for months. Jack too is in the neap tide.— Hand to the oar! —

All Europe is in a state of disturbance, of

[1] See *Letters*, i. 249. " *Teufelsdreck*, that is the title of my present *Schrift*." *Id.* 237.
[2] Had gone to *Fraser* first, then? [T. C. 1866.]

Revolution. About this very time they may be debating the question of British 'Reform,' in London : the Parliament opened last week, our news of it expected on Wednesday. The times are big with change. Will *one* century of constant fluctuation serve us, or shall we need two ? Their Parl. Reforms, and all that, are of small moment; a beginning (of good & evil) nothing more. The whole frame of Society is rotten and must go for fuel-wood, and *where* is the new frame to come from ? I know not, and no man knows.

---

The only Sovereigns of the world in these days are the Literary men (were there any such in Britain), the Prophets. It is always a Theocracy; the King has to be anointed by the Priest, and now the Priest (the Goethe for example) will not cannot consecrate the existing King, who therefore is a usurper, and reigns only by sufferance. What were the bet that King William were the last of that Profession in Britain, and Queen Victoria never troubled with the sceptre at all ? Mighty odds; yet nevertheless not infinite; for what thing is certain *now ?* No mortal cares twopence for any King, or obeys any King except thro' *compulsion:* and Society is *not* a Ship of war, its Government *cannot* always be a Pressgang.

What are the Episcopal Dignitaries saying

to it? Who knows but Edward Irving may yet be a Bishop! They will clutch round them for help, and unmuzzle all manner of Bulldogs when the thief is at the gate: Bulldogs with *teeth;* the generality have no teeth in that Kennel.

Kings *do* reign by divine right, or not at all. The King that were God-appointed, would be an emblem of God, and could *demand* all obedience from us. But where is that King? The BEST MAN, could we find him, were he. Tell us, tell us, O ye Codifiers and Statists and Economists, how we shall find him and raise him to the throne:— or else admit that the science of Polity is worse than unknown to you.

Earl (*Jarl, Yirl*), Count, Duke, Knight, &c. &c. are all titles derived from *fighting:* the honour-titles, in a future time, will derive themselves from *knowing* and well-*doing*. They will also be conferred with more deliberation, and by better judges. This is a prophecy of mine.[1]

---

God is above us! Else the figure of the world were well nigh desperate. 'Go where we may the deep HEAVEN will be round us.'

---

Jeffrey is Lord Advocate and M. P. Sobbed and shrieked at taking office, like a bride going

[1] Cf. *Sartor Resartus*, Book iii. ch. vii.

to be married. I wish him altogether well; but reckon that he is on the wrong course: Whiggism, I believe, is all but forever *done*. Away with Dilettantism and Machiavelism, tho' we should get Atheism and Sanscullotism in their room! The latter are at least substantial things, and do not build on a continued *wilful* falsehood.—

But oh! But oh! Where is Teufelsdreck all this while?— The Southwest is busy thawing off that horrible snow-storm; Time rests not: thou only art idle. To pen! to pen! (I shall have *Benvenuto Cellini* at night.)—

Feby 14th   *Ay de mi!* Another week gone, painfully and lazily and no work done!—

*Benvenuto Cellini* a very worthy Book, gives more insight into Italy than fifty Leo-Tenths would do.[1] A remarkable man Benvenuto and in a remarkable scene. Religion and Art with Ferocity and Sensuality; polished Respect with stormful Independence; faithfully obedient subjected to Popes who are not Hierarchs but plain scoundrels! Life was far sunnier and richer then; but a time of change (loudly called for) was advancing,— and but lately has reached its crisis.—Goethe's Essay on Benvenuto quite excellent.—

[1] The *Autobiography of Benvenuto Cellini*, compared with Roscoe's *Life of Leo X.*

## THOMAS CARLYLE.

Pope's Homer's *Odyssey*, surely a very false and tho' ingenious and talented yet bad translation. The old Epics are great because they (musically) show us the *whole world* of those old days: a modern Epic that did the like would be equally admired, and for us far more admirable. But where is the genius that can write it? Patience! Patience! he will be here one of these centuries.

Is Homer or Shakespeare the greater genius? Were hard to say. Shakespeare's world is the more complex, the more spiritual, and perhaps his mastery over it was equally complete. 'We *are such* STUFF as Dreams are made on': there is the basis of a whole Poetic universe; to that mind all forms, and figures of men and things, would become ideal.—

What is a *Whole ?* Or how, specially, *does* a Poem differ from Prose? Ask not a definition of it in words, which can hardly express common Logic correctly; study to create in thyself a *feeling* of it: like so much else, it cannot be made clear, hardly even to thy thought(?) — Alas, 'white men know nothing.'

I see some vague outline of what a *Whole* is: also how an individual Delineation may be 'informed with the Infinite'; may appear hanging in the universe of Time & Space (partly): in which case is it a Poem and a Whole? Therefore, are the true Heroic Poems of these times to be written with the *ink of Science?* Were a correct philosophic Biography of a Man (meaning by philosophic *all* that the name can include) the only method of celebrating him? The true History (had we any such, or even generally any dream of such) the true Epic Poem?—I partly begin to surmise so.—What after all is the true proportion of St. Matthew to Homer, of the Crucifixion to the Fall of Troy!

---

On the whole I wish I could define to myself the true relation of moral genius to poetic genius; of Religion to Poetry. Are they one and the same, different forms of the same; and if so which is to stand higher, the Beautiful or the Good? Schiller and Goethe seem to say the former, as if it included the latter and might supersede it: how truly I can never well see.—Meanwhile that the *faculties* always go together seems clear. It is a gross calumny on human nature to say that there ever was a mind of surpassing talent that did not also surpass in *capability* of virtue; and *vice versa;* nevertheless in both cases there are 'female geniuses" too, minds that admire and receive, but can hardly create; I have observed in these also the taste for Religion and for Poetry go together. The most wonderful words that I ever heard of being uttered by man are those in the four Evangelists, by Jesus of Nazareth. Their intellectual talent is hardly inferior to their moral. On this subject, if I live, I hope to have much to say.

---

And so ends my first Notebook, after nigh eight years,—here at Craigenputtock, at my *own* hearth, and tho' amid trouble and dispiritment enough, yet with better outlooks than I had then. My outward world is not much better (yes it is, though I have far less money), but my inward *is ;* and I can promise myself never to be *so* miserable again. Farewell ye that have fallen asleep since then; farewell, tho' distant perhaps near me! Welcome the Good and Evil that is to come, thro' which God assist me to struggle wisely! What have I to look back on? Little or nothing. What forward to? My own small sickly force amid wild enough whirlpools! The more diligently apply it then. Νὺξ ἔρχεται.[1]

[1] "The night cometh." *John* ix. 4.

Alfred Jones Aqua Fortis
from a photo. of a daguerreotype taken 1846.

# SECOND NOTE BOOK.

BEGUN IN LONDON.

August 4th 1831.  Left Craigenputtock,[1] and my kind little wife, Alick[2] driving me, at 2 o'clock in the morning. Shipped at Glencaple [3]: hazy day: saw Esbie [4] in the steerage; talked mysticism with him during six weary hours we had to stay at Whitehaven. Reimbarkment there, amid bellowing and tumult and fiddling unutterable: all like a spectral vision — '*she* is [not] there.' St. Bees Head. Man with the Nose. Sleep in the steamboat cabin: confusion worse confounded. Morning: views of Cheshire, the Rock, Liverpool and steamboats. Boy — Man.

[1] For a long contemplated visit to London in the hope of finding a publisher for *Sartor Resartus*, which had just been completed.
[2] His brother.
[3] Five miles beyond Dumfries.
[4] An old acquaintance, described in a letter of 27 Nov., 1818, to Mr. Robert Mitchell, as a "double-refined travelling tutor."—*Early Letters*, i. 191.

NOTE BOOK OF

5th   7½ in the morning. Land at Liverpool: all abed at Maryland street.[1] Boy Alick[2] accompanies me over Liverpool. Exchange-Dome: dim view there. Dust, toil; cotton-bags, hampers, repairing ships, disloading stones. Carson[3] a hash. Melancholy body of the name of Sloan. Wifekin's assiduity in caring for me.[4]

6th (Saturday)   taken to one Johnstone a Frenchified Lockerby man, who leads me to 'Change; place in ' the Independent Tallyho, Sir! ' — See George Johnstone, Surgeon, whom I had unearthed the night before. Patient of his. He dines with us. Walk on the Terrace near the Cemetery. Have seen the Steam-coaches[5] in the morning. Liverpool a dismembered aggregate of streets and sandpits. Market-hubbub.

[1] Home of Mrs. Carlyle's uncle, Mr. John Welsh, "a most munificent, affectionate and nobly honorable kind of man." *Reminiscences* i. 156; see also pp. 166–168.
[2] Son of Mr. John Welsh.
[3] A Liverpool doctor. See *Letters*, ii. 367.
[4] "Delightful it was" Carlyle writes to his wife on August 11, "on opening my trunk to find everywhere traces of my good 'coagitor's' [coadjutor's] care and love. Heaven reward thee, my clear-headed, warm-hearted, dearest little Screamikin!" *Life*, ii. 165.
[5] The Steam-coaches were still novelties; the first experimental trip with a steam engine was on the Liverpool & Manchester railway in October, 1829. The celebration of the opening of the road for regular steam travel and traffic was on Sept. 15, 1830, a memorable event made tragic by the death of Mr. Huskisson.

## THOMAS CARLYLE.

8th [1] *Oleum ricini.* Go out to find Esbie: he calls on me. Confused family dinner; do. tea. G. Johnstone again. Talk: to bed.

9th Off on Monday morning. Shipped thro' the Mersey; coached thro' Eastham, Chester, Overton (in Wales) Ellesmere, Shrewsbury, Wolverhampton, Birmingham: attempt at tea there. Discover (not without laughter) the villainy of the Liverpool Coach-Bookers. Henley in Arden; Stratford on Avon (horses lost there); get in to sleep. Oxford at 3 in the morning. Out again there: chill but pleasant. Henley, Maidenhead &c. Arrive full of sulphur at the Wh[ite] Horse Cellar, Piccadilly: dismount at the Regent Circus, and am wheeled (not whirled) hither,[2] about half past 10; poor Jack waiting all the while at the Angel, Islington. Talk together when he returns; dine at an Eatinghouse among Frenchmen, one of whom ceases eating to hear me talk of the St. Simonians. Leave my card at the Lord Advocate's,[3] with promise to call next morning. Sulphurous enough.

[1] The dates from the 8th to the 14th inclusive are wrong by a day in advance.
[2] To 6 Woburn Buildings, Tavistock Square, the dwelling of Edward Irving's brother George, where Dr. John Carlyle lodged.
[3] Jeffrey.

NOTE BOOK OF

11th (Wednesday)   Go to the Advocate's: am kindly received, the A. looking better than I expected: a Dr. Baron there (whom I knew not as such till after he was gone). Napier's Letter in the hands of the Postman.¹ Am advised to try Murray with my MS. rather; get a letter to him; see him with difficulty; send over my Papers, to have the answer affirmative or negative next Wednesday. A tall squinting man; not of the wisest aspect; seems to know me, and smiles on my description of *Dreck*² (the dog! I fear he will make me *greet* on it yet): the favour of the Ministry, through Jeffrey's interest, buoys me up with him. See the Badamses that evening (B. had already called on me very shortly after my arrival): poor B. seemed flushed and to have been drinking; his Wife a true soul, talented, true, but girlish; her mother a gigantic French-woman, now Wife of one Kenny a Playwright. Look in upon the Montagues as I return: Procter standing at the door;³ Mrs. M. in the dusk, colder

[1] Napier was Jeffrey's successor as editor of the Edinburgh Review. His letter enclosed one of introduction of Carlyle to Mr. Rees, of the publishing house of Longman & Co.   [2] " Dreck," that is, *Teufelsdreck*.

[3] The Basil Montagus; Procter, the poet who wrote under the pseudonym of Barry Cornwall, was their son-in-law. Carlyle's relations with the Montagus had begun during his visit to London with the Bullers in 1824. See *Life*, i. 120; *Reminiscences*, ii. 112, 127-130.

than might have been expected, yet with professions enough.¹

12th (Thursday)  Go out to see about a Sealcutter at Mrs. M.'s; am by her detained with a most vituperative history of the *Badams Bankrupt*, or a cheat discovered. Seems to me all overcharged; at best common-place, vindictive, nowise magnanimous. Speaking of John, almost get provoked, yet do not. Alas! 'all things go round and round' there: old friends utterly gone there; I too am no longer necessary. The people to be pitied; the 'noble lady' is *alone*, with her so shewy *Iety*.² Can say nothing of the Seal; and now I have hardly

¹ See for the filling out of this and the preceding entries the letter to Mrs. Carlyle of that date. *Life* ii. 164. Carlyle had become acquainted with Mr. Badams, a friend of Irving, in 1824, and had spent two months with him in that year at Birmingham. "This man, one of the most sensible, clear-headed persons I have ever met with, seems also one of the kindest," is what he writes of him to his mother. *Life*, i. 229. "A most inventive, light-hearted, and genially gallant kind of man; sadly *eclipsed* within the last five years, ill-married, plunged amid grand mining speculations, which were and showed themselves *sound*, but not till they had driven him to drink brandy instead of water, and next year to die miserably overwhelmed." *Reminiscences*, i. 93.

² The 'Noble Lady' was Edward Irving's epithet for Mrs. Montagu. Irving had introduced Carlyle to the Montagus in 1824, and in his "Reminiscences of Irving" Carlyle gives a vivid description of the Montagu household. *Reminiscences*, ii. 123–134.

NOTE BOOK OF

time remaining to write a most confused Letter to my Own, which I do in all sorrow at such loss of time, and the sight of such havoc and dismemberment as 6 years have brought. The Montagues are *wünderliche Menschen ;* [1] worth what?

13th (Friday)   Out to Longman's with my Napier Letter. State to them my *German Lit. History:* they "decline the article," civilly enough. Shall I try them with *Dreck* if Murray fail? *Schwerlich.*[2] On to the India House: see Strachey[3] and talk consentaneous Politics: invited to Sh[ooter's] Hill for Saturday. Returning call on Bowring,[4] he is in the country, but coming and going. Steer over to Allan Cunningham's[5] at night. (Have a Letter from my little Hermitess which makes me glad and sad.) Allan as of old: full of honesty and loud talk; I promised

---

[1] 'Strange people.'     [2] Hardly.
[3] The Stracheys were old acquaintances. Mrs. Strachey was the sister of Mrs. Buller. Mr. Strachey was a Somersetshire gentleman, ex-Indian, an examiner in the India House. See *Reminiscences*, ii. 49, 102, 124 *et al.* Often mentioned in *Life*.
[4] Dr., afterward Sir John, Bowring, a well-known radical and man of letters; described in a letter to Mrs. Carlyle, *Life*, ii. 172.
[5] At this date more or less a London celebrity, "a genuine, interesting man." "Solid Dumfries mason, with a surface polish," and a touch of native genius. For description of him, see *Reminiscences*, i. 175; ii. 169. See also *Life*, i. 220.

something of dining there next week. Have bought this *Book* in the mg.

14th Write to Goethe, to Buller, to Fraser. Off to Shooter's Hill. See Mrs. Badams by the way. She has engaged Godwin to meet us at tea; and countermanded him, and again talks of countermanding him for still a *new* night. Shooter's Hill looks as well as ever [1]: Strachey as talkative and full of vivacity as ever: his wife has an unhealthy, faded air; looks rather afraid of me, yet friendly and earnest. Kitty [2] is Mrs Phillips, a mother, and almost a widow (as I hear). Foolish Miss —— whom the Unregenerate demolishes with a shovel-hat.[3] Awake in the country with rooks (on the 15th or Sunday), beautiful morning; views of the Thames and Essex; talk, dinner; return (forgetting my umbrella) by Woolwich, Greenwich and the river to Tower Stairs; thence home, where a Letter lies from Bowring 'to breakfast on Tuesday.' Shave, wash, drink tea; argue on the everlasting 'spirit of the time' with Jack;

[1] "I have seldom seen a pleasanter place, a panorama of green, flowery, clean, and decorated country all round; an umbrageous little Park, with roses, gardens; a modestly excellent House." *Reminiscences*, ii. 124.

[2] Kitty Kirkpatrick, cousin of Mrs. Strachey, with whom she had been living at the time of Carlyle's visit to London in 1824. She is described charmingly in *Reminiscences*, ii. 117, 125.

[3] Cf. letter to Mrs. Carlyle, *Life*, ii, 170.

bolt off, and write thus far: will now read my Goody's Letter again, and therewith *Gute nacht!* (15<sup>th</sup> 10¾ o'clock at night — up stairs.) —

15<u>th</u> (believe I misdated on Sunday, and that *Monday* was the 15<u>th</u>) Went to breakfast with the Jeffreys: all very kind. The Adv. entered in his yellow night-gown, with his greyish face, clear roguish eyes, and said: " Why Charly [1] I've got cholera I believe." *Nichts weiter passirt* [2], except that I got a frank for Goody. Empson[3] not at home. The Seal-cutter not to be found (in Warwick Court). Write to my Jeannie and my Mother: barely in time for the Post. Go to Irving's to tea; talk of St. Simonism, etc.; Irving at heart the old friend. To dine with Drummond [4] (Banker) in his company on Friday. Off for Southampton Row to meet Godwin. Eheu! find there the French woman with Mrs. Godwin, presently afterwards the Badamses. Then a multifarious collection of Dilettanti, Play-

---

[1] His wife Charlotte.    [2] "Nothing further occurred."
[3] Jeffrey's son-in-law. See *Reminiscences*, ii. 269; and *Correspondence of Goethe and Carlyle*, p. 282.
[4] Henry Drummond, a worldly mystic, the most important figure in the sect that grew up around Irving, and the chief of the Apostles of the Catholic Apostolic Church, which still (1898) survives with a faint and what seems like an expiring life in America and in Germany, as well as in England. See *Reminiscences*, ii. 187, 198; *Life*, ii. 177.

## THOMAS CARLYLE.

wrights and Nondescripts: G. has in the meanwhile arrived. A little thickset man, with bushy eyebrows (white), grey open eyes, large coarse nose and chin; bald, hoary, yet brisk, and hearty of aspect, tho' old. He speaks little: what he says has a certain epigrammatic effect-character. Ask him, after some skirmishing about the bush, what he thinks of Literary London now as compared with the same object of old. He answers that old men always prefer the bygone time; that many of *his* friends are now gone; but that on the whole the old *was* the best. ' Deeper questions were mooted.' I describe to him somewhat of my notions about coöperation, proselytism and so forth: he looks gratified, seems beginning to talk, when they force him up to — play whist, and I only see him for the rest of the night! A furious jingle of pianos ensues; Rossini's operatic melodies almost driving me deaf; and so from amid the chaotic jargoning, I glide off, seeing symptoms of a *Supper* in the other room. Godwin has not impressed me with very high notions of him: yet I still see him with his quick short laugh (in the end of which lies a *chirl*, as there did in Gilbert Burns's), parson's black coat, firm position in his chair, and general *handfest*[1] appearance. Will try to see him again under better circumstances.—He drinks

[1] "Sturdy."

'strong green tea' by himself.— After ten at night, John brings up a certain young Mr. Glen, of whom much might be made: a figurative mind, eager for insight; self-helping: but very talkative and confused; hovering as yet between light and darkness.[1] Bed at twelve.

16th (whereon I now write). Awoke some time before seven; sickish, unslept; must have *drugs:* am for breakfasting with Bowring. Not very well.

27th Have some time ago discontinued this Journal-writing; my Wife's Letters[2] being properly a Journal. This afternoon I am just returned from Enfield.[3] Bibliopolic speculation languid enough: 'nothing moving upon wheels': *ach Nichts!*

Is all Education properly an *unfolding:* does all Knowledge already exist in the mind, and Education only uncover it? There is something in this: but not what is here (so ill) expressed.

[1] "Glen was a young graduate of Glasgow, studying law in London, of very considerable though utterly confused talent. Ultimately went mad, and was boarded in a farmhouse near Craigenputtock, within reach of us, where in seven or eight years he died." *Life,* ii. 200, n. See also pp. 225, 278, 403, and *Letters,* i. 336.
[2] His letters to his wife.
[3] Where the Badams's lived.

## THOMAS CARLYLE.

Vision of *all* the suits of "Clothes" you have ever worn! —

---

October 10th
Wife arrived ten days ago; we here quietly enough (in 4 Ampton Street), and the world jogging on at the old rate.[1] Jack must be by this time in Paris. *Teüfelsdreck*, after various perplexed destinies, returned to me, and now lying safe in his box. There must he continue, till the Book-trade revive a little; if forever, what matter? The Book contents me little; yet perhaps there is material in it: in any case I did my best.— To see Gustave d'Eichthal [2] the St. Simonian this night!

[1] " The beggarly history of poor *Sartor among the Blockheadisms* is not worth my recording . . . In short, finding that whereas I had got £100 (if memory serve) for *Schiller* six or seven years before, and for *Sartor* ' at least thrice as good,' I could not only *not* get £200, but even get no ' Murray' or the like to publish it on ' half profits,' . . . I said, 'We will make it *No* then ; wrap up our MS. ; wait till this ' Reform Bill ' uproar abate; and see, and give our brave little Jeannie a sight of this big Babel, which is so altered since I saw it last (in 1824-25)! ' —She came right willingly; and had, in spite of her ill-health, which did not abate but the contrary, an interesting, cheery, and, in spite of our poor arrangements, a really pleasant winter here. We lodged in Ampton Street, Gray's Inn Lane, clean and decent pair of rooms, and quiet decent people . . . reduced from wealth to keeping lodgings, and prettily resigned to it; really good people." *Reminiscences*, i. 92.

[2] " The most interesting acquaintances we have made," wrote Mrs. Carlyle in December, 1831, " are the St. Simonians . . . Gustave d'Eichthal is a creature to

Their *Reform Bill* lost (on Saturday morning at six o'clock) by a majority of 41.[1] The Politicians will have it, the people must *rise*. The People will do nothing half so foolish — for the present. London seems altogether quiet (however, I will go out and see); here they are afraid of Scotland, in Scotland of *us*. ' Spanish banditti ' — the sign of a general *apprehensiveness*.— Poor Jeffrey very ill, but not dangerously.

On Saturday saw Sir J. Macintosh (at Jeffrey's), and looked at and listened to him tho' without speech. A broadish, middle-sized, gray-headed man; well dressed and with a plain courteous bearing; grey intelligent (unhealthy yellow-whited) eyes, in which plays a

---

love at first sight — so gentle and trustful and earnest-looking, ready to do and suffer all for his faith." *Life*, ii. 224.

Gustave d'Eichthal had a friendly acquaintance with Emerson as well as with the Carlyles. See *Letters*, ii. 113.

On Emerson's first visit to Carlyle, at Craigenputtock, in 1833, he brought to him from Rome a letter from d'Eichthal. See Emerson's *English Traits*, p. 18, where, however, the name of d'Eichthal is not mentioned.

[1] It was between seven and eight o'clock, in the morning of Saturday, the 8th of October, after an exciting debate for five successive nights, that the House of Lords rejected the Reform Bill, which had passed the Commons on the 21st of September, by a majority of one hundred and nine. Carlyle's lack of interest in a matter of such grave concern to the nation, and one which was stirring the people more deeply than they had been stirred for many years, is noticeable as an illustration of his engrossment with things of still deeper import.

## THOMAS CARLYLE.

dash of *cautious vivacity* (uncertain whether Fear or latent Ire; remember old Dr. Fleming's [1]); triangular unmeaning nose; business mouth and chin: on the whole, a sensible, official air, not without a due spicing of hypocrisy and something of Pedantry — both no doubt involuntary. The man is a whig Philosopher and Politician, such as the time yields, our best of that sort,— which will soon be extinct.— He was talking mysteriously with with other "Hon. Members," about "what was to be done."— Something *à la* Dogberry the thing looked to me; tho' I deny not that it is a serious conjuncture; only believe that *any* change has some chance to be for the better, and so see it all with composure.

---

Meanwhile *what* were the true duty of a man; were it to stand utterly aloof from Politics (not ephemeral only, for that of course, but generally from all speculation about social systems &c. &c.); or is not perhaps the very want of this time, an infinite want of Governors, of Knowledge how to govern itself? — Canst *thou* in any measure spread abroad Reverence over the hearts of men? That were a far higher task than *any* other. Is it to be done by Art; or are men's minds as yet shut to Art, and open only at best to ora-

[1] "A good old Dr. Fleming, 'a clergyman of mark' in former years in Edinburgh." *Reminiscences*, ii. 103.

tory; not fit for a *Meister*, but only for a better and better *Teufelsdreck; Denk' und schweig!*[1]

The stupidity I labour under is extreme. All dislocated, prostrated, obfuscated; cannot even speak, much less write. What a dogged piece of toil lies before me, before I get afoot again! Set doggedly to it then.

When Goethe and Schiller say or insinuate that Art is higher than Religion, do they mean perhaps this: That whereas Religion represents (what is the essence of Truth for men) the Good as *infinitely* (the word is emphatic) different from the Evil, but sets them in a state of *hostility* (as in Heaven and Hell),— Art likewise admits and inculcates this quite infinite difference; but *without* hostility, with peacefulness; like the difference of two Poles which *cannot* coalesce, yet do not quarrel, nay should not quarrel for both are essential to the whole? In this way is Goethe's morality to be considered as a *higher* (apart from its comprehensiveness, nay universality) than has hitherto been promulgated?— *Sehr einseitig!*[2] Yet perhaps there is a glimpse of the truth here.

Mary Wollstonecraft's Life by Godwin:

[1] "Think and be silent."
[2] "Very one-sided," or "partial" view.

an Ariel imprisoned in a brickbat! It is a real tragedy, and of the deepest: sublimely virtuous endowment; in practice misfortune, suffering, death,—by Destiny and also by Desert.—An English Mignon; Godwin an honest Boor that loves her, but cannot guide or save her.—Ever wondrous is the pilgrimage of man!—

---

*Shall* I write about Müllner?—Gott weiss.[1]

---

11th October. Last night, saw Mill and d'Eichthal (Brother of Gustave the St. Simonian), and discoursed largely upon men and things. M. continues to please me.—

Strange tendency everywhere noticeable to speculate on *Men* not on *Man*. Another branch of the Mechanical Temper. Vain hope to make mankind happy by Politics! You *cannot* drill a regiment of knaves into a regiment of honest men, enregiment and organise them as cunningly as you will. Give us the honest men, and the well-ordered regiment comes of itself. Reform one man (re-

---

[1] "God knows." Carlyle had already, in his article on "German Playwrights," 1829, written at considerable length about Müllner, of whom he had said, "no Playwright of this age makes such a noise as Müllner" . . . but "we must take liberty to believe . . . that he 'is no dramatist.'"

form thy own inner man), it is more than scheming out reforms for a nation.[1]

———

Hear talk of a "Convention of Delegates" about to assemble from all the four winds here at London, to expedite the Reform Bill. — Some noises in the streets last night; but as yet no reports of rioting: general or serious rioting for the present I do not expect.

———

Now to Müllner; not to write upon him; he is not worth that: but to scrawl upon him and get him off my hands. *Allons!—Eheu!*

———

22nd October. The principle of *Laissez-faire* fast verging, as I read the symptoms, to a consummation. *Let people go on*, each without guidance, each striving only to gain advantage for himself, the result will be this: Each, endeavouring by "competition" to outstrip the others, will endeavour by all arts to manufacture an article (not better) only *cheaper* and *showier* than his neighbour. As we see in all things! A newly built house is more like a tent than a house; no Table that I fall in with here can

[1] "To reform a world, to reform a nation, no wise man will undertake, and all but foolish men know that the only solid, though a far slower reformation, is what each begins and perfects on himself." With these words Carlyle had ended his paper on "Signs of the Times," in 1829.

stand on its legs; a pair of good Shoes is what I have not been able to procure for the last ten years. The Tradesman, in every department, has become an *eye-servant;* and could not help it, without being a *martyr,*— as indeed all men should be.

Hence too comes the so incessant fluctuation in the modes of things. Is the taste of the article better? Its durableness increased? Its end more completely answered? Its utility in *any* way extended? No: generally altogether the reverse. The childishness of men (often it is their *bad* passions) must be ministered to; *that* is the surest course for getting payment: so the workman turns his whole effort in that direction.

But if such is the condition of things in regard to the Useful which is said to promote *itself*, what will it be in regard to the Beautiful, the Moral, which is of *no* value till once it be had *possession* of! Look round on all hands and see — in the Church, in the Arts, in Literature. (*This* last part due to Mill.)

---

Expect not a pair of tolerable "shoes" (even tolerably made ones) here![1] They are

[1] Even in later life Carlyle used to complain humorously that no tolerable shoes could be found in London; and to declare that his only pair of well-made shoes came from an old shoemaker in Dumfries, that he had worn them for years, 'had them upper-leathered and under-leathered,' and they would last a long while yet.

all made incalculably too wide in the instep: thou puttest them on (and payest for them) *easily;* they pinch and becorn thy toes all the time thou wearest them; and daily thou growlest over the " Competition Principle," exemplified here, as in all other provinces lowest and highest.—Important remark!

---

One problem lies before man in all ages and places; Ascertain what thou canst do, and *do it.* Here in London, lies a second problem often harder than the first: having done thy work, *convince the world that thou hast done it.*

John told me of having seen in Holborn a man walking steadily along with some six Baskets all piled above each other, his Name and Address written in large characters on each, so that he exhibited a stature of some twelve feet, and so by the six separate announcements had his existence sufficiently proclaimed. The trade of this man was Basket-making; but he had found it needful to study a quite new Trade, that of walking with six (or twelve) baskets on his head in a crowded street.

In like manner: Colburn and Bentley the Booksellers are known to expend Ten thousand pounds annually (I had this from Dilke,[1]

---

[1] Editor and proprietor of the *Athenæum*, father of Sir Charles Dilke.

who had it from their man of business) on what they call "advertising," more commonly called *puffing*.

Puffing (which is simply the *second* trade, that of Basket-*carrying*) flourishes in all countries; but London is the true scene of it; having this one quality beyond all other cities: a quite immeasurable size. It is rich also, stupid and ignorant, beyond example; thus, in all respects, the true Goshen of Quacks.

Every man I meet with mourns over this state of matters; no one thinks it remediable; you must do as the others do, or they will get the start of you, or tread you under foot. "All true, Mr. Carlyle; BUT"—I say: "All true, Mr. Carlyle; AND"—The first beginning of a remedy is that some *one* believe a remedy possible; believe that if he cannot *live* by truth, then he can *die* by it. Dost *thou* believe it? Then is the new Era begun!¹

In a better time this huge monster of a city will contract itself into some third part of its

[1] Of Dilke "I have little to say, except that the man is very tolerant, hospitable; not without a sense for the good, but with little power to follow it, and defy the evil. That is the temper in which I find many here; they deplore the prevalence of dishonesty, quackery, and stupidity; many do it (like Dilke) with apparent heartiness and sorrow; but to believe that it can be *resisted*, that it will and shall be resisted, herein poor *Teufelsdreck* is well-nigh singular." *Letters*, i. 319.

present bulk. The Landed People have almost no business here except incidentally; they should be *governing* in their respective districts; not here flaunting and flirting. Were the quite superfluous population of London shipped off, it would shrink to the third part of its bulk, and be still large enough.

Potatoes (one penny per lb.) are exactly *ten* times the price they are in Annandale. (Of their quality I say nothing.) So is it in all things, in a less or greater ratio: so many mortals living together hamper and hinder one another in innumerable ways.

How men are hurried here; how they are haunted and terrifically chased into double quick speed; so that in self-defence they *must not* stay to look at one another! Miserable is the scandal mongery and evil idle speaking of the country population: more frightful still the total ignorance and mutual heedlessness of these poor souls in populous city pent. " Each passes on, quick transient; regarding not the other or his woes." Each must button himself together, and take no thought (not even for *evil*) of his neighbour. There in their little cells divided by partitions of brick or board, they sit strangers, unknowing, unknown; like Passengers in some huge

## THOMAS CARLYLE.

Ship, each within his own cabin: Alas! and the Ship is Life, and the voyage is from Eternity to Eternity!

Everywhere there is the most crying want of GOVERNMENT, a true all-ruining anarchy: no one has any *knowledge* of London in which he lives; it is a huge aggregate of little systems, each of which is again a small Anarchy, the members of which do not *work* together but *scramble* against each other.

The Soul, what can properly be called the Soul, lies dead in the bosom of man; starting out only in mad ghastly Nightwalkings (e. g. " the gift of tongues [1] ") : Ignorance eclipses all things with its owlet wings; man walks he knows not whither; walks and wanders till he walk into the jaws of Death, and is there devoured.— Nevertheless, *God is in it*: here, even here, is the Revelation of the Infinite in the Finite; a majestic Poem (tragic, comic or epic), couldst thou but read it and recite it! Watch it then; study it, catch the secret of it, and proclaim the same in such accent as is given thee.— Alas! the spirit is willing, but the flesh is weak.

---

*Müllner* is not written or perhaps worth writing; however the rude materials of it are

[1] " In the course of the winter, sad things had occurred in Irving's history. His enthusiastic studies and preach-

on paper, and lie tied up with packthread, abiding their time.— I am now to write *something* (*what* thing?) for the Edin<sup>r</sup> Review. Two subjects I have; both distant, both vague. Sad struggle I shall have! "On man," "On Authors": which? Or neither?

---

Serious thoughts are rising in me about the possibility of attempting a *Course of Lectures* here.[1] The subject should be "Things in general" (under some more dignified title): but as yet the ground is quite unknown to me; the whole process *towards* the *cathedra*, even much of the process *there* lies hidden. Let me look and study.—

What are the uses, what is the special province of *oral* teaching at present? Wherein superior to the written or *printed* mode, and when?— For one thing, as I can see, London is fit for no higher *Art* than that of Oratory: they understand nothing of Art; scarcely one of them anything at all.— But hast *thou* any Eloquence? *Ja wohl, ein klein*

ings were passing into the practically 'miraculous'; and to me the most doleful of all phenomena, the 'Gift of Tongues' had fairly broken out among the crazed weakliest of his wholly rather dim and weakly flock." *Reminiscences*, ii. 204.

[1] It was not till the spring of 1837, nearly six years after the date of the entry, that Carlyle gave his first Course of Lectures in London. His "Things in General" had dwindled to "German Literature." See *Life*, iii. 97-105.

## THOMAS CARLYLE.

*weniges*,[1] were my tongue once *untacked. Ach, dass es so wäre!*[2]—

Have been reading in Hazlitt's *Table Talk:* an incessant *chew-chewing,* the Nut never cracked, nothing but teeth broken and bleeding gums. The man has thought much; even intently and with vigor: but he has discovered nothing; been able to *believe* nothing. One other sacrifice to the Time![3] — Ritson's *Fairy Tales* and *Old Ballads* worth almost nothing: thickheaded discourteous boor of an Editor, and almost nothing of the smallest moment to edit.—

—On Thursday night last (this is Monday, the 24$^{th}$ Oct$^r$ 1831) dined with Fonblanque Editor of the *Examiner.* An honourable Radical; might be something better: London-bred; limited, by education more than by nature.—Something metallic in the tone of his voice (like that of the Professor Austin): for the rest, a tall, loose, lankhaired, wrinkly, wintry, vehement looking flail of a man. I

[1] " Perhaps so, a little bit."
[2] " Ah, would it were so!"
[3] " How many a poor Hazlitt must wander on God's verdant earth, like the Unblest on burning deserts: passionately dig wells, and draw up only the dry quicksand; believe that he is seeking Truth, yet only wrestle among endless Sophisms, doing desperate battle as with spectre-hosts; and die and make no sign." ' Characteristics.' *Essays,* iv. 28.

reckon him the best of the Fourth Estate now extant in Britain.—Shall see him again.[1]

Allan Cunningham with us, last night. Jane calls him a genuine Dumfriesshire mason still; and adds that it is delightful to see a genuine man of any sort. Allan was, as usual, full of Scottish-anecdotic talk. Right by instinct; has *no* principles or *creed* that I can see: but excellent old Scottish *habits* of character: an interesting man.—
—Walter Scott left Town yesterday on his way to Naples. He is to proceed from Plymouth in a Frigate, which the Government have given him a place in. Much run after here (it seems); but he is old and sick and cannot enjoy it: has had two shocks of Palsy, and seems altogether in a precarious way.— To me he is and has been an object of very minor interest for many many years; the Novel-wright of his time, its favourite child, and *therefore* an almost worthless one. Yet is there something in his deep recognition of the worth of the Past, perhaps better than anything he has *expressed* about it: into which I

[1] Cf. *Letters*, ii. 359. Albany Fonblanque was editor of *The Examiner* from 1830 to 1847. He was in the main a disciple of Bentham; and by his wit and vigorous intelligence he secured a wide hearing. His *England under Seven Administrations* (3 vols. 1837), a selection of his editorial articles, is a good record of current opinion during the reign of William IV.

## THOMAS CARLYLE.

do not yet fully see.—Have never spoken with him (tho' I might sometimes, without great effort); and now probably never shall.

---

What an advantage has the Pulpit, where you address men already arranged to hear you, and in a vehicle which long use has rendered easy: how infinitely harder when you have all to create, not the ideas only and the sentiments, but the symbols and the mood of mind! Nevertheless in all cases, where man addresses man, on his spiritual interests especially, there is a *sacredness*, could we but evolve it, and think and speak in it.—Consider better what it is thou meanest by a *symbol;* how far thou hast insight into the nature thereof.—

—Is *Art* in the old Greek sense possible for man at this late era? Or were not (perhaps) the Founder of a Religion our true Homer at present?—The *whole Soul* must be illuminated, made harmonious: Shakespeare seems to have had no religion, but his Poetry.—

—Where is Tomorrow resident even now? Somewhere, or somehow, it *is*, doubt not of that. On the common theory thou mayest *think* thyself into madness on this question.

---

Society I have for some years been wont to divide into four classes: Noblemen, Gentlemen, Gigmen, and Men. When is the *Defensio Gigmanica* to make its appearance? [1]

---

Priest-ridden, wife-ridden, plague-ridden,
Who escapes his lot?
Bearing, forbearing, paying, obeying,
Will ye, will ye not.
Child-ridden, tremble at my Doll's pouting:
Fortune, spare me that!

---

Richard Brothers (1798); a most wonderful madman; believes himself to be the promised Deliverer of the Jews; writes a " Letter to Miss Cott the recorded Daughter of King David and Future Queen of the Hebrews." (which I see to-day in the Brit. Museum.)— Deals exceedingly in study of the Scriptures. —" Dated from Islington Madhouse March the 18$^{th}$ 1798."—What became of him ultimately? [2]

[1] The notion of the gigman, "one who kept a gig," as the type of British Respectability and Philistinism had struck Carlyle's sense of humour, and recurs often about this time in his writing. The source of it is given in a note in his essay on Richter (1830). "In Thurtell's trial (says the *Quarterly Review*) occurred the following colloquy: ' *Q*. What sort of person was Mr. Weare. *A*. He was always a respectable person. *Q*. What do you mean by respectable? *A*. He kept a gig.' Since then we have seen a ' *Defensio Gigmanica*, or apology for the Gigmen of Great Britain' composed not without eloquence, and which we hope one day to prevail on our friend, a man of some whims, to give to the public." *Essays*, iii. 32; cf. *id*. iv. 150.

[2] Brothers was born in 1757, and lived, maintaining

## THOMAS CARLYLE.

November 2ⁿᵈ. How few people speak for Truth's sake, even in its humblest modes! I return from Enfield, where I have seen Lamb &c &c. Not one of that class will tell you a straightforward story, or even a credible one, about any matter under the sun. All must be perked up into epigrammatic contrasts, startling exaggerations, claptraps that will get a plaudit from the galleries! I have heard a hundred anecdotes about W. Hazlitt (for example); yet cannot, by never so much cross-questioning even, form to myself the smallest notion of how it really stood with him.— Wearisome, inexpressibly wearisome to me is that sort of clatter: it is not walking (to the end of time you would never advance, for these persons indeed have no WHITHER); it is not bounding and frisking in graceful natural joy; it is dancing — a St. Vitus dance. Heighho!—

Charles Lamb I sincerely believe to be in some considerable degree *insane*. A more pitiful, ricketty, gasping, staggering, stammering Tom fool I do not know.[1] He is his character as madman, enthusiast, and prophet, till 1824. According to the *Dictionary of National Biography* (1886), "the believers in Brothers are not yet extinct."

[1] Time did not change Carlyle's judgment of Lamb (see *Reminiscences*, i. 94), but added to it, "yet something too of humane, ingenuous, pathetic, sportfully much-enduring."

witty by denying truisms, and abjuring good manners. His speech wriggles hither and thither with an incessant painful fluctuation; not an opinion in it or a fact or even a phrase that you can thank him for : more like a convulsion fit than natural systole and diastole. — Besides he is now a confirmed shameless drunkard; *asks* vehemently for gin-and-water in strangers' houses; tipples till he is utterly mad, and is only not thrown out of doors because he is too much despised for taking such trouble with him.[1] Poor Lamb! Poor

[1] Knowing what we now know of Lamb's life this judgment appears unsympathetic and hard. But it was not unjust to Lamb as he displayed himself to Carlyle. In October of this year, 1831, Carlyle and his wife went to stay for three or four days with Mr. and Mrs. Badams at Enfield. Mr. Alexander Carlyle narrates in a letter to me an incident which took place during this visit: "Lamb was present one evening at supper. The Carlyles were supping on oat-meal porridge, their usual dish. Lamb began to quiz Mrs. Carlyle about her queer dish, and ended by dipping his spoon into her bowl, saying 'Let us taste the stuff anyhow.' Mrs. Carlyle, greatly annoyed at such ill-breeding and familiarity on the part of a person she had not met before, gave him a cutting retort to the effect that, 'your astonishment at my porridge cannot exceed my surprise at your manners,' and had her bowl removed." In writing to her mother soon afterward, she said, "Some of them [London literary men], C. Lamb for instance, would not be tolerated in any society out of England." Carlyle, too, referred to the incident in a letter to his brother, Dr. Carlyle, 13 Nov., 1831, "He [Lamb] also loudly criticized our Scotch porridge that evening, and being swept away, as a troublesome insect should, got more and more obstreperous."

## THOMAS CARLYLE.

England where such a despicable abortion is named genius!— He said : There are just two things I regret in English History ; first that Guy Faux's Plot did not take effect (there would have been so glorious an *explosion*); second, that the Royalists did not hang Milton (then we might have laughed at them) : &c. &c. *Armer Teufel!* [1]

---

News of wild riots from Bristol: many lives lost, much mischief much scandal perpetrated. The Noodles, if they mind not, will have an old house about their ears. Sir C. Wetherell affirmed and re-affirmed that "there was a reaction, that the people had ceased to care for reform " &c. &c.: argument, evidence, was of no use; the man's brain was not to be reached that way ; so the Rascality took another: that of knock-

---

In a letter now in my possession, undated, but written probably not far from this time, from Mrs. Procter to Mrs. Jameson, is the following narrative: "Charles Lamb dined here on Monday at five, and by seven was so tipsy he could not stand. Martin Burney carried him from one room to the other like a sack of coals, he insisting upon singing ' diddle, diddle, diddle dumpty, my son John.' He slept until ten and then awoke more tipsy than before, and between his fits of beating Martin Burney kept saying, ' please God I never enter this cursed house again.' He wrote a note the next day begging pardon, and asking when he may come again. — Poor Miss Lamb is *ill.*"
[1] " Poor devil."

ing it in with clubs.¹ — O the wondrous wild ways of this world: how knaves and noodles rise to the summit, and huge movements of society must depend on *their* good pleasure, on *their* best insight!— *Farvâ sapientiâ*,² indeed! Why it is *Dementia;* even with that it will go on.

———

Dull, Dull! yet have a "striking Article" to write! I mean to try if I can write a true one, let it *strike* or not: would I were able. The fight must be unspeakable first. *Gott hilf mir!*

———

All the world is in apprehension about the

¹ Sir Charles Wetherell, Recorder of Bristol, had been a determined opponent of the Reform Bill in the House of Commons. This had made him unpopular in Bristol, where on the 29th of October he opened the City Sessions. The Mansion House where he took up his residence was attacked by a mob. Dealt with too timidly at first, the violence of the mob increased, and for two days Bristol was given over to arson and plunder.

² These words are from Chancellor Oxenstiern's famous saying to his son, as it is usually cited, *I, mi fili, vide quam parva sapientia mundus regitur*, " Go, my son, see with how little wisdom the world is governed." The correct form of the saying seems to be, *An nescis, mi fili, quantilla prudentia mundus regatur?* " Do you not know, my son, with how little good sense the world may be governed?" The son was hesitating, on account of his inexperience, to accept a mission to which he had been appointed. Buchmann, *Geflügelte Wörte*, 1884, S. 310.
'Thou little thinkest,' said Selden, 'what a little foolery governs the world.'

## THOMAS CARLYLE.

*Cholera* Pestilence;[1] which indeed seems advancing towards us with a frightful, slow, unswerving constancy. For myself I cannot say that it costs me great suffering: we are all appointed once to die; Death is the grand sum-total of it all.— Generally now it seems to me as if this Life were but the inconsiderable portico of man's Existence, which afterwards in new, mysterious environment were to be continued without end. I say, 'seems to me;' for the proof of it were hard to state by Logic; it is the fruit of Faith; begins to show itself with more and more decisiveness, the instant you have dared to say: Be it *either* way! The *hohe Bedeutung des Entsagen*.[2] — But on

[1] This was the last great visitation of cholera to England. It was a blessing in disguise, for it compelled attention to the public health, which led to the sanitary measures that have gradually made England the best protected country in the world against pestilence and epidemic disease. For the wisdom by which these measures were devised and carried out, England is mainly indebted to the venerable, still living, Sir John Simon, K.C.B., who had charge of them as the Medical Officer of the Privy Council.

[2] "The deep significance of renunciation." 'The great doctrine of *Entsagen*,' as Carlyle calls it in his essay on Novalis (1829) was one that he had learned for himself from life, but for which Goethe had given him the word. " Well did the wisest of our time write: 'It is only with Renunciation (*Entsagen*) that Life, properly speaking, can be said to begin." *Sartor Resartus*, Book ii. ch. ix. This word *Entsagen* Carlyle had cut upon a seal, which he and his wife frequently used. An engraving of the

the whole, our conception of Immortality (as Dreck too has it)¹ depends on that of *Time ;* which latter is the deepest belonging to Philosophy, and the one perhaps wherein modern Philosophy has earned its best triumph. Believe that there properly *is* no Space and no Time, how many contradictions become reconciled! — ²

———

"Sports" are all gone from among men: there is now no holiday either for rich or poor. Hard toiling, then hard drinking, or hard fox-hunting: this is not the era of sport, but of martyrdom and persecution. Will the new morning never dawn? — It requires a certain vigour of the imagination, and of the social faculties before Amusement, popular Sport, can exist; which vigour at this era is all but total inanimation. Nay, you have to argue and redargue (with most men) before they will admit that it is not total.— Do but think of the Christmas Carols and Games; the Abbots of Unreason, the Maypoles &c &c! Then look at your Manchesters on Saturday; and on Sunday! —

———

"Education" is beyond being so much as

seal is in *Early Letters of Jane Welsh Carlyle*, etc. Edited by David G. Ritchie, London, 1889.
  1 In Book iii. ch. viii of *Sartor.*
  2 "Time and Space are but quiddities, not entities." *Essays,* i. 143.

despised: we must praise it when it is not *De*ducation, or an utter annihilation of what it professes to foster. The best-*educated* man you will often find to be the Artizan, at all rates the man of Business. For why? He has put forth his hand, and operated on Nature; *must* actually attain some true insight or he cannot live.— The worst-educated man is usually your man of Fortune. *He* has not put forth his hand upon anything, except upon his Bell-rope. Your scholar proper, generally too your so-called man of Letters, is a thing with clearer vision — thro' the hundredth part of an eye. A Burns is infinitely better educated than a Byron.—[1]

Authors must *unite;* must form themselves into a Corporation, into a Church. It is one of my prophecies that they one day *will*. In this present race there is not virtue enough to form a Drinking Club. But what then? Other races and innumerable centuries are coming.—

A common persuasion among serious ill-informed persons that the *end of the world* is at hand: Henry Drummond, E. Irving, and all that class.— So was it at the beginning of the Christian era; say rather, at the *termination* of the Pagan one.

---

[1] The thoughts in the preceding paragraph are developed in a passage near the beginning of Carlyle's article on "Corn-Law Rhymes," which appeared in the *Edinburgh Review* in 1832.

NOTE BOOK OF

Which is the most ignorant creature of his class even in Britain? Generally speaking, the Cockney, the London-bred man; and for reasons. He has no Libraries, no schools, no clergy: nothing but a workshop, *where* indeed he is the expertest of men.—In literature, think of Heraud, Lamb, P.,[1] &c. &c.—What does the Cockney boy know of the muffin he eats? Simply that a hawker brings it to the door, and charges a penny for it. The country youth sees it grow in the fields, in the mill, in the Bake house. Thus of *all* things, pertaining to the Life of man.

November 4th 1831. Yesterday reading Strutt's *Games* and Brand's *Popular Antiquities* in the British Museum. Both good solid serviceable Books.— Playing-cards commonly said to have been introduced in the time of Charles VI. (the mad Dauphin & King) of France; to appearance erroneously; for they are mentioned by some court-officer of his predecessor. The *first* law against them is in Spain. *Primero* a Spanish name; *spades* was originally *espada*, and had the figure of a *sword*. Probably came from the East in the Crusade times; as Chess then or earlier did.— Strange old inventions! *who* was the author of them?— Merelles called also (in Shakespeare for

[1] The initial probably stands for Procter.

instance) *nine men's morrice* is the game I have played at fifty times in boyhood under the title of *Corsicrown* (cross i' the crown); or rather our poor *Corsicrown* played with only three men, was but the first portion of the game.—Vauxhall was once Spring Gardens (in the Spectator's time); Ranelagh was the Earl of R's House; Sadler's Well (in London?) was once a sacred *Holywell;* then walled in at the Reformation, and subsequently discovered by the successor of one Sadler.[1] Could any Well or Rock, or other natural Product, but relate its history!—Will look at Brand today, when my work (strenuous no-work!) is done here. Meanwhile to it thou *Taugenichts!*[2] Gird thyself, stir, struggle, forward! forward! Thou art bundled up here, and tied as in a sack? On then, as in a sack-race. " Running not raging." *Gott sey mir gnädig!*—[3]

12 November. Have been two days as good as idle! Am far from any approximation to health; hampered, disturbed, quite out of sorts. As it were quite stranded; no tackle left, no tools but my ten fingers,

[1] Peter Cunningham, in his "Handbook of London" says: "Discovered by one Sadler, in 1683, in the garden of a house which he had newly opened as a public music-room."
[2] "Do-nothing."
[3] "God be gracious to me."

nothing but accidental drift-wood to build even a raft of. "This is no my ain house." — Art thou aware still that no man and no thing but simply thy own self can permanently keep thee down? Act thou on that conviction.—

How sad and stern is all Life to me! Homeless, Homeless! Would my *Task* were *done:* I think I should not care to die; in real earnestness should care very little: this earthly Sun has shown me only roads full of mire and thorns. Why cannot I be a kind of Artist! Politics are angry, agitating, for the present little productive business: what have I to do with it? Will any Parliamentary Reform ever reform *me?*—

On the 10th, the beginning of my Idleness, breakfasted with a Mr. Taylor,[1] and various parliamentary diplomatic young men in Grosvenor street. Men of pleasant, easy manners; a rather pleasant party. Hyde Villiers gave me a frank, and I wrote a long stupid letter to my mother[2]; accompanying John's (from Turin).— Yesterday, sick enough, and was visited by Glen: a perfect refining furnace, chaotically melting and weltering, in which

---

[1] Henry, later Sir Henry, Taylor, "author of *Artevelde* and various similar things." In his *Reminiscences*, ii. 278, Carlyle records the "early regard, constant esteem, and readiness to be helpful and friendly" of this "solid, sound-headed, faithful" man.

[2] See *Letters*, i. 360.

there is yet nothing *cast*, nor any *mould* to cast in. Advised him to establish forthwith a few "great Possibles"—as poor Davie Halliday, when mad, had established certain "great Impossibles," and was wont in hunting down his theological chimeras, from proposition out of proposition, to exclaim at length: "*that* is one of the great Impossibles!" and so terminate the chase.— Poor Glen's Life, as I told him, has been a *soliloquy;* he has not yet acquired the gift of communicating, and chiefly therefore, not of practically understanding—*Was wird von ihm werden? Weiss nicht; hoff' doch.—Was wird von Dir? Ach Gott!*[1]

This I begin to see, that Evil and Good are everywhere like Shadow and Substance: inseparable (for man); yet not hostile, only opposed.[2] There is considerable significance in this fact—perhaps the *new* moral principle of our Era. (*How?*)—It was familiar to Goethe's mind.—

———

Everywhere and Everywhen lie the materials of Art: these waggons and Drivers in

[1] "What will become of him? I know not, but have hope. What will become of thyself? Ah, God!"
[2] "Evil . . is precisely the dark, disordered material out of which man's Freewill has to create an edifice of order and Good." "Characteristics," (1831). *Essays*, iv. 25.

Holborn are a Dance of Death,— also of Life. Man and his ways reach always from Heaven to Hell. But *where*, O where is the Artist that can again body this forth! — Not yet born? —

———

Cholera Morbus arrived at Sunderland.— If men are united no other way, contagion and pestilence unite them.— Poor Ricker is dead of it at Berlin; poor Dickenson dead (also of infection) at Edinburgh. Death's thousand doors stand open. *Eheu!*

———

But now, to thy Sheet! Complain not, still more, *zürn'* not. As the saints say: " Pray to the Lòrd," rather (in such dialect as thou canst); also handsomely and heartily *set thy shoulder to the wheel!* HEAVE-OH!

The nobleness of Silence. The highest melody dwells only in silence (the Sphere melody, the melody of Health); the eye cannot see Shadow, cannot see Light, but only the two combined. General Law of Being. (Think farther of this. Nov$^r$. 17$^{th}$).—

As it is but a small portion of our Thinking that we can articulate into Thoughts, so again it is but a small portion, properly only the outer surface of our morality that we can shape into Action, or into express Rules of Action. Remark farther that it is but the correct coherent shaping of this outer surface, or the incorrect incoherent monstrous shaping of it, and nowise the moral Force which shaped it, which lies under it, vague, indefinite, unseen, that constitutes what in common speech we call a moral conduct or an immoral. Hence too the necessity of tolerance, of insight, in judging of men. For the correctness of that same outer surface may be out of all proportion to the inward depth and quantity; nay often enough they are in inverse proportion; only in some highly favoured individuals can the great endowment utter itself without irregularity. Thus in great men, with whom inward and as it were latent morality must ever be the root and beginning of greatness, how often do we find a conduct defaced by many a moral impropriety; and have to love them with sorrow! Thus too poor Burns must record that almost the only noble-minded men he had ever met with were among the class named Blackguards.[1]

---

Extremes meet. Perfect Morality were no more an object of consciousness than perfect Immorality, as pure Light cannot any more be seen than pure Darkness.—

[1] "I have often courted the acquaintance of that part of mankind, commonly known by the ordinary phrase of *blackguards* . . . I have yet found among them, in not a few instances, some of the noblest virtues." Burns, "Common Place Book," March, 1784. In Cromek's *Reliques of Burns*, 1817, p. 323.

NOTE BOOK OF

The healthy moral nature loves virtue; the unhealthy at best makes love to it.[1]

Friday  
23d December.

Finished the *Characteristics*, about a week ago; baddish, with a certain beginning of deeper insight in it.
Reading the *Corn Law Rhymes*.[2] "Balaam's Ass has not only stopt, but begins to *speak!*" Witness Detrosier too.— [3]
Byron we call "a Dandy of Sorrows, and acquainted with grief." That is a brief definition of him.

13th January 1832.

*London still.*— Have spent nearly three weeks in reading Croker's Boswell's Johnson; on which I have now (and had) some purpose of writing an Essay. I mean to try whether I cannot get into a more *currente calamo* style of writing; for magazines and the like, it were far more suitable: whether also for me and my objects? The *Charac-*

[1] The thought in this and the preceding entry is worked out in the "Characteristics."
[2] By Ebenezer Elliott. These poems furnished the text of the article with the same title.
[3] Detrosier was a "Manchester Lecturer to the Working Classes," brought by John Mill to Carlyle. "The Saint Simonians, Manchester, Detrosier, etc., were stirring and conspicuous objects in that epoch, but have now fallen all dark and silent again." T. C. 1866. *Life*, ii. 224, n.

*teristics* was written with almost intolerable difficulty, and is ill written, I fear no one will understand it. We shall see in a week or two, for it is coming out.—

Have made a kind of engagement with Lardner of the *Cabinet Cyclopedia* to furnish him a *Zur Geschichte*[1] of German Literature; incorporating my Papers in the Foreign Review &c, 170 pages of original writing: do not yet above three-fourths see my way thro' it; am to have it ready next November. No list of "Books wanted" yet made out; this should be my first task. The work will serve me perhaps pretty tolerably thro' the summer; I shall get done with German Literature; a little money too (£300) for my two volumes, and pay off that £60,[1] my only debt which sometimes grieves me a little.— I have been sick of a kind of cold; and am still in rather uncomfortable health; but do not mind it very much.

Plenty of Magazine Editors applying to me; indeed sometimes pestering me. Do not like to break with any; yet must not close with any. Strange state of Literature, periodical and other! A man must just lay out his manufacture in one of those Old-

[1] A book "on the history" of German Literature. See *Letters*, i. 389.
[2] Money lent by Jeffrey to Carlyle's brother John. See *Letters*, i. 314. It was paid in August, 1832. See *Id.*, ii. 64.

Clothes shops, and see whether any one will buy it. The *Editor* has little to do with the matter, except as Commercial Broker; he sells it and pays you for it.— Lytton Bulwer [1] has not yet come into sight of me: is there aught more in him than a Dandiacal Philosophist? Fear, not.— Tait the Bookseller about beginning a new Magazine, on the Radical side of things: my feeling is that the chances are greatly against him; for my own share I have nothing to do with him or it as yet, my hands full otherwise. Then of the infatuated Fraser, with his Dog's-meat Cart of a magazine, what? His pay is certain, and he means honestly; but is a goose. It was he that sent me Croker's Boswell: am I bound to offer *him* the (future) Article? — Or were this thy Rule in such cases: "Write thy best and the Truth; then publish it where thou canst best"? An indubitable rule; but is it rule enough? —

Last Friday, saw my name in large letters at the Athenaeum Office in Catherine street Strand; hurried on with downcast eyes, as if I had seen myself in the Pillory. Dilke (to whom I had entrusted *Dreck* to read it, and see if he could help me with it) asked me for a scrap of writing with my *name:* I could not quite clearly see my way thro' the business (for he had twice or thrice been civil

[1] Then editor of the New Monthly Magazine.

to me, and I did reckon his *Athenaeum* to be the bad best of literary Newspaper syllabubs, and tho! I might harmlessly say so much); gave him *Faust's Curse*, which hung printed there. Incline now to believe that I did wrong; at least imprudently. Why yield even half a hair's-breadth to Puffing? Abhor it, utterly divorce it, and kick it to the Devil! — This little adventure, however, *hat nichts zu bedeuten ;* [1] so trouble not thyself with it.

---

On Tuesday last (10<sup>th</sup> Jan<sup>y</sup>) wrote to John in Rome;[2] from whom I am getting impatient for a Letter.

Have an Article in prospect (still within myself) on ·the Radical plebeian who writes Cornlaw Rhymes. Wish to do the poor soul a justice and a kindness.

---

Singular how little wisdom or light of any kind I have met with in London. Do not find a single creature that has communicated an idea to me; at best one or two that can understand an idea. Yet the sight of London works on me strongly; I have not perhaps *lost* my journey hither.[3]

*Dreck* unpublished, to all appearance unpublishable. One Tilt of Fleet-street (a triviality) " glanced over it," then " regretted "

[1] " Is really insignificant."
[2] See *Letters*, i. 382.    [3] See *Id.*, i. 391.

&c. Dilke had no light to throw on the business, and I think will have none: the MS at this moment in the hands of Charles Buller. Glen, Mill and he have all read it; apparently, not without result: it was *intended* for such, therefore seems not wholly *verfehlt*.[1] As for the publication of it, I grow indifferent about that matter; indeed the whole concern is becoming unimportant to me. What is true today will be true tomorrow and next day.— We can wait,— forever.[2]

Hayward, of the Temple,[3] a small but active and vivacious 'man of the time,' by a strange impetus, takes to me; the first time, they say, he ever did such a thing, being one that lives in a chiaro-scuro element of which goodhumoured contempt is the basis. I met him at Mr Gray's, where also was one Dr. Bach, a German zealously kind to me: Hayward started this scheme of the Germ. Lit. Hist., and made it all *ready* for me.[4] Singular enough. (Lardner *ein Langöhriger*).[5] Dined

[1] "A failure."     [2] See *Letters*, i. 391.
[3] Mr. Abraham Hayward, translator of the first part of *Faust*, editor of *Autobiography, Letters*, etc. of Mrs. Piozzi, 1861, writer of a multitude of gossiping papers. He died in 1884.
[4] Cf. *Letters*, i. 389.
[5] Dr. Dionysius Lardner, "a long-eared" man of science, of some transient repute, editor of the *Cabinet Cyclopaedia*, in which this *History* was to appear. He afterward became sadly notorious. He died in 1859.

in his rooms (once Dunning's [1]!) with a set of Oxonian Templars: stupid (in part), limited (wholly), conceited, obscene. A *dirty* evening; I at last sunk utterly silent. Bernays (a German Professor — in the "King's College" here) understood what I was saying: but could *say* little, tho' in many words. Am to go thither today, and meet a certain Sir Alexander Johnston: small things expected of *him*. He has been in China, and knew Schiller.— [2]

I have never again seen Bowring or Fonblanque. Mean to see at least the latter. None of the great personages of Letters have come in my way here; and except as *sights*, they are of little moment to me. Jeffrey says he "praised me to Rogers," who, &c. &c : it sometimes rather surprises me that his Lordship does not think it would be kind to show me the faces of those people: something discourages or hinders him; what it is I know not, and indeed care not.— The Austins, at least *the* (*la*) Austin I like; [3] *eine*

[1] " The great lawyer," as Johnson called him in a letter to Boswell, July 22, 1777; afterward the first Lord Ashburton.

[2] Sir Alexander Johnston had as a young man, near the beginning of the century, studied at Göttingen, and probably then saw Schiller. A large part of his life was passed in Ceylon, where in the organization and administration of the government he did excellent service.

[3] The John Austins were living at Hampstead. "Mrs. Austin is described by Carlyle, after first seeing her, as

*verständige, herzhafte Frau*.¹ Empson a diluted, goodnatured, languid *Anempfindler*. ² The strongest young man, one Macaulay (now in Parliament, as I from the first predicted), an emphatic, hottish, really forcible person; but unhappily without *divine idea*.³ Perhaps he could play the part of a Canning; were the scene now the same, which however it is not. Rogers (an *elegant*, politely malignant old *lady*, I think ⁴) is in Town (and probably I might see him) : Moore is I know not where,— a lascivious triviality, of great name. Bentham is said to have become a driveller, and garrulous old man : perhaps I will try for a look of him; he is or was a forcible product. — I have much to see, and many things to

' the most enthusiastic of German Mystics I have ever met with : an exceedingly vivid person, not without insight, but enthusiastic, as it were astonished, rapt to ecstasy with the German apocalypse, and as she says herself *verdeutscht* " (Germanised). *Letters*, i. 320. Author of *Characteristics of Goethe*, 3 vols., 1833. The friendly acquaintance begun at this time continued through later years.

1 "An intelligent, resolute woman."
2 " Adopter of the sentiments of another."
3 Macaulay had distinguished himself greatly in the debate in the House of Commons on the Reform Bill. One of his speeches was said by Jeffrey to put him "clearly at the head of the great speakers, if not the debaters of the House." Cockburn, *Life of Lord Jeffrey*, i. 324.
4 " Rogers was a kindly old man, excepting when he was bilious." Tennyson reported by Mr. Locker-Lampson. *Life of Tennyson*, ii. 72.

wind up in London, before we leave it — in March.

I went one morning searching for Johnson's *places of abode*. Found, with difficulty, the house in Gough (Goff) Square where the Dictionary was composed:[1] the landlord, whom Glen and I incidentally inquired of, was just scraping his feet at the door; invited us to walk in; showed us the garret rooms &c. (of which he seemed to have the obscurest traditions; taking Johnson for a schoolmaster!); interested us much; but at length (dog of a fellow!) began to hint that he had all these rooms to let as lodgings! — I saw also Savage's Birthplace (Foxcourt, Brook st. & Gray's Inn Lane) one of the horridest holes in London.— Must speak with old Smith of the Museum, on the subject.—

London is of all the places I ever walked and inquired in, that where you oftenest have the answer: "Don't know." A quite anarchic place in *all* respects. The men that could tell you, *exist*, but where? You cannot even find a Library to borrow Books from.[2] Were

---

[1] Cf. article on Johnson. *Essays*, iv. 112.

[2] After Carlyle settled in London, and especially when he was at work on Cromwell, this want of a lending library in London was pressed home upon him, and he set earnestly at work to supply the need. He interested people of influence in the matter, and mainly through his efforts the invaluable London Library was estab-

## NOTE BOOK OF

it not for the Museum one where you have a certain help, the obstruction were total.

Biography is the only History:[1] Political History, as now written and hitherto, with its Kings and changes of *Taxgatherers*, is little (very little) more than a mockery of our want. This I see more and more.

———

The world grows to me evermore as a Magic Picture, a true Supernatural Revelation; infinitely stern, but also infinitely grand. Shall I ever succeed in *copying* a little therefrom.

———

"What I gave I have; what I spent I had, what I left I lost." Epitaph at Doncaster (?) from Johnson's Letters.[2] The first, and only

---

lished. He wrote to Emerson, 8 Feb., 1839, "We have no Library here, from which we can borrow books home; and are only in these weeks striving to get one: think of that!" In the course of the year the Library was opened. Carlyle was for many years its President. See *Life*, iii. 152, 188.

[1] Cf. 'Biography,' *Essays*, iv. 53.

[2] Carlyle cites this epitaph in his fine essay on Johnson. The epitaph varying slightly in form is found on several tombs. Gibbon in his History cites from Cleaveland's *Genealogical History of the Family of Courtenay*, 1735, p. 142, the epitaph of Edward, the blind Earl of Devon of the 15th century, which is in the words given by Carlyle, except for having 'we' in the place of 'I.' The epitaph at Doncaster which Johnson cited was on the tomb of one Robyn of Doncaster and ran:

"That I spent, that I had;
That I gave, that I have;
That I left, that I lost."

## THOMAS CARLYLE.

true, clause of it was long ago a perception of my own.

*Dies irae, dies illa:* where shall I find that old chant? Must investigate. (Now enough for one morning!) —

1.
Dies irae, dies illa
Solvet saeclum in favillâ:
Teste David cum Sybillâ.

2.
Quantus tremor est futurus
Quando Judex est venturus,
Cuncta stricte discussurus!

The tomb perished in the fire that destroyed the church in 1853. See *Letters of Johnson*, edited by G. Birkbeck Hill, 1892, i. 224, n. In the church of St. Peter at Verulam (St. Alban's), Bedfordshire, there is, or was at the beginning of the century, a brass plate engraved with a similar epitaph in Latin, with an English translation, the two in concentric circles, the outer circle being formed of the English words, the inner of the Latin. The English, modernized, ran thus:

Lo all that ere I spent, that sometime had I;
All that I gave in good intent, that now have I;
That I neither gave nor lent, that now abie I;
⁎ That I kepte till I went, that lost I.

The Latin was as follows:

Quod expendi habui,
Quod donavi habeo,
Quod negavi punior,
Quod servavi perdidi.

See *Beauties of England and Wales*, 1808, vii. 100, where is an engraving of this curious plate.

### 3.

Tuba, mirum spargens sonum
Per sepulchra regionum,
Coget omnes ante thronum.

### 4.

Mors stupebit et natura,
Cum resurget creatura,
Judicanti responsura.

### 5.

Liber scriptus proferetur,
In quo totum continetur,
Unde mundus judicetur.

### 6.

Judex ergo cum sedebit,
Quidquid latet, apparebit:
Nil inultum remanebit.

### 7.

Quid sum miser tunc dicturus,
Quem patronum rogaturus,
Cum vix justus sit securus?

### 8.

Rex tremendae majestatis,
Qui salvandos salvas gratis,
Salva me, fons pietatis.

### 9.

Recordare Jesu pie,
Quod sum causa tuæ viæ;
Ne me perdas illâ die.

## THOMAS CARLYLE.

### 10.

Quaerens me, sedisti lassus;
Redemisti crucem passus:
Tantus labor non sit cassus.

### 11.

Juste Judex ultionis,
Donum fac remissionis,
Ante diem rationis.

### 12.

Ingemisco tanquam reus,
Culpâ rubet vultus meus,
Supplicanti parce, Deus.

### 13.

Qui Mariam absolvisti,
Et latronem exaudisti,
Mihi quoque spem dedisti.

### 14.

Preces meæ non sunt dignæ;
Sed Tu bonus fac benigne
Ne perenni cremer igne.

### 15.

Inter oves locum praesta,
Et ab haedis me sequestra,
Statuens in parte dextrâ.

### 16.

Confutatis maledictis,
Flammis acribus addictis,
Voca me cum benedictis.

17.

Oro supplex et acclinis,
Cor contritum quasi cinis :
Gere curam mei finis.

18.

Lachrymosa dies illa
Quâ resurget ex favillâ
Judicandus homo reus.
Huic ergo parce, Deus.

*Pie Jesu Domine dona eis requiem.—Amen.*

[Copied from the " Mass for the Dead on the Day of decease or burial " in the *Romish Missal* (London, 1806 p. 512) this 14th Jany: long sought for; found by Jane, last night accidentally.]

— Did not see the Sir A. J. yesterday ; and cared less than nothing.—Invited to see Hogg (the Ettrick Shepherd) for Friday next.

Books to be looked after.
Grose's Olio.— The Foundling Hospital of Wit.
Arnold on Insanity. Carleton's Memoirs (of the Duke of Ormond ? — 17th century. Republished 1808).
Psalmanazar's Memoirs. Wool's Life of Warton.
Moore's Life of Smollett (worth anything?)

# THOMAS CARLYLE.

Hardy's Life of Charlemont. Pennant's London.
Cradock's Memoirs (when? who?)
Spence's Anecdotes. Davies's Life of Garrick.
Life of Goldsmith (by Sir Joseph Mawbey?)
Maty's Life of Chesterfield. Leland's Itinerary.
Seward's Anecdotes of Eminent Persons.
Nichols's Anecdotes. — Miss Hawkins's Memoirs.

These works are noted down from Croker's edition of Boswell's Johnson; which work I have just been earnestly reading; and now propose writing some kind of Essay upon.— January 18th, 1832.—

---

Parson Hackman (Narrative of) in " Love & Madness; " a foolish, partially indecent, altogether frothy Book. He killed M's[1] mother (Lord Sandwich's mistress, a Miss Ray) at the door of the Theatre, and was executed at Tyburn in 1779 (his *Trial* was 16th April).[2]—What stuff men are made of! It is very true that a madman lies within every sane man; is the material whereof the sane man fashions himself.

---

Hazlitt's *Liber Amoris* read for the first

[1] Basil Montagu, born 1770, died 1851, husband of the 'Noble Lady' (see ante, p. 195), and not without other claims to remembrance.

[2] Cf. *Reminiscences*, ii. 126; and see Boswell's *Johnson*, edited by Dr. Birkbeck Hill, iii. 383.

time: quite an enchantment, like one of those in the *Midsummer Night's Dream ;* a most hairy-faced, long-eared Bottom the weaver! No 'Confession' perhaps ever exhibited a a man in more despicably pitiable, ludicrously abominable light, since confessions first came into fashion.

Il volto sciolto, i pensieri stretti. (*This* is Wotton's word.)[1]
Campbell's *Hermippus Redivivus* (gives account of the Hermetic Philosophy).— Lives of the Admirals by the same. This was he who "always pulled his hat off when passing a church."[2]

Came upon Shepherd, the Unitarian Parson of Liverpool, yesterday for the first time, at Mrs. Austin's. A very large purply flabby

[1] "At Siena I was tabled in the house of one Alberto Scipioni, an old Roman Courtier in dangerous times . . . and at my departure toward Rome . . . I had won confidence enough to beg his advice how I might carry myself securely there, without offence of others, or of mine own conscience. *Signor Arrigo mio* (sayes he) *I Pensieri stretti, e il viso sciolto:* That is, *Your thoughts close, and your countenance loose*, will go safely over the whole World." Letter to Master —— *Reliquiæ Wottonianæ, 1651,* p. 434. The letter was to Milton; see *Notes and Queries,* July, 1852, p. 5.

[2] See Boswell's *Johnson* (ed. Hill), ii. 418. Dr. Campbell was but the translator of the *Hermippus Redivivu,* the author was Dr. J. H. Cohausen of Coblentz, See *Id.,* iii. 427, note, for an account of the book.

man; massive head with long thin grey hair; eyes *both* squinting, both overlapped at the corners by a little roof of brow; giving him (with his ill-shut mouth) a kind of lazy, eating, goodhumoured aspect. For the rest, a Unitarian Radical; clear, steadfast, but every way limited. . . . He said Jeffrey did not strike him as "a very taking man." Lancashire accent, or some provincial one.—Have long known the Unitarians *intus et in cute ;* and *never* got any good of them; or any ill.

---

Was the building of St. Paul's or the writing of Paradise Lost more necessary to England? The one cost us £150,000, the other £15.— Literature *cannot* be rewarded in money : it is priceless.— Have an Essay "on Authors" in my eye.

---

Franklin, I find twice or thrice in Boswell, defines man as "a Tool-making Animal." Teufelsdreck therefore has so far been anticipated.[1] *Vivant qui ante nos nostra dixerunt !*

---

Saturday 21st January. Yesterday sat scribbling some stuff, close on the borders of nonsense, about Biography, as a kind of introduction to "*John-*

[1] "'But on the whole,' continues our eloquent Professor, 'Man is a Tool-using Animal.'" *Sartor*, Book i. ch. v. See Boswell's *Johnson* (ed. Hill), iii. 245 for the citation of Franklin's definition.

*son.*"[1]   How is it to be?   I see not well; know only that it should be light, and written (by way of experiment) *currente calamo.*   I am sickly, not dispirited, yet sad.   As is my wont: when did I laugh last?   Alas, 'light laughter, like heavy money, has altogether fled from us.'   The reason is we have *no communion;* company enough, but no fellowship.   Time brings roses.   Meanwhile, the grand perennial COMMUNION OF SAINTS is ever open to us: enter, and worthily comport thyself there!

Nothing in this world is to me more mournful, distressing and in the end intolerable, than mirth not based on Earnestness (for it is false mirth); than wit, pretending to be wit, and yet not based on wisdom.   Two objects would reduce me to gravity had I the spirits of a Merry Andrew: a Death's Head and a modern London Wit.   The besom of destruction should be swept over these people; or else perpetual silence (except when they needed victuals or the like) imposed on them.

In the afternoon, Jeffrey, as he is often wont, called in on us: very lively, quick and — light.   Chatted about "cholera;" a subject far more interesting to him than it is to us.   Walked with him to Regent street; in

[1] It was printed as an independent paper in Fraser's Magazine.

hurried assiduous talk. Shiel (the Irish orator) had been once, he said, *convicted of a lie:* it was some story he had told, of Police tortures or such like, in the Catholic Association; having been that very day *convinced* that it was not true. O'Connell I called a real specimen of the almost obsolete species *Demagogue.* (Why should it be obsolete, this being the very scene for it? Chiefly because we are all Dilettantes, and have no heart of Faith, even for the coarsest of beliefs.) His " cunning" the sign, as cunning ever is, of a *weak* intellect, as of a weak character.— Very few Irish Appeals come to the House of Lords; a far greater proportion of Scotch. Why? The Irish Courts are identical with the English; their decisions little apt to be reversed: in any Scotch case, from the Chancellor's ignorance, there is a *chance* (like the throwing of dice) that he may decide either way. Eldon often decided palpably wrong. Nevertheless not above 1 case in 70, even of those decided in the Scotch Inner House, is appealed from. Of those that stop in the Outer House, "perhaps not one in 500." *All* causes that go from the Outer to the Inner House go thither in the shape of appeal. Scotch law, Jeffrey agrees, is much better than English. *He* tells, what so few here can do, an intelligible tale about what he is working in. Seemed to admit with me that the whole system of English Law has provoked not unjustly a fixed spirit of revolt in the minds of all men, and that it must be totally new-made. 'In my younger days, it was said if you had a contention about £30, let it go either way, do not enter Court at all: *now* the £30 has become £80, and the advice is repeated with that variation. Very bad.'—I have an immense appetite for statistics; but can get *no* proviant of that kind.

At my return home, whom should I find standing but Gustave d'Eichthal the Saint-Simonian! A little, tight, cleanly pure lovable *Geschöpfchen* :[1] a pure martyr and apostle, as it seems to me; almost the only one (not 'belonging to the Past') whom I have met with in my pilgrimage. Mill goes so far as to think there might and should be martyrs: this *is* one. He spoke French and English. His ideas narrow, and sore distorted; but his mind open, his heart noble. I have pleasure in the prospect of meeting him again.—

Soon after, Arthur Buller called with a " *mein bester Freund!* " A goodish youth; affectionate, at least attached: not so handsome as I had expected, tho' more so than enough. He walked with me to Fraser's Dinner in Regent street; or rather to the

[1] 'Little creature.'

door of Fraser's house, & there took leave with stipulation of speedy re-meeting.[1]

Enter thro' Fraser's Bookshop into a backroom, where sit Allan Cunningham, W. Fraser[2] (the only two known to me personally), James Hogg (in the easy-chair of honour), Galt, and one or two nameless persons; patiently waiting for dinner. Lockhart (whom I did not know) requested to be introduced to me. A precise brief active person, of considerable faculty, which however had shaped itself *gigmanically* only. Fond of quizzing, yet not *very* maliciously. Has a broad black brow indicating force and penetration, but a lower half of face dwindling into the character at best of distinctness, almost of triviality. Rather liked the man, and shall like to meet him again.[3] — Galt looks old, is deafish; has the air of a sedate Greenock Burgher;

---

[1] In a letter to his mother, 22 Jan., Carlyle said, "The Bullers are here, both parents and sons all in the friendliest relation to me . . . The two boys are promising fellows and may one day be heard of in the world" (as, indeed, they were). *Letters*, ii. 10.

[2] James Fraser was the proprietor of the Bookshop, and publisher of *Fraser's Magazine*. William Fraser was for some time editor of the *Foreign Review*, to which Carlyle was the most important contributor.

[3] In 1839 Carlyle's acquaintance with Lockhart was renewed, and he wrote to his brother, 'Had a long interview with the man [Lockhart] yesterday, found him a person of sense, good breeding, even kindness.' *Life*, iii. 163. After this their relations continued on terms of mutual respect and friendliness.

mouth indicating sly humour, and self-satisfaction; the eyes old and without lashes, gave me a sort of *wae* interest for him. He wears spectacles, and is hard of hearing: a very large man; and eats and drinks with a certain west-country gusto and research. Said little; but that little peaceable, clear and *gutmüthig*.[1] Wish to see him also again.[2] — Hogg[3] is a little, red-skinned, stiff, sack of a body, with quite the common air of an Ettrick shepherd; except that he has a highish tho' sloping brow (among his yellow-grizzled hair), and two clear little beads of blue or grey eyes, that sparkle if not with thought yet with animation. Behaves himself quite easily and well. Speaks Scotch, and mostly narrative absurdity (or even obscenity) therewith. Appears in the mingled character of Zany and raree-show: all bent on bantering him, especially Lockhart; Hogg walking thro' it, as if unconscious, or almost flattered. His vanity seems to be immense, but also his

[1] 'Good-natured.'
[2] John Galt, 1779–1839, a busy and prolific man of letters, whose 'Annals of the Parish' are still worth reading as a true picture of rustic Scotch life; liked and praised by Scott.
[3] The 'Ettrick Shepherd,' eternized not so much by his own works, as by Scott's goodness to him, and Wordsworth's verses upon his death. "He was undoubtedly," wrote Wordsworth, in the note prefixed to his 'Extempore Effusion,' "a man of original genius, but of coarse manners and low and offensive opinions."

goodnature: I felt interest for the poor 'Herd Body'; wondered to see him blown hither from his sheepfolds, and how, quite friendless as he was, he went along cheerful, mirthful and musical. I do not well understand the man: his significance is perhaps considerable. His poetic talent is authentic, yet his intellect seems of the weakest, his morality also limits itself to the precept: Be not angry. Is the charm of this poor man chiefly to be found herein, That he *is* a real product of Nature, and able to speak *naturally*— which not one in the thousand is? An 'unconscious talent,' tho' of the smallest; emphatically *naïve*. Once or twice in singing (for he sung of his own) there was an emphasis in poor Hogg's look, expressive of feeling, almost of enthusiasm. The man is a very curious *specimen:* Alas he is a *Man;* yet how few will so much as treat him like a *specimen*, and not like a mere wooden *Punch* or *Judy*[1]*!* — For the rest our talk was utterly despicable. Stupidity, insipidity, even not a little obscenity (in which all save Galt, Fraser and myself seemed to join) was the only outcome of the night.[2] Literary *men!* They are not worthy to be valets of such. Was a

[1] Cf. *Letters*, ii. 9.
[2] 'The conversation was about the basest I ever assisted in," wrote Carlyle to his brother John, 18 Febr. *Life*, ii. 263.

# NOTE BOOK OF

thing said that did not even solicit in mercy to be forgotten? Not so much as the attempt or wish to speak profitably. *Trivialitas trivialitatum; omnia trivialitas!* —I went to see, and I saw; and have now *said*, and mean to be silent, or try if I can speak elsewhere.— Enough for once.

\* \* \* \* \*1

[What follows was written under another binding; and is now slit out, and sewed in here, another better Note book having come to hand. 15th May.]²

March (about 8th) 1832 — Finished a *hastened* Paper on *Johnson;* which now (15th) lies at Press. Perhaps not wholly without

---

1 On the 22 January Carlyle's Father died, and the remaining pages of the original Note Book (pp. 52–76), and an addition sewed into it of forty-two pages, are occupied with Carlyle's Reminiscences of his Father. They begin: "On Tuesday, January the 24th 1832, I received tidings that my dear and worthy Father had departed out of this world." And a few pages further on Carlyle writes: 'I purpose now, while the impression is more pure and clear within me, to mark down the main things I can recollect of my Father.' This record of his Father's life, one of the most impressive biographical sketches in the language, is printed in *Reminiscences*, i. 1–52. The date at its close is 'Sunday night, 29th January 1832.'

2 "What follows" occupies an addition to the Notebook, of which the pages are numbered 119–152.

## THOMAS CARLYLE.

worth: we shall see.—[Have been interrupted, and no time is left at present.] —

*British Museum* (Saturday, S$^t$ Patrick's day for I saw Irishmen with shillelahs!) Came hither to look after *Diderot*, whereof here is what lies in the Biog. Universelle: He translated Stanyan's History of Greece (1743). Dict. de Médecine (1746). Essai sur le Mérite et la Vertu (1745) half-translated out of Shaftesbury— Pensées Philosophiques (1746) made much noise — Lettre sur les aveugles for the use of those that see (1749): sent to Vincennes in consequence. Encyclopéd. (1751) the two first vol.— and excited attention — 1752 it was suspended (de par le roi) for 18 months. Stopt again in 1759 when d'Alemb. retired: Dider. exerted himself (honour of the nation, advantage to trade, &c.); the Direct. de la librairie (who? what?) and duc de Choiseul granted a *protection* (7 vol. already out); and the rest of the work was published with the entirest freedom, each striving who should emit the most "philosophical idea": hastily got up too: Diderot was alone in it; took such workmen as he could get.—

In the fidélité conjugale ne voit qu'un *entêtement* et un *supplice*. Supplem. to the voyage of Bougainville.— Obscene novels (vols. 10, 11, 12 of Naigeon[1]) *very* obscene it

[1] Naigeon was the editor of the Works of Diderot, in

is said.—*Eleuthéromanes* (Liberty-mad), these two lines (qu'on lui a tant reproché)

Et ses mains ourdiraient les entrailles du prêtre,
A défaut d'un cordon, pour étrangler les rois.[1]

—Vol. 4. contains his pièces de théâtre.

---

Bishop Douglas[2] (Dr Johnson's) came from Pittenweem in Fife! The son of a 'merchant' (*négociant*) there: wrote against Hume and on Politics.

---

*Home*.[3] (This appears to be the 17th of March). Have just finished with Lardner about the Lit. Hist. of Germany; and am OFF WITH HIM, *einmal und immermehr*.[4] 'Tis as well, perhaps better. A *History* will *grow*

15 volumes, published in 1798, and reprinted often afterwards. He inserted in the text passages of an atheistic character, without indication that they were his own, and not Diderot's. See Sainte-Beuve, *Causeries du Lundi* (1851), Tome iii. p. 227.

[1] Carlyle cites and comments on these verses "surpassing all yet uttered or utterable in the Tyrtaean way" in his article on Diderot. *Essays*, v. 43.

[2] Dr. John Douglas, Bishop of Salisbury, 1721–1807; a member of the Literary Club, noted for his exposure of Lauder's forgeries, commemorated by Goldsmith in *Retaliation*,—
 " Here Douglas retires from his toils to relax,
 The scourge of impostors, the terror of quacks."

[3] '*Home*,' that is, the lodgings in Ampton Street; the last entry having been made at the British Museum.

[4] ' Once and forever.'

## THOMAS CARLYLE.

among my hands (by Review Articles) into a fitter shape; and may, one day, be published on its own foundation,— if the world require it; if not, *not*. Meanwhile, I have other work to seek for myself: The Sheffield Radical,[1] Diderot, Authors, Lessing, Thomasius, Fichte; plenty of them!

---

Settled yesterday, with Fraser, about the dividing of *Johnson*.[2] A foolish vehicle his scavenger-cart of a Magazine is: but what then? We *must* speak; if not by one organ, then by another.— Make not so much of those pitiful lucubrations of thine: *cast* them forth; *wirf sie schweigend in die ewige Zeit!*[3] They are but rubbish,— as all Time-things are: do thy best with them; then let the world do *its*.

---

Bookselling (as I told Lardner, much to his surprise) is in the state of 'delirium before death': the more needful is it that *thou* walk wisely thro' the middle of it.

---

We are both (Weibchen and I) considerably hurt in health, and longing to be home; which we expect soon. The climate of this

---

[1] Ebenezer Elliott.
[2] By the separation of the introductory pages on Biography in general, to form an independent article.
[3] "Cast them silently away for ever."

place is among the most detestable on Earth : otherwise, the place has been wholly agreeable to us.

Yesternight I saw Sir Nicholas Harris Nicolas Knight of the Guelphic Order, Antiquarian and what not; a good-natured, rattling, small rather than *thick*-headed mortal : he said (coming home with me thro' Chancery Lane), " I believe I have ruined (or done more to ruin) more Booksellers than any man living : no Book of mine ever paid its expenses."

The evening before (at W. Fraser's), I had seen this Knight, and another of the same,[1] ᴜ. David Brewster! B. is still full of projects and purveyor-activity : for the rest, has become a Whig and Reformer, and speaks about *this* Chancellor[2] exactly as about *the* Chancellor; whose sublime mind (he took pains to say) had included even *me* in its contemplations. A tough, vivacious man! Not without kindness, at least great sociality, of disposition ; and for his practical opinions :

> O wonder, O wonder! enter and see :
> A weathercock's head where his tail sh[d] be.

Leigh Hunt and I have come into contact by occasion of the *Characteristics :* he sought me out, and has been twice here; I once with

[1] 'Another of the same' is a phrase from the Scotch version of the Psalms, in frequent use in Scotland. A. C.
[2] Lord Brougham.

## THOMAS CARLYLE.

him. A pleasant, innocent, ingenious man; filled with *Epicurean Philosophy*, and steeped in it to the very heart. He has suffered more than most men; is even now bankrupt (in purse and repute), sick, and enslaved to daily toil: yet will nothing persuade him that Man is born for another object here than *to be happy*. Honour to tenacity of conviction! *Credo quia impossibile.*— A man copious and cheerfully sparkling in conversation; of grave aspect, never laughs, hardly smiles; black hair shaded to each side; hazel eyes, with a certain lifting up of the eyebrows that has no archness in it, rather sentient, well-satisfied self-consciousness. He is a real lover of Nature, and even singer thereof; and, for the rest, *belongs to London in the opening of the 19th century.*—[1]

The 'Cockney School' will one day be historically significant; in a small way. Its chief character is even this Epicurism; half-vision it had, but then *only* half. . . . Not *Stare super antiquas vias*, thencefrom to look out for *new ways*, and walk thereon; but simply to *leap the hedges*, and so sink in quagmires: this has been their method. They knew the wrong, not the right: worst of all, they did not *care* properly to know it, but

[1] The acquaintance with Hunt was renewed when Carlyle settled in London in 1834. See *Reminiscences*, i. 104, 174; *Letters*, ii. 150, 701, et al.

sought only *self*. We shall see them all better one day.

Wrote to John at Rome (a double Letter, which would go off yesterday).—

Schlegel is here: I left my card; and hope not, and care not, to see the old fool. His usual wig is blond; his face he paints! *Ach!* Finally, he is a literary *Gigman*. They are to give him a dinner at the "Literary Union" to-day: *who?* One Hayward (the "cleverest of the second-rate men," who has been much here), and Dionysius Lardner!— The day of small things.—

"Dr. Maginn" was at Fraser's with the two *Sirs*.[1] A rattling Irishman, full of quizzicality and drollery, without ill-nature, without earnestness, certainty of conviction or purpose in regard to *any* subject, except this one: *Punch is Punch*. A shortish thickset man (looks upwards of forty) with a fine (almost genial) gray eye; wears a wig. Is the proper Palinurus and originator of *Fraser's Magazine;* wherein, and in the *Standard* Newspaper, he finds his chief threshing-floor at present. I understand he "works mostly for the *dead horse*."

---

[1] William Maginn (1794—1842) was one of the most prolific and versatile magazine-writers of his time; he had cleverness, wit, and a store of miscellaneous learning. But he wrote little or nothing of permanent value.

THOMAS CARLYLE.

Fraser's Magazine took being *first* in the head of William Fraser; has, or had no Editor, Aim, or Principle: a chaotic, fermenting, dunghill heap of compost (as all these things are); of which I have at last succeeded in forming to myself some comprehensible notion. Its circulation only is still obscure to me; the methods of circulating it. One day I will jot down what I know: such things will rather *soon*, I think, be *strange*. The Bookseller is *no knave:* that is perhaps the only merit of the whole.

———

*What* have I *to do* now, before quitting London? Let me consider well, and have a *plan* of it, for next week, and *attain* something. — For once, enough![1]

———

[*Times.*] London, Monday, April 2, 1832.

"These papers announce a death which may almost be considered an event in politics as well as in literature,— the celebrated GOETHE died at Weimar on the 22d ult. He expired, without any apparent suffering, in his armchair, having a few minutes previously called for paper for the purpose of writing, and expressed his delight at the arrival of spring. He had, however, for the last two years en-

[1] The Carlyles left London on the 25th March, and after a few days in Liverpool and Dumfries returned to Craigenputtock in the middle of April.

joyed little of his usual health, and had fallen off greatly in personal appearance. We believe that he had passed his 82d year. All Europe knows the literary era of Germany which commenced with this distinguished man, which ends with him, and which may be considered as identified with his personal history."

This came to me at Dumfries, on my first return thither. I had written to Weimar, asking for a Letter to welcome me home; and *this* was it. My Letter [1] would never reach its *address:* the great and good Friend was no longer *there;* had departed some seven days before.— Craigenputtock, 19th April, 1832.

---

Tribula was a kind of threshing-machine; a chest roughened with wood-bars, or iron or flint notches on the bottom, and so trailed by cattle back and forward over the ears of corn till the grain was hustled out of them. The driver sat on it; and (as among the modern Turks) might have a *ladle wherein to catch the dung!*

*Tribulatio* is from this word; and so originally signifies something like what we Scotch mean by a *Heckelling* (Hatchelling): use has made it honourable.

---

The Fuller's was a great craft among the

[1] In regard to this letter see *Correspondence of Goethe and Carlyle,* p. 298, n.

Romans, for they had no shirts (?), and on gala-days dressed all in white woolen. The smell of the *Fullones* was not the pleasantest: they were sent to work, therefore, in fields, remote from the nostrils of men. Their use of a certain Liquor was great: they had pots or jars set at street-corners to tempt the Public to produce it, at least to yield it freely. Thus instead of "Whitbread's Entire" might there be a sign-post of quite inverse quality: Somebody's "Effete."— Consider also the Chinese; and sniff not at the wants and the ingenuity of poor man.

It is proof of the height to which Antiquity also had carried the art of Taxation, that Vespasian laid a Duty on these same Fuller's Pots; so that whoso was pleased to set forth his urinal to the world must pay the Prince for it.— It was on occasion of Titus' reproaching him with this meanness, that old V. bid him smell a piece of the money produced thereby, and said: *Dulcis odor lucri ex re qualibet.*[1]— Works of the Learned (or rather Repub. of Letters). v. I. (150 &c) where lies some curious matter.

---

Caxton printed in the Almonry of West-

[1] Vespasian's words, according to Suetonius, in his Life of the Emperor, c. xxiii, were *Atqui e lotio est.* It is Juvenal who wrote:
　　. . . Lucri bonus est odor ex re
　Qualibet. *Sat.* xiv. 204.

minster Abbey (why *there* specially is not known): hence, say some, our English Printers still call their workshop a *Chapel*.— (do. elsewhere)—

I squelched my finger-nail (curing smoke in company with Pate Easton, at Scotsbrig; and *effectually*, I believe!): the nail is quite black, but sticks there until a new white one be formed under it; the old black nail dead and worthless, yet performing a worthy sort of service: how like many a Social Institution of these days! But, indeed, so it is ever; as I have often enough remarked.

A sneering, jeering Review of Hume's *Essay on Human Nature* in Repub. Lett.[1] for November 1739: to be farther looked into. The poor Reviewer no doubt imagined he had done a feat. How the Tables turn!

Saturday, April 22nd[2] Have now been here for a week: quite sickly, lazy, lost, stranded in a *Juan Fernandez;* do not remember that I have passed many more

[1] "The present State of the Republick of Letters," London, 1723–1736, was the chief literary journal of its time. In 1736 it was united with the "Literary Magazine," and published as "The History of the Works of the Learned." This ran from Jan., 1737, to Dec., 1743, and it was in it that the review of Hume's Essay appeared.

[2] In 1832 Saturday was the 21st of April.

despicable or unjoyful or unprofitable weeks in my life. No work will forward with me. What a week!—A day of it, this day, yet remains for thee: To work! To work!— Repent not uselessly; only *amend*.—I have fasted (from bread) this breakfast time: may that be the beginning of better things.—Now for the "Sheffield Radical."

---

Sunday morning. Yesterday quite down-pressed, over-powered (with bodily obstruction chiefly) and worthless, or next to that. Did no work, that can be shown; tho' I rather zealously attempted it. Again endeavour! Times *will* mend.

The whole thing I want to write seems lying in my mind; but I *cannot get my eye on it*. The Machine is lazy, languid; the motive Principle cannot conquer the inertia.

---

A question arises, whether there ought to be, in a perfect society, *any* class of purely speculative men? Whether all men should not be of active employment and habitude; their speculation only growing out of their activity, and incidental thereto?—

The grand Pulpit is now the Press; the true Church (as I have said twenty times of late) is the Guild of Authors. How these *two* Churches and Pulpits (the velvet-cushion one and the metal-type one) are to adjust their mutual relations and cognate workings: this is a problem which some centuries may be taken up in solving. It is the deepest thing to be solved in these days.

———

Every man that writes is writing a new Bible; or a new Apocrypha; to last for a week, or for a thousand years: he that convinces a man and sets him working is the doer of a *miracle*. [Strange language this: but it is as in the immigration of the Northmen, or any other great world-revolution, *two* languages must get *jumbled together*, and old words get new meanings; all things for a time being confused enough.]

———

*Ought* any writing to be transacted with such intense difficulty? Does not the True always flow *lightly* from the lips and pen? I am not clear in this matter; which is a deeply practical one with me. Consider the following also:

The *True* indeed flows lightly; but how stands it with the *mixture* of True and Untrue (or Unknown), wherein the latter element has to be continually eliminated, and elaborated, or rejected?—

One thing, at all events, is plain: Take not *too* much care about thy writing, or about aught else that belongs to thee. Know that it is intrinsically *trivial* (as thyself art) and will *soon* perish,— let vanity whisper what she may. Quick, then; thro' with it! Learn to do it *honestly* (learn what that means); *perfectly* thou wilt never do it.

Time flies; while thou balancest a sentence, thou art nearer the *final* Period.

Cast thy thought forth (so soon as thou hast *thought* it) with some fearlessness: *let* it sink into the great mass of Action (under which rolls Eternity!): *let* it sink there, since such was its allotment. *Dissolved* (what we call Dead), the *Life* of it will still go on working there. *Deny* THYSELF; whatsoever is *thyself*, consider it as nothing.

This, however, I must say for myself: It is seldom or never the Phraseology, but always the Insight, that fails me, and retards me.

On, then; on! why stand describing how thou *shouldst* move; forward, and move, in *any* way.

---

April 28th (Saturday). Finished the day before yesterday a *Leichenrede* on Goethe.[1] Stiff and starched, and a poor expression of my feelings.

Yesterday wrote to John, &c. To-day am for these villainous " Corn Law Rhymes " again: a task that is beginning to get hate-

[1] "Funeral discourse," 'Death of Goethe,' published in the 'New Monthly Magazine'; *Essays*, iv.

ful to me; so small, so unmanageable—in the way I have taken it up.

N. B. Be very cautious how you *take up* anything. I have a strange reluctance to renounce the road I have entered on, how stony soever, how roundabout soever. You do not like to turn back: On then!

———

Thus does a Time pass, and with the time its man. The man who can live and work thro' two Times, and welcome a Palingenesia after mourning for a Death, is rarely to be met with— *T[iec]k*.

———

When the State Cauldron leaks, there is nothing but a hissing, and foul ashy steaming and sputtering; the social Cookery can no longer be carried on. It must be mended, then; let it be mended. Easy to say, difficult to do! There are Tinkers that in mending one hole make a couple. But especially, if your whole Cauldron has ceased to be metal at all, and become one thick laminated mass of rust and corrugation, without heart or solidity anywhere, how then is the soldering-iron to be applied; what Tinker so cunning as to operate with effect there. They do it in this way: *mend with putty*. Each mending lasts for a week, and the outbreaks get more and more frequent. At last when the mending has become a daily and hourly matter, and per-

## THOMAS CARLYLE.

petually there is a puttying and never an end of leakage, but ever as the puttying proceeds on the one hand, the dripping and hissing proceeds on the other,— some indignant State-Tinker says, Putty will no longer do, but they must have metal cloutings; and so sets him to rivet and to solder, and smites resolutely with hammer and punch on the old rust cauldron : what is the issue then ? Ask Earl Grey with his *Reform Bill*[1]

GOTF$^D$ SAUERTEIG.[1]

---

Sometime about the 4$^{th}$ of May, finished, rapidly enough, a Paper on the Corn Law Rhymer, very little to my mind. It still lies here; intended for Napier, who however may well be excused for rejecting it, so intensely " speculative-radical " is the whole strain of it. Perhaps times may have a little changed with him, even during the last fortnight.—

Purposed next to draw up an Encyclopedia

[1] *Gottfried Sauerteig* ("Leaven," "Yeast") is one of the names, like Teufelsdröckh, invented by Carlyle, as a transparent symbolic cloak for his own individuality. In his Essay on *Biography*, he thus introduces this personage. 'Here, however, . . . we may as well insert some singular sentences on the importance and significance of *Reality*, as they stand written for us in Professor Gottfried Sauerteig's *Æsthetische Springwürzel* [*Aesthetic Castor-oil plant*]; a work, perhaps, as yet new to most English readers. The Professor and Doctor is not a man whom we can praise without reservation. . . Nevertheless in his crabbed, one-sided way he sometimes hits masses of the truth.' *Essays,* iv. 55.

memoir of Lord Byron (for N. and *purely* in compliance with his request); had accordingly jotted down some pages of it: but now an uncertainty arises whether my service (as I explained the possibility of rendering it) is wanted; which uncertainty will soon become a certainty that said service cannot be had. I had no manner of call to speak *there* about Lord Byron; and had much rather eschew it. —I am now for a long Essay on Goethe to be printed in the *Foreign Quarterly Review:* do not in the least see any way thro' it; feel only that there is much to be said, or repeated. Have been idle (from the *pen*) for twelve days, and must alter very soon.— Bulwer Lytton [1] writes me, euphuistically announcing that the *Leichenrede,* on 'our Greatest that has departed' is at press, and will be forwarded as Proofsheet soon: I partly expect it to-night. Very unsatisfactory was the whole to me. *On,* however, taking small heed of it!—

Went down to Scotsbrig on Thursday to settle about family affairs there. All was already clear for settlement, by the wise prudence of him who had left us. His last Will I read over, with a sad and obstructed feeling, yet as a necessary task. All was methodical, just, decisive. He divides his property equally among the five children who had helped by their toil to earn it. At first, I

[1] Bulwer was editor of the New Monthly Magazine.

can remember he was for introducing John and me also; but I dissuaded him, inasmuch as *our* share was already received, I having been *educated*, and John thro' me. A sad and earnest look was the answer to this proposal: but I now found, for the first time, that it had been complied with.— All the immovable property (some Houses in Ecclefechan, yielding between twenty and thirty Pounds annually) are left in life-rent to my Mother; reverting finally to the other five. — My two Brothers valued what was at Scotsbrig, I acting as Umpire and Father on the occasion; the whole was managed last Saturday, not without some study and discussion, yet in a spirit which ought to satisfy me; without covetousness or ill-nature appearing on any side, which in such cases I understand usually do appear violently enough. The valuation was somewhere near the verge of £600 : James and his two Sisters made an arrangement, which is to last on trial for a year; our good Mother, who however is independent, will stay with them, and keep them together. They are not foolish, far from it, as people go; but they are young; and no community can subsist without a *governor*.— Scotsbrig is much changed for me; yet the place where of all others I feel among my loved ones. At home here, I am with my loved *one*, and among my *tools :* otherwise it has never yet become homelike to me. Let us be content; let us hope. *Der Mensch ist eigentlich auf Hoffnung gestellt.* This is the ' Place of Hope.'—[1]

On Sunday evening I went over with Alick and Jamie to see our " Aunt Fanny." Found her in a miserable hut (named Knowehead, or some such thing); a vehement, fiercely-assiduous and fiercely-thrifty old woman; very dirty in apparel and environment; not without a touch of antique courtesy; and much flattered by the visit. She is now in her eightieth year; the last survivor of the past Time. Her memory seemed excellent, but she would not talk to questions. A natural garrulity had become heightened to endless copiousness by old age. She described to me when and where she first saw her Husband; stepping Middlebie Burn, with a blue jacket and doe-skin breeches, a proper man to look upon.[2] Also, with infinite minuteness, her journey to Peebles, rencontres and adventures at the Crook Inn; all which stood perfect in her memory as things of yesterday. It was in 1773 that she was wedded. The beginning of the apprentice-

[1] "' Man is properly speaking based upon Hope,' he has no other possession but Hope; this world of his is emphatically the Place of Hope." *Sartor Resartus,* Book ii. ch. vii.

[2] Her husband's name was William Brown. See *Reminiscences,* i. 32.

ships she could not date with accuracy. She was six years older than my Father. In such a scene and with so many auditors there was little to be gathered from her. I partly calculate on seeing her again, when her son and she have removed to their Farm. He ("Wull," a strange, half-inspired, half-idiotic character, miserly, rich, to be wondered at and laughed at) stands in the strictest subjection to her; is not without awe of her, as of a really superior mind. In all points spiritual, the withered old woman is clearly stronger than the lumpish, pausing, prosing man.

---

On Monday morning I came off hither. Vague rumours of the loss of the Reform Bill had been circulating in our remote circle; these at Dumfries were made clear certainties.[1] The people have been burning (in effigy) their Patriot King; a Butcher at Annan had been put in jail for beheading him. All the things were in a flutter and fluster at Dumfries, politically speaking; one of those *tout est perdu*'s, which occur often enough in

[1] On the 7th of May the new Reform Bill was before the House of Lords, and the Ministry were defeated on an amendment. On the 9th Lord Grey and his colleagues resigned. Then followed the Duke of Wellington's ineffectual attempt to form a ministry. On the 15th Lord Grey resumed office, and on the 4th of June the Bill was finally carried in the House of Lords by a majority of eighty-four.

men's affairs. *Rien n'est perdu ; il n'y avait rien à gagner.*

Poor M'Diarmid[1] amused me with his soap-bubble frothing. A wild little man; dark in the face; anger and vehemence, trepidation, indignation, indetermination; a look too as if he still were not angry *enough:* wholly as if a posse of sheriff's officers had come upon him, and were selling his bed. Three times, tho' sad enough in heart under the chill May moonshine, in driving home, I laughed outright to remember him. The foolish Editor that he is! A snuff drop hanging at his nose, *smoke* (not fire) in his eye, distraction in his aspect: and all for what? Because a batch of Incapables had been turned to the street, and a batch of Capables, perhaps a shade more knavish than the other had been substituted in their room.— Our withers are unwrung.

---

The question now arises which no one is prepared to answer: what will follow next; what is to be done next? I comforted poor Mac that " King Arthur " (so he would name poor Wellington) would *not* try governing by the bayonet; would study to seat himself firmly on the coachbox, and then drive — whither the people forced him: at all events would *drive;* not sit flourishing the whip and

[1] Editor of *The Dumfries Courier.*

stirring no hair's breadth, as the others had done for eighteen months long. To me (who know nothing whatever of these latest doings) it seems not unlikely that Arthur will pass a Bill, perhaps very like the other, perhaps better. Let him take his own mind: me or mine he cannot help much or hinder much. One great comfort I shall have: *talk* will be changed into *action;* the country will not die of starvation, but at worst by grapeshot and gunshot.—

So then our "Friends" are all on the pavement; ousted in one short week! One Tuesday M'Diarmid crows stout defiance, triumphant note of victory; next Tuesday, the crow has become a screaming cackle; a kite has pounced down and eaten up the sun. Lord Chancellor Brougham, that virtuous man Viscount Althorp, the incomparable Earl Grey, Lord Advocate and all the rest — must take the road in such weather as chances to be blowing.— For Jeffrey (to whom alone the slightest interest attaches me) I rather esteem it a happiness. Brougham but "bides his time;" and, if he live, will come again, not whig but radical. Earl Grey deserves his fate: he set the interests of England and those of his own small fractional (unjustifiable) *part* of England on the same level; would in his own way save both or neither; has in consequence lost only himself. Can the man not see that Lordhood is becoming obsolete, that Manhood is henceforth the only order? Be he reputed *honest* (I believe him to be so, whiggishly speaking): and with that character let him retire from the public scene forever and a day.

---

Or is this the state of it? Granting the King to be an Imbecile and Nonentity, has he changed so much for the worse? He gets a professed Dugald Dalgetty or Soldier of Fortune, able to fight, ready to fight on any side, for his pay: he parts with a 'Soldier of Principle,' but who unhappily did not know what his principle was, or who had two incompatible principles, and so stood ready to fight on some side, could he have seen which; but unable to fight on any.—

---

Poor "Patriot King"! I never cheered him or heeded him; only once laughed at him (as I witnessed his Coronation procession); and now do not upbraid him. The wisest man in the world might pause in that situation: what shall the foolishest do?

---

The only Reform is in *thyself*. Know this O Politician, and be moderately political.

---

For me I have never yet done any one political act; not so much as the signing of a petition. My case is this: I comport myself wholly like an alien; like a man who is not in his own country; whose own country lies perhaps a century or two distant. When the time comes, should it ever come, that I can do *any good* in such coming forward, then let me not hang back. Meanwhile pay thy taxes to his Majesty and the rest, so long as they can force thee; the instant they can*not* force thee, that instant cease to pay. This has been my political principle for many a year. The passing or the failing of innumerable Reform Bills might not alter it much : money is paid to him who does a service worth money; obedience is due to him who governs: to him who wears the governor's *mask*, the *mask* of obedience,— as to the ass in lion's skin (who in any case could kick) — while you are near him.—

And now a truce to Politics. All this I have written down, this Wednesday, May 16th, 1832 years : knowing that it is trivial; also that some day even these transitory phrases will have meaning.

Reminiscence. Two nights before leaving London I went down to the House of Commons with W. Fraser, who however could not get admittance for himself and me; a thing I partly rejoiced at. We went to a Club house in S<sup>t</sup> James's, the first and only one I was ever in. Waited also afterwards a while in the Lobby of the " House ": while here saw Macaulay (Thomas Babington) come out, and buy two oranges; a sign, Fraser said, that he was going to speak; which accordingly next day showed that he had done. Macaulay, whom I noted strictly, is a short squat thickset man of vulgar but resolute energetic appearance. Fair-complexioned, keen gray eyes, a large cylindrical head set close down between two strong round shoulders; the brow broad and fast-receding, the crown flat — perhaps it was baldish. Inclines already to corpulence, tho' I suppose he is not five-and-thirty, of which age or a somewhat higher he wore the air. The globular will one day be his shape, if he continue. I likened him, in my own mind, to a managing Ironmaster (I know not well why); with vigorous talent for that or some such business (on what *scale* fortune may order); with little look of talent for anything higher. He is the young man of most force at present before the world. Successful he may be to great lengths, or not at all, according as the times turn: meanwhile, the limits of his worth are discernible enough. Great things lie not in him. It is a fatal circumstance that he rests satisfied with being *a Critic*, feels not the want of any force belonging to himself, wherewith he might *do* somewhat; has yet attained to no *belief*, and apparently is not wretched for not having any. The moral nature of the man I take to be intrinsically common; hence, if no otherwise, were his intellectual nature marked as common also. He is the only young man of any gift, at this period, who is a whig; another characteristic. He may be heard of, and loudly; but what is being heard of? Whosoever beats a drum is heard of. Let us hope too that M. will gain better insight, a clear, manly foundation, and be what he might be: "a man among clothes-screens."

As for Fraser's Clubhouse, it was a splendid mansion, with dining-rooms (where whiskered hungry people, Irishmen mostly, sat devouring viands and drinking champagne), drawing-rooms full of sofas, pier glasses, periodicals &c &c. We went and lounged in one for a quarter of an hour. It is called the Windham Club, I think. The house had belonged to some dissipated distracted Irish Nobleman, who had married a woman of infamous character, still living, and sinning, her husband having made the world rid of him some years before.

The Clubs are a curious feature of London: the principle of Sociality being quite gone, that of Gregariousness is there in full action. Men combine together, *professing* no other object than that they may have cheaper food and drink and accommodation than separately could be come at. They have all grown up since I was in London before. A more significant phenomenon than is usually recognized in them.

---

But here, my paper being done, let me close. Joy and sorrow; irreparable losses; toils fruitless or fruitful: a share of all lies noted in this little Tome. Onwards are we going, ever onwards: Eternity alone can give back what Time daily takes away. I am Fatherless now, (thank God, not yet Motherless): be all that remains the dearer. Improve, cherish, laudably work with whatever Time gives and leaves. *Gedenke zu leben!*[1] Farewell ye loved ones! I have still *zu leben.*

[1] "Resolve *to live!*"

*Autograph Letter.*

Chelsea, 25 june, 1862

"Seekest thou great things, seek them not!" I cd do no good with your "tragedy" after ever so much endeavour; it depends on Playhouse Managers &c &c;— and is, I must say, likely to have been an unreasonable, tho' innocent attempt, on the part of a young man, inexperienced in life, much more in the special ways of

Delineating and Expounding what life is and of? ends.

Forgive my plainness of speech. But it is my standing advice to all young persons who trace in themselves a superior capacity of mind, to select, beyond all other conditions, a silent course of activity; — and to disbelieve totally the babble of reviews and newspapers, and bad clamour of Names everywhere prevalent, that "Literature" (every one were qualified) is the truly noble human career. For older, very few! since you ask my opinion the greatest minds I have known, or have authentically heard) of, have not been the Shockings boys at all, — much less in these bad times; raging with helpless, and with so little else, from sea to sea! —

In my great haste (wishing you well, not ill),

T. Carlyle

*Chelsea, 25 June, 1862.*

"*Seekest thou great things, seek them not!*"

I could do no good with your "*Tragedy*," after never so much endeavour, it depends on *Playhouse Managers, etc. etc.;* — and is, I must say, likely to have been an unreasonable, tho' innocent attempt, on the part of a young man, inexperienced in Life, much more in the suitable ways of Delineating and Expounding what Life is and should be.

Forgive my plainness of Speech. But it is my standing advice to all young persons who trace in themselves a superior capacity of mind, to select, beyond all other conditions, a silent *course of activity;* — and to disbelieve totally the babble of reviews and newspapers, and loud clamour of Nonsense everywhere prevalent, that "*Literature*" (even if one were qualified) is the truly noble human career. Far other, very far! since you ask my opinion. The greatest minds I have known, or have authentically heard of, have not been the speaking ones at all, — much less in these loud times; raging with palaver, and with so little else, from sea to sea! —

In very great haste (*wishing you* well, *not ill*),

*T. Carlyle.*

# INDEX

# INDEX.

Action and Morality, 228
Actions, great, sometimes historically barren, 171; smallest, sometimes very fruitful, 171
Adam, fable concerning, 81, 82
Advertising, Carlyle upon, 208, 209; amount spent by two booksellers annually in, 208
Aikin, Lucy, "Memoirs of Queen Elizabeth," 4
Air, always hope in the, 106
Age, every, full of vicissitudes to its people, 141
Alexander, remark by Carlyle concerning, 7; compared with Hambden, 7; expedition of, compared with St. Paul's mission, 171
Alfieri, on genius, 30
Alison, Rev. Archibald, "Essay on Taste," 84; criticism of, 84
"Anatomy of Melancholy," extracts from, 85; anecdote concerning, 98
Antimachus Clarius, on Plato, 124
Areopagitica, Milton's, Carlyle on, 29, 30
Aristocracy, a true, wanted, 179
Aristotle, as to Action and Thought, 81; upon solitude, 122 (*note* 2); "Philosophy" of, contrasted with "Sermon on the Mount," 171
Arlesford, Battle of, defeat of Royalists at, 9; location of, 9
Art, is, higher than Religion? 204; possibility of, at this era, 215; materials of, everywhere, 227, 228
Ascham, Roger, birth and death, 89; tutor to Queen Elizabeth, 89; his chief and other works, 89; life of, by Dr. Johnson, 89; "a good sort of man and well worth study," 89

Bacon, on solitude, 122, 123
Badams, friend of Irving, calls on Carlyle, 194; described by Mrs. Montagu 195 (see *note* 1)

Ballhorn, stanza from Golden A B C, 118 (for trans. see p. 177)
Barclay, John, 25 (see *note*)
Bardili, his "Rational Realism," 112; similar to Malebranche? 112
Baretti, short account of, 130, 131; adventure of, in London, 131; his works and character, 131 (see also *note*)
Beaumont (and Fletcher), dramatists, disappointing to Carlyle, 31; criticism of 31, 32
Bentham, Jeremy, significance of, 171; senility of, 236
"Benvenuto Cellini," criticism upon, 186
Berkenhout, Dr., his "Literary History of England," 147
Biography, the only history, 238
Böhmen, ex-king of, comes to London, takes Covenant, and receives pension, 11
Book, by Carlyle, description of projected, 29
Books (French), to be read, 52, 53; where met with, 52; (German) recommended in Herder, 75, 76, 77; recommended by Mr. Aitken, 121; more, to be read, 123, 127; more, to be seen, 142, 143; list of English, 146; list of, copied from Croker's Boswell's Johnson, 242, 243
Boscovich, Kant reminds Carlyle of, 112; died mad, 130
Bossuet, "Oraisons funèbres," 10
Bouterwek, his "System of Virtuality," 112
Bowring, Sir John, meets Carlyle, 196 (see *note* 4)
Bradock-Down, Battle of, 6; location of, 6; defeat of the Parliament at, 6; indifferently described, 6
Brandes, Johann Christian, "Autobiography," 121
Brentford, Royalist general, defeated at Arlesford by Waller, 9; rescued from Donnington, 10

19      289

# INDEX.

Brerewood, what of? 25
Brewster, Sir David, meets Carlyle, 256; Carlyle's opinion of, 256
Brothers, Richard, 216 (see also *note* 2)
Brougham, Lord, Carlyle prophesies concerning, 273
Browne, Sir T., his "Religio Medici," "Urne Burial," and "Vulgar Errors," 67; Carlyle's opinion of, 68; midway between poet and orator, 69; his "Religio Medici" most readable, 69; errs in giving himself too good a character, 69; account of, 90; knighted by Charles II, 90
Bruyère, La, characterization of, of, 126
Buller, Mrs., verses to, by Dr. Leyden, 65
Burgess, Dr., who was? 1
Burns, contrasted with Scott, 127; Carlyle finishes a paper on, 129
Burrow, Sir J., 29
Burton, quotations from, 85, 86; little to be learned about him, 90; short account of, 90; firm believer in Astrology, 90; anecdote of his life at Oxford, 91; quotations from, 97; Carlyle's characterization of, 99
Byron, a "kraftmann," at his death, 17; Carlyle's opinion of him, 71 (see also *note*); a brief definition of, 230

Cabbage, the, characterization of, 105
Caesar, remark by Carlyle concerning, 7; compared with Hambden, 7; Hadrian's epitaph on, 123
Capel, Lord, 17
Carisbrook Castle, Charles I confined in, 15; treaty with Scots signed by Charles in, 15
Carlyle (Mrs.), Jane Welsh, arrives in London, 21 (see *note* 1)
Carlyle, Thomas, begins first notebook while reading Clarendon's History, 1; invokes fortune, 1; finishes third volume of Clarendon, 19; ill health of, 54; despondency of, 55; rejection of suicide by, 56 (see *note*, p. 57);

Carlyle, Thomas — *continued*.
estimate of true affection, 58; to leave Kinnaird, 58; hopes of Wilhelm Meister (translation), 58; Schiller, Part II, sent to London, 54; Schiller, Part III, begun, 59; effect of drugs on, 59; scribbling, not writing Schiller, 59; anxiety about Schiller (the book), 59; farewell to 1823, 59, 60; has trouble with the introduction to Schiller, 60; at Hoddam Hill, 64; despondency of, 64, 65, 66; marries, 67; finishes "Anatomy of Melancholy," 98; doubtful what to say concerning it, 98; sums up Burton and his book, 98, 99; on a diseased liver, and virtue as its own reward, 103; finishes article for "Edinburgh Review," 140; to see Jeffrey at Dumfries, 141; thinks seriously of discussing Martin Luther, 142; proposes to write an essay on Metaphors, 142; criticizes Political Economists, 144; is occupied writing a "History of German Literature," 147 (see *note*); comments on his difficulties in doing so, 148; rebukes himself, 148, 149; on the origin of quarrels, 149, 150; has "done with the Germans," 150; inquires how much truth is in them, 150; gets rid of Materialism, 151; inquires into the nature of a miracle, 151; asks what is poetry, 151; laments his lack of memory, 151; doubts if he shall succeed, 152, cannot judge of his own talent, 152; writes letter to Dumfries "Courier," 153 (see *note*); gets on badly with a speculation on History, 154; is asked to write a life of Goethe, 154 (see *note*); also of Luther, 154, 155; his sentiment as regards a life of Luther, 155; is offered an annuity by Jeffrey, but refuses, 155 (see *note*); comments upon this, 155; confesses his error about independence, 156; begins second volume of "German Literary History," 156; his impression concerning

# INDEX.

Carlyle, Thomas—*continued*.
it, 156; on the death of his sister Margaret, 157; on the Saint-Simonians, 158 (see also *note* 2); failure of project as to "History of German Literature," 163; reproaches himself, 163 (see *note* 2); has glimpses of the power of spiritual union, 164; exhorts himself to be up and doing, 165, 166; writes "The Beetle," 170; undefined aim of, 170; criticizes "Fraser's Magazine," 170; refers to John Wilson ("Christopher North"), 170; declares printing not to be the symbol of literature, 170, 171; compares great and small actions, 171; quotes examples, 171; compares moral and intellectual nature of man, 171; defines the significance of Christ, 171; defines the place of Jeremy Bentham, 171; pities England, 172; contrasts Utilitarians and Whigs, 182; has no patience with Dilettanti, 172; defines the Sin of the age, 172; condemns the idle, 172; visit of the Jeffreys to, 173 (see *note*); criticizes Jeffrey at length, 173, 174, 175; begins "Sartor Resartus," 176; on Seclusion and Meditation, 176; on Silence, 176; as to Words, 176; as to Silence and Speech, 177; as to Secrecy, 177; "On Clothes," 177; receives the ornamented "Schiller" from Goethe, 177 (see *note* 1, p. 178); sends the "Clothes" to Fraser, 178 (see *note* 2); comments on political state of England, 178, 179; divine right of squires equal to that of kings, 179; as to property, 179; as to Art and Poetry, 180; the logical import of life, 180; analyzes his condition, 181; hears from his brother John, 182; criticizes Taylor, 182; on a stanza by Mrs. Carlyle, 182; trouble with "Teufelsdreck," 183 (see *notes* 1, 2); refers to Goethe, 183; literary prospects of, 183; on the state of Europe, 183; on the state of England,

Carlyle, Thomas—*continued*.
184; on the frame of society, 184; as to the only sovereigns of the world, 184; as to divine right in kings, 184, 185; the derivation of honor-titles, past and future, 185; reliance on God, 185; comment on Jeffrey, 185; criticizes Benvenuto Cellini, 186; on Pope's "Odyssey of Homer," 187; Homer or Shakespeare the greater? 187; inquires as to constitution of a Whole, 187; as to the true Heroic Poems, 188; seeks the true relation of moral to poetic genius, 188; characterizes the words of Jesus, 189; ends the first Note-book at Craigenputtock, 189; exhorts himself, 189; leaves Craigenputtock for London, 191 (see *note* 1); account of journey, 191, 192, 193; calls on the Lord Advocate, 193; is advised to try Murray with "Sartor" and sees him, 194; comment on the meeting, 194; meets the Badamses, 194; renews acquaintance with the Montagues, 194 (see *note* 3); calls on Mrs. Montagu, 195 (see *notes* 1 and 2); calls on Longman's with Napier's letter, 196; meets with refusal of "German Literary History," 196; renews acquaintance with the Stracheys and Bowring, 196; sees Allan Cunningham, 196; writes to Goethe, 197; visits Shooter's Hill, 197 (see *note* 1); breakfasts with the Jeffreys, 198; sees Edward Irving, 198; appoints to dine with Drummond, 198 (see *note* 4); meets Godwin, 198; characterization of Godwin, 199; ill health of, 200; journal writing discontinued by, 200; inquiry as to education, 200; notes the arrival of Mrs. Carlyle, 201; comments on "Sartor Resartus," 201 (see *note* 1); meets Gustave d'Eichthal, the Saint-Simonian, 201; notes loss of Reform Bill, 202; notes illness of Jeffrey, 202; meets Sir J. Macintosh and describes him, 202,

# INDEX.

Carlyle, Thomas — *continued.*
203; refers to Dr. Fleming, 203 (see *note* 1); inquires as to the true duty of a man, 203, as to Reverence the need of men, 203; complains of stupidity, 204; inquiry into dictum by Goethe and Schiller that art is higher than religion, 204; notes tendency to speculate on men, not man, 205; comments on the general condition of things, 206, 207: complains that good shoes cannot be had in London, 207 (see *note*); states the universal problem of man, 208; notes a harder problem, to be found in London, 208; upon advertising or *puffing*, 208, 209; calls London the Goshen of quacks, 209; on how to remedy things, 209; on the size of London, 209, 210; notes extravagant price of potatoes, 210; comments on the hurry of life in London, 210; notes the isolation of life in London, 210; on the want of Government in, 211; on the torpidity of the Soul, 211 (see *note* 1); to write for the "Edinburgh Review," 212; as to a course of lectures in London, 212 (*note* 1); inquires as to province of oral teaching, 212; avers London to be ignorant of art, 212; as to eloquence in himself, 212; upon Hazlitt's "Table Talk," 213 (see *note* 3); dines with Fonblanque, 213; describes him, 213; receives Allan Cunningham, 214; analyzes him, 214; as to Sir Walter Scott, 214; upon the advantage of the pulpit, 215; as to the meaning of symbol, 215; on the possibility of Art at this era, 215; "where is tomorrow?" 215; classifies society, 215, 216; note on Richard Brothers, 216; meets Charles Lamb at Enfield, 217; opinion of Lamb, 217, 218, 219 (see *note* 1, p. 217, and *note* 1, p. 218); on the difficulty of obtaining the truth, 217; notes wild riots in Bristol, 219 (see *notes* 1,

Carlyle, Thomas — *continued.*
2, p. 220); has a "striking article" to write, but finds it "unspeakably" difficult, 220; general apprehension of cholera unshared by, 221 (see *note* 1); as to "Life" and "Existence," 221; the "hohe Bedeutung des Entsagens," 221 (see *note* 2); conception of Immortality depends on that of Time, 222; laments the absence of "Sports," 222; upon education, 222, 223; upon the best and the worst educated man, 223; prophesies the union of authors, 223; as to the end of the world, 223; the Cockney the most ignorant creature of his class, 224; on the date and origin of playing cards, 224; on "Merelles," 224, 225; idle and out of sorts, 225; relates origin of Sadler's Well, 225; finds life sad and stern, 226; longs for the end, 226; meets Mr. (later Sir Henry) Taylor, 226; visited by Glen, 226; characterization of, and advice, to Glen, 226, 227; inseparability (for man) of evil and good, 226, 227; finds materials of Art everywhere, but not the artist to embody them, 227, 228; notes arrival of cholera at Sunderland 228; urges himself to work, 228; "the nobleness of Silence," 228; as to Thinking and Thoughts, 228; as to Morality and Action, 228, 229; perfect morality not an object of consciousness, 229; finishes the "Characteristics," 230; his opinion of it, 230; defines Byron, 230; reads Croker's Boswell's Johnson, 230; purposes an essay on it, 230; difficulty in writing the "Characteristics," 230, 231; engages with Lardner to furnish a "History of German Literature," 231; difficulty concerning it, 231; pestered by magazine editors, 231; comments on the strange state of literature, 231, 232; as to Bulwer Lytton, 232; feeling as to Tait and his new Radical

# INDEX.

Carlyle, Thomas —*continued.*
magazine, 232; as to Fraser and his magazine, 232; a rule for writing, 232; writes for the "Athenaeum," 232; dislikes being advertised, 232; blames himself for writing for Dilke, 233; writes to his brother John in Rome, 233; proposes article on the author of the Corn Law Rhymes, 233; remarks scarcity of ideas in London, 233; "Sartor" still unpublished, 233; indifferent as to the publication of it, 234; meets Abraham Hayward, 234; Hayward's service to, 234; dines with Hayward, 235; describes the evening, 235; meets Sir Alexander Johnston, 235; characterizes Macaulay, 236; epitomizes Rogers, 236; opinion of Moore, 236; on Bentham, 236; seeks to visit Dr. Johnson's places of abode, 237; difficulty of finding places in London, 237; notes the need of a lending library in London, 237 (see *note* 2); sees that biography is the only history, 238; the aspect of the world to, 238; quotes epitaph from Johnson, 238 (see *note* 2); quotes "Dies Irae," 239 *et seq.*; comments on Parson Hackman, 243; reads Hazlitt's "Liber Amoris," 243, 244; ridicules it, 244; as to Dr. Campbell, 244; meets Mr. Shepherd (Unitarian parson), 244; describes him, 245; characterizes Unitarians, 245; St. Paul's or "Paradise Lost" the more necessary? 245; finds Franklin's definition of man in Boswell, 245; avers literature to be priceless, 245; writes unsatisfactory introduction to essay on Johnson, 245, 246; sadness of mirth not based on earnestness, 246; receives Jefrey, 246; as to O'Connell, 247; as to the Scotch, English, and Irish courts, 247; convinced that English law must be re-made, 248; meets Gustave d'Eichthal again, 248; opinion of him, 248; sees Arthur Buller, 248; dines

Carlyle, Thomas —*continued.*
with Fraser in Regent Street, 248; meets Allan Cunningham, James Hogg, and Lockhart, 248; describes Lockhart, 249; describes Galt, 249; describes Hogg (the "Ettrick Shepherd"), 250; condemns the evening spent with Fraser, 251, 252; chronicles death of his father, 252 (see *note* 1); finishes paper on Johnson, "not wholly without worth," 252; investigates Diderot, 253; quotes concerning Diderot from the "Biographie Universelle," 253; as to Bishop Douglas, 254; breaks with Lardner, 254; settles with Fraser about essay on Johnson, 255; criticizes "Fraser's Magazine," 255; as to the state of bookselling, 255; longs (with Mrs. Carlyle) to be home, 255; likes London, but not the climate, 256; quotes remark of Sir N. H. Nicholas as to booksellers, 256; describes Sir David Brewster, 256; meets Leigh Hunt through "Characteristics," 256; describes him, 257; writes to John Carlyle at Rome, 258; calls on Schlegel, but hopes not to see him, 258; terms Schlegel a literary Gigman, 258; meets William Maginn, 258; describes him, 258 (see also *note*); as to the origin of "Fraser's Magazine," 259; leaves London, 259 (see *note*); hears of the death of Goethe, 259; realizes his last letter to Goethe would arrive too late, 260; describes the Tribula, 260; comments on the fuller's craft among the Romans, 260, 261; as to Vespasian and the fuller's craft, 261; "squelches" his finger-nail, 262; philosophizes on it, 263; complains of ill health, 262, 263; as to the true pulpit and true Church, 263; upon the right of speculative men to exist, 263; on writers, 264; should writing be difficult? 264; cautions himself as to writing, 264; exhorts himself to honesty

# INDEX.

Carlyle, Thomas — *continued.*
in writing, 265; defines his difficulty in writing, 265; finishes funeral discourse on Goethe, 265 (see *note* 1); takes up Corn Law Rhymes, 265; his reluctance to renounce a road once entered on, 266; reflects on the tinkering of the State, 266, 267 (see *note*, p. 267); finishes a paper on the Corn Law Rhymer, 267; purposes memoir of Lord Byron for "New Monthly Magazine," 268; projects essay on Goethe for "Foreign Quarterly Review," 268; is idle for twelve days, 268; hears from Lytton about the Goethe funeral discourse, 268; goes down to Scotsbrig to settle family affairs, 268; gives an account of the settlement of his father's will, 268, 269; as to his Aunt Fanny and her son, 270, 271; hears rumors of loss of New Reform Bill, 271; on the political situation, 272, 273, 274; on the *only* Reform, 274; his alienation from politics, 274; his political principle, 275; goes with Fraser to House of Commons, but fails to get in, 275; sees Macaulay in lobby of House, 276; describes Macaulay, 276, 277; visits Windham Club with Fraser, 277; describes Windham Club, 277; on clubs in general, 277; farewell reflections, 278
Carnwath, Earl of, anecdote of, at Naseby, 12
Chalgrove-field, skirmish at, between Thame and Oxford, 6
Champollion, inventor of phonetic characters, 111; well received in Italy, 111
Chapel, origin of the word, as used by printers, 261, 262
Character, national, the description of a, tends to realize itself, 134
Characters, phonetic, well received in Italy, 111
Charles I, seizes members of Commons "accused of Treason," 2; eludes Waller at Worcester, 10; rejoins Queen at Oxford, 10;

Charles I — *continued.*
fights at Cropredy-bridge, 10; follows Essex into the West, 10; defeats him at Lostwithiel, 10; is beaten at Newbury, 10; retires to Oxford, 10; retires to Chepstow after Naseby, 13; thence to Cardiff, etc., 13; inclines to join Montrose, 13; sends Lord Digby north to Dumfries, 13; at Oxford in 1646, 14; surrenders to Scotch army at Newark, 14; seized at Holmby by Cornet Joyce, 14; brought to Newmarket, 15; Henderson attempts to convert, to Presbyterianism, 15; signs treaty with Scots in Carisbrooke, 15; beheaded, 16; Carlyle's opinion of, 16
Charles II, "getting settled in Scotland," 3; Milton's fear concerning, 3; stanza on, 5; goes to Scilly in 1646, 14; at the Hague, 16
Charles III, of Spain, last years of, most illustrious, 109
Chaucer, Godfrey, his house Donnington, near Newbury in Wilts, 8
Chillingworth, Mr., taken at Arundel, 9; illtreatment of, 9
Cholera, apprehension of, not shared by Carlyle, 221
Christ, Jesus, the significance of, 171; the words of, characterized, 189
Christianity, introduced into England about A. D. 180, 23
Church, the true, 263
Cicero, anecdote of Antimachus Clarius, 124
Cockney, the, the most ignorant man of his class, 224
Coleridge, on talent and genius, 46; on ideas, 78
Comley Bank, 67 (see *note*)
Conduct, 31, *note*
Confessio fidei (of Wallensteins Jäger), translation of, 61, 62, 63
Cookery, the ultimate object of, 71
*Cor ne edito*, 165 (see *note*)
Corniani, "Secoli della Let. It.," 130
Cote, 31, *note*
Courtesies, of polished life, Carlyle on the, 126

# INDEX.

Craft, the fuller's, among the Romans, 260, 261
Critics, German, curious people, 33; comparison of, with English and Scotch, 33; favorable to Germans, 33
Cromwell, Oliver, remark to Lord Falkland touching The Remonstrance, 1; chosen to command force under Manchester, 9; his "iron band" at Marston Moor, 10; proposes "self denying ordinance," 11; general in the West, 14; orders Joyce to seize Charles I, 14; secretly doomed to the Tower, but escapes to the army, 15; defeats Scotch under Duke of Hamilton, 16; Carlyle comments upon, 17; dissolves the Parliament by force, 18; summons Barebone's Parliament, 18; declared Protector, 18; prosecutes Lilburn, 18; death, 19; Carlyle to ascertain more clearly the aims of, 31; a life of, desirable, 93
Cunningham, Allan, meets Carlyle in London, 196; visits the Carlyles, 214; meets Carlyle at Fraser's, 249

Dante, commentators on, 111
"Defensio Gigmanica," the, 216 (see *note* 1)
D'Eichthal, Gustave, the Saint-Simonian, meets Carlyle (see *note* 2); acquainted with Emerson, 201 (see *note* 2)
Delegates, Convention of, to expedite Reform Bill, 206
Delusion, popular, as to, 105, 106
Denovan, Denny, 59
Descartes, founds all truth on God, 100; differs from the English, who found God on truth, 100
Desideratum, the great, in society, 152
Didot, F., French printer, number of volumes produced annually by, 110
Digby, Lord, advises king to seize members of the House of Commons, 2; despatched north by Charles I, 13; deserts his army at Dumfries, 13

Dilettantism, the Sin of the age, 172
Dilke, C. W., 208, 209 (see *notes*)
"Dumfries Courier," the, Carlyle writes letter to, 153 (see also *note* 2)
Dunoyer, writer on Industrialism, 113
Drake, various quotations from, 146 (see also *note* 2)

Ebel, Dr., 107
Economists, Political, error of, 143; Carlyle's query as to, 143, 144; the whole philosophy of, 144; uselessness of, 144; should collect statistical facts, 160
Economy, Political, as to, 100; present science of, requires little intellect, 160; though young, is decrepit, 160
Edgehill, Battle of, 5; location of, 6
Education, Carlyle upon, 222, 223 (see *note* 1, p. 223)
Elizabeth, Queen, men of her time the Romans or Greeks of English history, 70; her literature the only true poetical literature of England, 70
Ellwood, reader of Latin to Milton, 21; his life of himself, 21; Carlyle's opinion of, 21; life of, why read by Carlyle, 21; description of, 21; compared with Alfieri, Goethe, Voltaire, 22
Emperors, Roman, anecdotes of 87
Empiricism, does it lead to Atheism? 102
Empirics, the, 102
England, Carlyle desires to *know*, 132; no precise history of, 132; the old literature of, 132; to understand her, one must understand her Church, 133; dearth of artists in, 133; dearth of musicians and painters in, 133; the characteristic strength of, 134; character of the people of, 134
English, the, found all truth on God, 100
Entsagen (Renunciation), 221 (see *note* 2)
Erasmus, characterization of, 118

# INDEX.

Esbie, Captain, "there is nothing like getting on," 104
Evil, inseparable (for man) from good, 227 (see *note* 2)
Existence, individual, a mystery, 161; social, still more, 161 (see *note*); speculations on, 161, 162; life only the portico of man's, 221
Eye, the spiritual and bodily, 136

Fable, 91; instruction communicated by, chiefly prohibitive, 92; the Conjurer (II), 93; as to the necessity of any man (III), 101; as to development of character (IV), 105
Fairfax, Lord, defeats Royalists at Naseby, 12; general in the West, 14; seizes Colchester, 16
Falkland, Lord, Cromwell's remark to, concerning The Remonstrance, 1; killed at Battle of Newbury, 8; Clarendon's opinion of, 8; Carlyle on, 8, 9; belonged to Lord Byron's regiment, 9
Fichte, a metaphysical atheist, 46; his "Transcendental Idealism," 112; pretended to have deduced his system from Kant, 112
Fleetwood, a trooper in the Guards, 5; sent by Essex to Shrewsbury, 5; son of Sir Miles Fleetwood, 19
Fletcher (and Beaumont), dramatists, disappointing to Carlyle, 31; criticism of, 31, 32
Fonblanque (editor of "Examiner"), entertains Carlyle, 213, 214 (see *note* 1, p. 214)
Foreign·minds and characters hard to judge truly, 92; exemplification, 92
Foscarini, Sebastian, Doge of Venice, inscription on tomb of, 89 (see also *note* 2)
France, printers, booksellers and authors in, 110; number of volumes printed annually in, 110; number of printing offices in, 110; number of active presses in, 110; amount spent annually in printing in, 110; number of booksellers in, 110; amount earned by authors annually in, 110

Franklin, definition of man by, 245; anticipates "Teufelsdreck" in it, 245
Fraser, James (publisher of "Fraser's Magazine"), entertains Carlyle at dinner, 249; settles with Carlyle about essay on Johnson, 255
"Fraser's Magazine," criticized by Carlyle, 170; characterized by Carlyle, 232; described by Carlyle, 259
Fraser, W. (brother to James Fraser), editor of "Foreign Review," 249 (see *note*); entertains Carlyle, 256; is denied admittance to the House of Commons with Carlyle, 275; takes Carlyle to the Windham Club, 275; sees Macaulay in lobby of House, 276; remark concerning Macaulay, 276
Friendship, not mentioned in New Testament, 106
Fuller, craft of the, among the Romans, 260, 261

Gall, borrows from Herder, 46
Gallicistes, the, 109
Galt, John, meets Carlyle at Fraser's, 249; described by Carlyle, 249, 250
Gassendi, as to the metaphysics of? 102; "the father of existing French Philosophy," 102
Gellert, anecdote of, 122
Genius, Alfieri on, 30; Coleridge's distinction between talent and, 46; the true relation of moral to poetic, inquired into, 188
"Genoveva," Tieck's, consideration of characters in, 73
Gherardini, translator and impugner of Schlegel, 111
Gleig, G. R., Rev., writes to Carlyle concerning Goethe and Luther, 154 (see *note*)
Glen, ——, 200 (see *note* 1)
Godwin, William, meets Carlyle, 198; characterized by Carlyle, 199; his life of Mary Wollstonecraft, 204; epitomized by Carlyle, 205
Goethe, on the spending of time, 31; Carlyle's query as to, 32

# INDEX.

Goethe — *continued*.
  effect of "Wilhelm Meister" on Carlyle, 32; his comprehension of Carlyle, 32; "a wise and great man," 32; last volume of life of, 32; meets Schiller, 36; wiser than Herder or Wieland, 46; Carlyle's approval of, 46; "again dangerously ill," 60; on idea and action, 81; called illbred by British critics, 126; Carlyle's opinion of, 127; on the sublime, 128; on his work, 129 (see *note*); death of, 259
Good, inseparable (for man) from Evil, 227 (see *note* 2)
Goring, Lord, the Parliament's guardian and betrayer, 11; afterward Royalist general of Horse, 11; "a very sufficient cozener," but "clever" and "very original," 11; "the dog," 13; misbehaves, 13; goes to France, 13
Göttingen, professors at, account of, 117; many men of note produced at, 147
Gowkthrapple, Dr., 102 (see *note* 2)
Grammarians, Italian, 110
"Grammont," Carlyle's desire to read, 53
Greenvil, Sir Dick, the Nabal, 13; levies enormous contributions, 13; is imprisoned, but escapes, 13
Grey, Earl, Carlyle on, 273, 274
Gries, translations by, 131
Grossi, Thomas, poet and Romantic, 111; said to surpass Tasso, 111
Grotius, his method of reading "Terence," 128
Gryph, Andreas, death of, 119
Guards, troopers of the, all gentlemen's sons, 19

Hacket, Bishop, Life of Abp. Williams, 2, *note*
Hackman, Parson, comment on, 243
Hadrian, epitaph on Cæsar, 123
Hambden, accused of treason, 2; killed at Chalgrove-field, 6; Carlyle's estimate of, 7; coupled with Washington by Carlyle, 7; portrait of, by Clarendon, 8

Hamilton, Duke of, defeated by Cromwell, 16; taken prisoner at Uttoxeter, 16; beheaded, 17
Harrison, conducts Charles I to Westminster, 16; origin of, 16
Hazelrig, accused of treason, 2
Hazlitt, Carlyle's opinion of, 213
Honor-titles, derivation of, past and future, 185
Heeren, biographer of Heyne, 116
Henderson, Mr., pitted against Bishop Steward, 11; "why does not McCrie write a life of?" 12; tries to convert Charles I, 15; dies of a broken heart, 15
Herder, Carlyle has good hopes of, 33; his "Nemesis," 33; account of and quotation from, 33, 34; compared to Hervey, 34; his essay about the decay of taste used by Madame de Staël, 34; quotation from Herder, 35, 36; hates the "new philosophy," 45; his "Ideen," 72; Carlyle's criticism of it, 72; Carlyle's desire to see more of, 73; a sort of "Browne redivivus," 73
Heyne, list of works of, 115, 116; birthplace of, 116; short account of, 116; "not great, but large," 117
Historian, the, disadvantage of, 124
Histrio-Mastix, Prynne's, 29
Hoddam Hill, 64 (see *note*)
Hogg, James (the "Ettrick Shepherd"), meets Carlyle at Fraser's, 249; described by Carlyle, 250, 251
Holland, Lord, 17
Hollis, accused of treason, 2; quarrels with Ireton, 15; pulls Ireton by the nose, 15
Homer, greater than Shakespeare? 187
Hooker, as to the "Mother of Error," 143
Hopton, defeats Parliament at Bradock-Down, 6; defeated at Arlesford by Waller, 9; fails to save Royalist cause after Naseby, 14
Hopton-heath, Battle of, 6; location of, 6; Parliament beaten at, 6

297

# INDEX.

Horace, on mastering things, 132 (see also *note*)
Hume, "Essay on Human Nature," 262 (see *note*)
Hunt, Leigh, seeks out Carlyle, 256; Carlyle's opinion of, 257
Hurry (a Scot), account of, 7

Individuality, as to intellectual, 114; as to moral, 114
Industrialism, historical sketch of, 113
Industrials, the, 113; Saint-Simon the chief of the, 113; political theories of the, 113
Institutions (or Laws), as to, 141
Immortality, conception of, depends on that of Time, 222
Ireton, Henry, quarrels with Hollis, 15; refuses to fight him, 15; dies of plague at Limerick, 18;
Iriarte, Tomas, Spanish writer, 109; Carlyle's opinion, 109
Irving, Edward, "may be yet a Bishop," 185

Jeffrey, resigns editorship of "Edinburgh Review," 140 (see *note*); to see Carlyle at Dumfries, 141; offers Carlyle an annuity, 155; visits Carlyle at Craigenputtock, 173; as viewed by Carlyle, 173, 174, 175; Lord Advocate and M.P., 185; emotion on taking office, 185; receives Carlyle in London, 193, 194
Johnson, Dr., Carlyle on, 60
Joyce, Cornet, seizes Charles I at Holmby, 14; his authority for doing so, 14, 15

Kant, Carlyle on, 41, 46; writers on, 112; his system of morality universal in Germany, 112; denies that Fichte made use of his system, 112; reminds Carlyle of Father Boscovich, 112
Katherine of Portugal (and Charles II), stanza on, by Swift or Rochester, 5
Kimbolton, Lord, 2
Kings, divine right of, 184, 185
Kinnaird, Carlyle at (1823), 50, 51
Kirchberg, Hartman von, his epitaph on himself, 156

Know, how to, what we are, 152
"Knox," McCries', of no immense weight, 5

Lacépède, Comte de, history of Europe by, 107; Carlyle's opinion of it, 107
Lacrételle, a superficial historian, 32; estimate of, 32; his "Religious Wars," 52; Carlyle's opinion of it, 52
Landsdown, Battle of, near Bath, 8; Parliament beaten at, 8
Language, all, except concerning *sensual* objects, figurative, 141, 142 (see *note*, p. 142)
Lardner, Dr. Dionysius (of the Cabinet Cyclopedia), seeks Carlyle's aid, 231 (see *note* 5, p. 234); a "Langöhriger," 234 (see *note*); loses Carlyle, 254
Leibnitz, locates truth, 100; reverse view by the English, 100
Lesly, David, defeats Montrose at Philipshaugh, 14
Leyden, Dr. John, verses to Mrs. Buller, 63
Life, logical import of, 180; the portico of man's Existence, 221
Lilburn, persecuted by Star Chamber, 18; taken at Brentford, 18; attacks Cromwell, 18; is prosecuted by Cromwell, but acquitted, 18; the Cobbett of those days, 18
Lilis, first wife of Adam, 82
Literature, the old English, spirit of better than that of ours, 69; touched with true beauty, 69; Elizabethan, the only truly poetical, of England, 70; printing not the symbol of, 170, 171
Literary men, the only sovereigns of the world, 184
Logau, T. von, couplet by, 118; couplet by, 119
London, as to the size of, 209, 210; hurry of life in, 210; Carlyle on the want of Government in, 211; description of, 211; difficulty of finding places in, 237; no lending library in London, 237 (see *note* 2)
Londonderry, wrested from the City of London by Star Chamber, afterwards restored, 2

# INDEX.

Longman & Co., Carlyle presents letter of introduction to, 196; refuse Carlyle's "German Lit. History," 196

Lostwithiel, Essex's foot capitulates at, 10

Ludlow, succeeds Ireton, 18; at Battle of Edgehill, 19; a trooper of the Guards, 19; his "Memoirs," 19; Carlyle's opinion of his "Memoirs," 19

Luther, asceticism of, 136; last words of, 137; Melanchthon's life of, 138; Seckendorf's history of, 138; other works concerning, 138; ancestry of, 138; monastic life of, 138; Motschmanus on, at Erfurt, 138; character of, as a monk, 138, 139 (see *note*, p. 139); chronology of life of, 139; character of, 139; attachment to music of, 139; Carlyle desires to write a life of, 140; such men as,. needed in each century, 140; Carlyle thinks seriously of discussing, 142.

McCrie, his "Knox," no immense weight, 5

McDiarmid (editor of "Dumfries Courier"), Carlyle describes, 272

Macaulay, T. B., Carlyle on, 236 (see *note* 3), 276; bought oranges before speaking in House of Commons, 276

Machiavel, comment on, 15

Maginn, William, meets Carlyle at Fraser's, 258; described by Carlyle, 258; the real originator of "Fraser's Magazine," 258

Man, history of a, like that of his world, 132; Carlyle's own experience as to the history of a, 132; a visible mystery, 136; is a spirit, 161; viewed in a mere logical sense, 163; the moral nature of, 164; is an apparition, 164; infinitely venerable to every other man, 166; Novalis on the body of, 166

Manchester, Earl of, defeats Rupert and Newcastle at Marston Moor, 10

Manzoni, poet and romanticist, 111; failure as a tragedian, 111

Massinger (dramatist), disappointing to Carlyle, 31; criticism of, 31, 32

Marshall, Mr., who was? 1

Marston Moor, Battle of, 10; Royalists defeated by Manchester at, "chiefly by Cromwell's iron band," 10; location of, 10

Meditation and Seclusion, Carlyle on, 176

Memoirs, various, list of, 128

Mendelssohn, the "Phädon" of, a half imitation of Plato's "Phaedon," 94; possesses beauty and simplicity, 94; divided into three dialogues, 95; summary of them, 95, 96

"Mercurius," newspaper, set on foot during Spanish Armada, 4

Merelles, same as Corsicrown, 224, 225; also called "nine men's morrice," 225

Metaphors, prodigious influence of, 142; essay on, needed, 142; Carlyle determines to write essay on, 142; "Sartor Resartus" to be regarded as the essay on, 142 (see *note* 1)

Michaud, "Histoire des Croisades," 118

Milan, number of journals in, 112

Mill, J. S., sees Carlyle, 205; pleases Carlyle, 205

Millot, work on the Troubadours, 131

Milton, Defensio Pop. Angl. ag! the Def. Reg. of Saumaise, 3, 5; Carlyle's analysis of, 3; "not a man of breeding," 3; wife of, said to "have worn the breeks," 3; life and writings of, by Birch, 8; adjt-gen'l. to Waller, 19; his history of Britain, 22; criticism of, by Carlyle, 22; some "agates" picked from it, 23; his first publication, "Of Reformation," 23; praise of it, by Carlyle, 24; examination of it, 24, 25; his second pamphlet, "Of Prelatical Episcopacy, 25; characterization of it, 25; his third pamphlet, "The Reason of Church Government," 26; examination of it, 26; praise of it, 27; Carlyle only beginning to

# INDEX.

Milton — *continued.*
understand Milton, 27; Symmons' life of, and Hayley's life of, characterized, 27; "Axle of Discipline," 27; account of the "Axle," 28; Carlyle's criticism of himself as a critic of, 28; last two pamphlets of 1641, "Animadversions on the Remonstrant's defense of Smectymnuus" and "Apology for Sm.," 28; criticism of both, 28; the "Areopagitica" of, 29; account and criticism of it, 29, 30; Brougham in comparison with, 29; Carlyle to ascertain more clearly the aims of, 31
Mind, compared with nature, 132
Montaigne, Carlyle's opinion of "Essais" of, 53
Montrose, secret history of, 12; defeated at Philipshaugh by Lesly, 14; execution of, a disgrace to Scottish Kirk, 17; character of, 17
Montrevil, a French agent, 14; negotiates surrender of Charles I to the Scotch, 14
Moore, Thomas, Carlyle's opinion of, 236
Morality, and action, 228; perfect, not an object of consciousness, 229
Moratin, L.-F. de, restorer of dramatic art in Spain, 108
Moratin, N-F. de, father of L-F. de M., writer of tragedy, 108
Müllner, German playwright, 205 (see *note* 1), 206, 211
Murray, offered "Sartor Resartus" by Carlyle, 194; described by Carlyle, 194
Musicians, earliest Italian, 131; German, 131
Mystery, every living man a visible, 136

Naharro, B. T., playwright of 16th century, 108
Napier, succeeds Jeffrey on the "Edinburgh Review" and gives Carlyle letter to Longman's, 194 (see *note* 1)
Napoleon, remark by Carlyle on, 7; compared with Hambden, 7

Narration, primary defect in the art of, 124; this understood by Carlyle, 124
Naseby, Battle of, King defeated at, 12; good description of, by Clarendon, 12; ruin of Royalist cause after, 13
Navigation, Act of, passed in anger at the Dutch, 17, its intent, 17; attributed by Raynal to King James, 17; was the beginning of the Dutch-English quarrel, 17
Nepenthe, Helena's, supposition concerning, 93
Newbury, Battle of, both sides claim victory, 8; Lord Falkland killed at, 8
Newcastle, Duke of, beaten by Manchester at Marston Moor, 10; flies beyond the sea, 10
Newspapers, in Milton's time, 4
Nicolas, Sir Nicholas Harris, 143; remark of, to Carlyle, concerning booksellers, 256
"No day without writing a line," 167
Note book (No. 1) begun while reading Clarendon's History (Edin. 1822), 1, *note*
Novalis, "Schriften" of, review of the, 135; review published, 140; Carlyle's opinion of, 140; upon religion, 149; on the body of man, 166

O'Connell, a real demagogue, 247
"Oceana," 29
Oxford, attempted treaty in 1643 at, 6

Pain, irremediable, alleviation to, 164; the measure of life and of talent, 169; a stone feels no, 169
Paley, Carlyle's criticism of, 103
Palm, the, legend of, 119
Paris, number of booksellers in, 110; number of printing houses in, 110; number of active presses in, 110
Passeroni, anecdote of, 130; his "Cicerone," 130; death of, 130
Peers, House of, abolished soon after King's death, 17
Pétrarquistes, the, 109; "the glorious Spanish Literature," 109

# INDEX.

Petronius, quotation from, 97
"Phädon," the, of Mendelssohn (see Mendelssohn)
Philosophy, Political, what it should be, 144; what it is, 144
Phonetic characters well received in Italy, 111
Plato, Antimachus Clarius on, 124
Playing cards, on the date and origin of, 224
Poem, does a, differ from prose? 187
Poems that live, birth of, 103; heroic, as to the true, 188
Poet, what a, should be, 48; the ultimate object of a, 124
Poetry, the ultimate object of, 71
Politeness, peculiar to the rich and well-born, 166
Politics, not Life but the house wherein Life is lead, 141; the noblest science, 165; Carlyle's alienation from, 274
Pope, and his school, pedagogical poets, 70
Potatoes, in London, exorbitant price of, 210
Principle, Carlyle's political, 275
Printing, not the symbol of literature, 170, 171
Problem, the eternal, of man, 208; a further and harder, found in London, 208; the deepest, in these days, 264
Profane, the, proportion of, to the sacred, 188
Prose, does it differ from a poem? 187
Proverb, German, a, 129 (see also *note* 2)
Pullus Jovis, etc., 85 (see *note*)
Pulpit, the, advantage of, 215; the true, 263
Pym, accused of treason, 2

Quincunx, the, 68; Carlyle on, 68.
Quixote, Don, philosophical indifference of Sancho Panza in, 145
Qualities, in man, the unhappiest, 127
Quarrels, origin of all, 149, 150
"Quarterly Review," the, Carlyle's opinion of, 143

Raleigh, Sir Walter, advice of, to his son, 69

Ranelagh, formerly the Earl of R.'s house, 225
Rationalists, 102
Reading (town), taken 1643, 6
Reading, a weariness of the flesh, 53
Reason, decisions of, superior to those of understanding, 83; relation of, to Understanding, 142; can never be extinguished, 142
Reform Bill, lost, 202 (see *note* 1); the New, carried, 271 (see *note*)
"Register, Literary Annual," prospectus for, 77–81
Reinhold (coupled with Fichte), 46
"Religio Medici," the, Carlyle's opinion of, 69; "made a mighty noise at its first appearance," 90
Religion, moral of the Christian, 150; easy to write, hard to practice, 150; the Christian, like some Nile, 158; the true element of, 164; the cement of Society, 179; is Art higher than? 204
Reluctance, to turn back, Carlyle's, 266
Remedy, the beginning of a, 209
Remonstrance, The, 1
"Revue Encyclopédique" (French magazine) worthy of imitation in Britain, 110
Richter, Jean Paul, quotation from the "Levana" of, 114; anecdote from the "Levana," 123; on salvation, 143
Ritson, "Fairy Tales" and "Old Ballads," 213
River, a, as to the right and left bank of, 122
Rochester (or Swift), stanza on Charles II and Katherine of Portugal, 5
Rogers, Samuel, characterization of, by Carlyle, 236 (see *note* 4)
Romantics *versus* Classics, 111
Roundway, Battle of, near Devizes, 8; Parliament beaten at, 8
Rupert, Prince, beaten by Manchester at Marston Moor, 10; goes southward, 10; son of ex-king of Böhmen, 10; Carlyle's estimate of, 10; defeated at Naseby by Fairfax, 12; "a fiery ettercap, a fractious chiel," 12; in command in Ireland, 16

# INDEX.

Ruthven ("a Scot"), defeated by Hopton at Bradock-Down, 6; afterward General Brentford, "dotard, drunkard, deaf," 10

Sachs, Hans, Carlyle on, 74
Sacred, the, to the profane, proportions of, 188
Sadler's Well, origin of, 225 (see *note* 1)
St. Paul's or "Paradise Lost" the greater necessity? 245
Saint-Simon, chief of the Industriels, 113; reputed to be mad, 113; descended from Charlemagne, 113
Saint-Simonians, write to Carlyle, 158; have strange notions, with a large spicing of truth, 158; are among the Signs of the Times, 158; answered by Carlyle, 158 (see *note* 2)
"Sandy," Uncle, death of, 147
"Sartor Resartus," the germ of, 136 (see *note* 2)
Saumaise, Defensio Reg., 3, 5; Milton's abuse of, 3; Voltaire's reference to, 4, *note*; his mode of reasoning, 4
Scaliger, Joseph Justus, professor at Leyden, 88; his works, 88
Scaliger, Julius Cæsar, quotation from, 87; his birth and parentage, 88; life and character of, 88
Schelling, his "System of Identity," 112
Schiller, birth and origin, 36; obligation to Madame von Wollzogen, 36; visit to Weimar, 36; sees Herder and Wieland, 36; joins "Teutsches Mercur," 36; visits Rudolstadt and meets his future wife, 36; sees Goethe, 36; various remarks on, 36, 37; description of, 37, 38; not inclined to noisy pleasures, 38; close connection with the theatre of, 38; strict demands upon the performers of his plays, 39; his benevolence and kindliness, 39; his upright conduct in business, 39; delineation of himself by, 40; Carlyle's summing up of, 40, 41; quotation from, 48, 49

Schlegel, A., called on by Carlyle, 258; dined by Hayward and Lardner, 258; a literary Gigman, 258
Schlegel, F., Carlyle on, 42; as to thought, 104; his "Philosophy of Life," 129; death of, 135; comment on, by Carlyle, 135
Scotland, nothing poetical in, but its religion, 133; Carlyle's attitude toward, 133; Carlyle's unequal knowledge of, 133; have the gentry of, lost their national character? 134; is the peasant of, the true Scotchman? 134; people of, compared with people of England, 135; music and songs of, 135; books on, to be consulted, 135; Scott's history of, not a history, 168; what history of, is like, 169; herself not there, 169; behavior of the nobles of, 169; progressed independent of her history, 169
Scots, "ran like collies (fidem detis?)" at Marston Moor, 10
Scott, Sir Walter, "the great Restaurateur of Europe," 71; what he might have been, and what he is, 71; his novels characterized, 71; Carlyle on some characters in, 126; the "gentlemen" of, Carlyle on, 127; as to his "Bonaparte," 127; his character-building contrasted with Burns's, 127; Carlyle on his "History of Scotland," 168; inference drawn from, by Carlyle, 168; leaves England for Naples on a Government ship, 214; in precarious health, 214; estimate of, by Carlyle, 214
Seclusion, and Meditation, Carlyle on, 176
Secrecy, the element of all Goodness, 177
"Self denying ordinance," proposed by Cromwell and Vane, 11; object of, 11
Shaftesbury, Earl of, his "Characteristics," 71; criticism of, 72
Shakespeare, how to prize, 32; revision of above as to Carlyle, 32 (see also p. 121); greater than Homer? 187

# INDEX.

Shepherd (Unitarian parson), Carlyle's meeting with and opinion of, 244, 245
Shiel (Irish orator), convicted of lying, 247
Shoes, good, not to be had in London, 207
Sickingen, Franz von, one of the noblest men of the Reformation period, 166; defended Ulrich von Hutten, 166; fought against Würtemberg, 166; the terror of evil-doers, 166; read Luther with Hutten, 166; good breeding of, 166; is killed fighting against the Bishop of Triers, 166; anecdote concerning death of, 166, 167; enemies weep at the funeral of, 167
"Siegwart," Miller's, the beginning of the sentimental period, 120
Silence, Carlyle on, 176; contrasted with Speech, 177; the nobleness of, 228
"Sister Margaret," death of, 156;
Society, a wonder of wonders, 165; division of, by Carlyle, 215
Sonata, Devil's, the, 130
South, quotation from, 97; Carlyle's opinion of, 97
Southey, Carlyle on the "Travels" of, 5
Spain, literature in, English ignorance of, 109
Speech and Silence, Carlyle on, 177
Spenser, quotation from, 49, 50; pleases Carlyle, 50; a *dainty body*, 50
Spirits, Wandering, the, 167
"Sports," Carlyle laments the absence of, 222
Stamford, defeated by Royalists at Stratton Hill, 8
Stanza (by Swift or Rochester), on Charles II and Katherine of Portugal, 5
Star Chamber, date of institution, 2
Steward, Bishop, "pitted against Mr. Henderson," 11
Stewart, "Aunt Mary," death of, 147
Strahan, defeats Montrose, 17
Stratton hill, Battle of, 8; Parliament defeated at, 8; location of, 8

Strode, accused of treason, 2
Swift (or Rochester), stanza on Charles II and Katherine of Portugal, 5; quotation from, 103; Carlyle's comment on, 103
Swinburne, travels of, explanation of the *aequo pulsat pede* in, 60

Tacitus, as to physicians, 86; as to astrologers, 122
Tait (bookseller), to start a new Radical magazine, 232
Talent, Coleridge's distinction between genius and, 46
Talma, seen in rôle of Œdipe, 98
Tartini, Giuseppe, anecdote of, 130
Tasso, Carlyle proposes a discourse on, 123 (*note* 3); his "Del Poema Eroico," Carlyle on, 125; his "Gerusalemme," 125; a mystic, 125
Teaching, is oral superior to the written mode of? 212
Temple, Sir William, Carlyle's opinion of, 84; no artist or philosopher, but man of action, 84;
"Terence," how Grotius read, 128
Themistocles, his gift of forgetting, 53 (see *note*)
Theology, curious division of, 124
Thinking and Thoughts, 228
Thought, is every, an inspiration, 166
Thoughts and Thinking, 228
Tieck, Runenberg, 66; his "Genoveva," 73; consideration of characters in it, 73; next to Goethe, Richter being dead, 74; quotation from, 81
Time, Goethe on the spending o., 31; conception of, determines the meaning of Immortality, 222
"Times," the, criticism of Schiller, Part II, by, 61; Carlyle's comment on, 61
Titus, reproaches Vespasian for imposing tax on fullers, 261
Tribula, described by Carlyle, 260
Tribulation, derivation of the word, 200
Truth, difficult to obtain the, 217

Ugoni, Camillo, his "History of Italian Literature," 130; its scope, 130

# INDEX.

Understanding, decisions of, inferior to those of Reason, 83; relation of, to Reason, 142
Union, spiritual, power of, 164, 165
Unitarians, Carlyle and the, 245
Universe, wonder of the, 142
"Upstart companions," Clarendon's epithet, 2
"Urne Burial," the best of Sir T. Browne's books, 67; Carlyle's criticism of, 67
Utilitarians, the crowning mercy of the age, 145; trend of, 145; contrasted with Whigs, 172
Uxbridge-treaty, graphically delineated, 11

Vane, Sir H., proposes "self-denying ordinance," 11
Vauxhall, formerly Spring Gardens, 225
Vespasian, lays a tax on fullers, 261; reproached by Titus for doing so, 261
Villemain, writer of "Mélanges," 107
Virtue, its own reward, why? 103; as regarded by a healthy or an unhealthy moral nature, 230
Vives, Ludovicus, comment on, 86; history of, 90
Voltaire, his philosophy characterized, 85; Carlyle finds difficulty in writing on, 135; Carlyle's paper on, 140

Wages, disparity of, 159
Waller, Sir W., Parliamentary general, beaten at Landsdown and Roundway, 8; retakes Arundel, 9; defeats Royalists at Arlesford, 9; loses king at Worcester, 10

Waller (the poet), betrayed to the Parliament, 6; arraigned by Parliament and banished to Bermuda, 6
Washington, coupled with Hambden by Carlyle, 7
Werner, Zacharias, life by Hitzig, 82; his "Mutter der Makkabäer," 82; his history, 82; Carlyle's opinion of, 83
Whigs, contrasted with Utilitarians, 172; the grand "Dilettanti," 172
Whole, as to the constitution of a, 187
Wieland, meets Schiller, 36; induces Schiller to join the "Teutsches Mercur," 36; opposes the "new philosophy," 45; his reason for doing so, 45, 46
Williams, Archbishop of York, "a very queer man," 2
Winckelmann, quotation from, 106; "the only two modern *Friends*, 106; Goethe's opinion of, 107; quotations from, 107
Wolff, most characteristic writing of, 119
Wollstonecraft, Mary, life by Godwin, 204; epitomized by Carlyle, 205
Wonder, the basis of worship, 162; the reign of, 162
Worcester, Scots defeated at, 17
Words, the strangest and most potent product of our nature, 176
Works Carlyle would like to see written, 119, 120
Writers, Spanish, 108, 109
Writing, Carlyle on, 136

"Youth, happy limitedness of," 128

PR
4420
.T8
1922